Homicide-Suicides in Romania

Ecaterina Balica

Homicide-Suicides in Romania

Statistical Data and Media Representations

PL ACADEMIC RESEARCH

Bibliographic Information published by the Deutsche Nationalbibliothek
The Deutsche Nationalbibliothek lists this publication in the Deutsche Nationalbibliografie; detailed bibliographic data is available in the internet at http://dnb.d-nb.de.
Library of Congress Cataloging-in-Publication Data
Names: Balica, Ecaterina, author.
Title: Homicide-suicides in Romania : statistical data and media representations / Ecaterina Balica.
Description: 1 Edition. | New York : Peter Langa, 2016. | Includes bibliographical references and index.
Identifiers: LCCN 2016012039 | ISBN 9783631667224
Subjects: LCSH: Homicide--Romania. | Suicide--Romania. | Suicide in mass media.
Classification: LCC HV6541.R65 B35 2016 | DDC 364.15209498--dc23 LC record available at http://lccn.loc.gov/2016012039

This work was supported by a grant of the Romanian Ministry of Education, CNCS - UEFISCDI, project number PN-II-RU-PD-2012-3-0414 "Homicide - Suicide in Romania: Incidence, Patterns and Risk Factors"

Coverimage: fotolia.de #26969307 | @ alexskopje

ISBN 978-3-631-66722-4 (Print)
E-ISBN 978-3-653-06285-4 (E-PDF)
E-ISBN 978-3-631-69576-0 (EPUB)
E-ISBN 978-3-631-69577-7 (MOBI)
DOI 10.3726/978-3-653-06285-4

PL Academic Research is an Imprint of Peter Lang GmbH.

Peter Lang – Frankfurt am Main · Bern · Bruxelles · New York · Oxford · Warszawa · Wien

This publication has been peer reviewed.

www.peterlang.com

Table of Contents

Introduction

In more than twenty years of experience my research has tried to identify risk factors in different types of interpersonal violence. Investigations centered on particularities of violent crimes (Balica 2008, Balica 2012) committed in Romania in the transition from dictatorship to democracy. I gradually added to the list of research themes: the intimate partner homicide (Balica and Banciu 2009, Balica 2012) maternal and paternal filicide (Balica 2009, Balica 2010), femicide (Balica 2016b) and homicide-suicide (Balica and Stöckl 2016, Balica 2016a). The passing from one type of homicide to another was due to the results of my investigations that allowed me to talk about new types of violence while I was trying to study more deeply the problem of risk factors specific to homicide in Romania. My contact with the most recent scientific studies, published by European researchers, and my connection with international networks of researchers, who were investigating certain types of homicide, created the context necessary for my involvement in research about types of homicide.

My interest in studying homicide-suicides became a real project only after three years of waiting and of weighing the possibilities of making some investigations in Romania. The year 2013 was essential to my desire to initiate a wide research project which could offer relevant information regarding homicide-suicides. In 2013, my research project regarding homicide-suicides in Romania managed to obtain financial support from the Romanian Ministry of Education, CNCS – UEFISCDI. The project's name is PNI-II-RU-PD-2012-3-0414, Homicide – Suicide in Romania: Incidence, Patterns and Risk Factors. In 2013 I also became a Member of the Management Committee and coordinator of the Femicide Romanian Network, for the project COST ISCH 1206, Femicide across Europe. The themes covered by the COST Femicide across Europe project, and the interest of researchers from the international network of the project for the South-Eastern European space, were the elements that molded my investigations about homicide-suicides. These made me pay special attention to femicide-suicide and intimate partner homicide-suicide and they also helped me identify the information level and the elements of researchers' interest regarding the problem of homicide in the Romanian space. What I am writing here is the result of my research from the last two years focusing on homicide-suicides and some subtypes of homicide-suicides: intimate partner homicide-suicides, femicide-suicides, familicide-suicides and filicide-suicides in Romania.

This book is the first about homicide-suicides from South-East Europe and it is also one of the few books in Europe focused on homicide-suicides. It is also the first book about homicide-suicides from a post-communist country. Furthermore, the book is unique as it includes a chapter about femicide-suicides and intimate partner homicide-suicides from a South-Eastern country. There is little information about homicide and criminality in general committed in South-East Europe because information is published in the national language, which makes it difficult to integrate data into the international scientific circuit. Working on this study I tried to counteract the lack of information regarding Romania as a part of South-East Europe. At the same time, the book includes an analysis of all the homicide-suicide cases committed in Romania in a long period of time, 2002–2013, a situation that allows the formulation of some pertinent conclusions regarding incidence, risk factors and particularities of homicide-suicides in a country that belonged to the Soviet bloc and had a communist dictatorship.

The literature review shows that, until now, only Portugal, the Netherlands, France, Germany, the United Kingdom, Finland, Switzerland, Poland, Denmark, Iceland and Spain had studies which collected complex data regarding homicide-suicide. In other countries (such as Greece, Turkey and Croatia) studies were made only from a forensic perspective at the regional level and these types of data only allow a limited analysis of the phenomenon. As it can be noticed, the European researches on the issue were limited mainly to countries located in Western, Central and Northern parts of the continent. Researchers from Eastern Europe and/or the Balkans had approached this topic only rarely in their scientific research (3 studies, in 3 countries, from a forensic perspective with a small samples of cases).

Taking into account this context, in 2013 I initiated a research project regarding the patterns and risk factors which lead to homicide-suicide acts in Romania, a Balkan country with a low economic level (in comparison with the other countries studied), a different culture and traditions, and a high migration flow to Western countries. Through this research project I tried to provide the missing information from that part of Europe and to explore the patterns and factors that are peculiar for the violent acts committed in South-Eastern Europe. Moreover, I tried to produce a database with information about homicide-suicide cases from Romania, which can be connected to the international database and which can be analyzed in a comparative manner with the existing data from other European countries.

When writing this book I was in fact trying to answer some questions: What is the incidence of homicide-suicide in Romania compared to the other European countries and countries all over the world where these types of murders were studied? Is the homicide-suicide rate in Romania bigger than in other European countries or not? What types of homicide-suicide are specific to a country from South-Eastern Europe? What are the risk factors that determine committing homicide-suicides in Romania compared to the other European countries or to other countries of the world? What are the motivations of homicide-suicides? Are there any cultural differences between motivations of homicide-suicides from Romania and from other European countries or other regions of the world? Are there any differences between aggressors who commit homicide and those who commit homicide-suicide? What are the particularities of these two types of violent acts?

The book is in two parts: Homicide – suicides in an Eastern European country: Romania (Part 1) and Homicide-suicides and Online Media (Part 2). In the first part of the book I present the results of the analysis of data regarding homicide-suicides registered in the Homicide-Suicides in Romania (2002–2013) database. In the four chapters I discuss the methodology of research, the particularities and risk factors of homicide-suicides and some types of homicide-suicide (intimate partner homicide-suicides, familicide-suicides and filicide-suicides). My decision to include some studies regarding the way in which the online media present homicide-suicides came step by step. This happened when I was trying to gather information regarding homicide-suicides from the online media and compare it with data from other two sources (data from police and data from parquets) used for the database. While I was analyzing the online articles I noticed that there were some particularities of the way in which the cases of homicide-suicide are presented compared to other types of violence. I also noticed some similarities and differences about the way in which journalists from other countries cover this type of violence. I wanted to draw attention to the way in which Romanian journalists talk about cases of homicide-suicide. This is why, in the second part of the book, I talk about the results of the analysis regarding the coverage of homicide-suicides between Romanian emigrants, femicide-suicides and homicide-suicides committed by police officers. I also tried to draw attention to the lack of involvement of Romanian journalists when writing some articles meant to: 1) inform the audience about the non-violent ways of solving some problems or interpersonal conflicts that they could face in their life, 2) inform the audience about the risk factors that can lead to the transformation of some conflictual situations into lethal violence and 3) inform the potential victims about institutions of support.

The general aim of the first chapter, *Homicide-suicides in Romania: incidence, risk factors and particularities* is to describe and explain the incidence, patterns, types and mechanisms of homicide-suicide and formulate preventive measures specific to Romania. In this chapter I present the risk factors – at individual (sex, age, level of education, marriage/cohabiting, health, suicide attempts), micro-social (conflicting intra-familial relationships, dysfunctional families following the departure of some members abroad; group of friends), community (level of development, level of unemployment, level of migration of the population abroad), societal (recent global economic crisis, policies regarding the firearms regime, legislation on domestic violence control and prevention) and situational level in Romania.

In the second chapter, *Intimate partner femicide versus intimate partner femicide-suicide in Romania* I describe the particularities of the intimate partner homicide-suicide in comparison with intimate homicide cases after two samples of subjects were analyzed: 40 men who committed homicide against their intimate partner and 40 men who committed intimate partner homicide-suicides. The methodology included interviews with 40 men who murdered their partners (interviews taken in six penitentiaries in Romania), an analysis of penal files, interviews with the staff of penitentiaries (psychologists, sociologists, social assistants) and also an analysis of data from from the Homicide-Suicides in Romania database (from which I took data regarding intimate partner homicide-suicide cases).

When the issue of gender violence is analyzed in the academic field, the discussion is, in general, centered on physical, psychological, sexual, economic and social violence, and on the consequences of those acts. Many researchers stressed that intimate partner homicide is the end of a long period of violence against the victims (Stöckl et al. 2013, Mucchielli 2012, Pritchard 2012, Adinkrah 2008, Adams 2007, Menzies 2005, Gauthier and Bankston 2004, Alvarez and Bachman 2003, Mercy and Salzman 1989, Daly and Wilson 1988). At the same time, there are few studies (especially in the European space) about the violence which ends with the death of the woman-victim (who is in an intimate relationship with her aggressor) and the death of her aggressor. The experts named this act of violence as "intimate partner homicide-suicide" or "intimate femicide-suicide" (Russell and Harmes 2001). Intimate femicide-suicide represents, as such, an act of violence which implies the killing of an intimate partner with intention (who can be wife, former wife, lover, former lover, concubine or former concubine) and, after that, the suicide of the aggressor (who is also the intimate partner of the victim).

There is not much research about intimate partner homicide-suicide violence or intimate femicide-suicide violence in Europe. Information regarding this type of violence is frequently presented within the broader context of homicide-suicide acts (Pereira et al. 2010, Weizmann et al. 2012, da Ponte Martins Graça de Matos 2013).

The third chapter of the book is centered on the intimate femicide-suicide acts recorded in Romania between 2002 and 2013. Information, regarding acts of violence between intimate partners, will be analyzed in such a way that the peculiarities of acts of violence committed in Romania, as compared with Western, Northern and Central Europe will be stressed and discussed. The comparative analysis of the data, regarding intimate partner homicide-suicide, is made, on one hand, on the basis of the set of data collected in Homicide-suicide in Romania: 2002–2013 database. On the other hand, the analysis is based on the data from existing literature in the field (scientific articles, research reports, books) in the case of other European countries.

I included in this chapter information about the evolution of the intimate femicide-suicide rate in Romania and the specific factors which influence intimate femicide-suicides in Romania. For example, Romania is a former socialist country with a political and social regime which changed from dictatorship to democracy. In our country someone could record the lack of efficient public policies regarding the prevention of violence between partners. The economic level is low and the level of Romanian migration towards the European and non-European spaces is high. At the same time, I presented the factors at the micro and individual level, and the information about the ways in which the violent acts were committed. I compared the information about the relation between the victim and the aggressor, the history of the intimate relationship, the length of the intimate relationship, the motives of violent acts and weapons used as those elements were recorded in Romanian cases and their occurrences in other countries. Where I thought it was necessary I included case studies to emphasize factors that determined the committing of violent acts.

Filicide-suicides and familicide-suicides were the themes of the fourth chapter where I will present information regarding two other types of homicide-suicide in the family space: filicide-suicide (maternal and paternal) and familicide-suicide. These two types of homicide-suicide are rare but, through their consequences, they affect the life of the families where they were committed for a long period. Particularities of cases will be presented and some case studies will be brought to discussion. Information regarding victims and aggressors, weapons used, risk factors and motivations of the violent acts will be also presented.

As previously mentioned, the second part of the book contains information regarding the way in which Romanian journalists presented the homicide-suicide cases in online articles. In the chapter *Femicide-suicides in the Romanian online media* I analyze the way in which the Romanian online media covered femicide-suicides in articles published in 2010–2015. The sample of articles was built up in an iterative way. First, the femicide-suicide cases were identified on Google.com using keywords. After that, articles published by aggregation sites (Hotnews.com, Ziare.com), news agencies, online national and regional newspapers (e.g. adevarul.ro, romanialibera.ro, ebihoreanul.ro) were selected. The units of analysis which were analyzed referred to the murder, suicide, victim and aggressor. A specific set of sub-themes were added to the aforementioned main themes: period of time in which the case was covered by media, the online newspapers and the presence or absence of photos. The results of the analysis made at the level of selected articles showed that the online media pay great attention to the femicide-suicide cases which appear among Romanian emigrants. The main actors of these cases are local leaders or personalities and their deeds are motivated by inter-ethnical conflicts (conflicts between the Romanian and Roma families). Previous studies made at the level of some small sample of cases drew the attention to the Romanian journalists' preferences for certain types of victims and aggressors (Balica 2016a, Balica 2016b), and the study published in this book addresses new arguments.

The sixth chapter discusses the way in which cases of homicide-suicide committed between Romanian emigrants were made known to the public. I gave the title of this chapter, *Facebook kills! A case study of intimate partner femicide-suicide between Romanian emigrants*, because of a case that succeeded in drawing the attention of specialists from Romania. What we all noticed was the way in which the aggressor killed his wife and the motivation of the violent act. At the same time the case drew attention to the message written with a red pen on the victim's chest: Facebook kills! Based on this case of homicide-suicide committed between Romanian emigrants, I decided to identify all the cases committed between emigrants and to also identify the way in which the Romanian press dealt with these cases.

The analysis of data regarding the cases of homicide-suicide in Romania showed that a significant percentage of persons who committed homicide-suicide were policemen, military personnel, security agents. These cases were extensively covered by mass media and journalists using various sources for presenting the cases with detailed information (even with photos) about the aggressors, victims and acts of violence. Almost all cases had as a purpose the homicide of the life partner, but there were also some whose victims were senior military personnel or other persons from the aggressor's proximity. Due to the fact that in the scientific literature there are few studies regarding violence committed by policemen, I decided to include the results of the analysis of information regarding homicide-suicide within families where one of the members worked for the police.

The last chapter of the book analyses the articles which covered the cases in which the suicidal-offenders were policemen or worked in the army. In the first part of the chapter I will present information regarding particularities, risk factors, motivations and characteristics of victims and aggressors. In the second part I will discuss how the online press takes over information about these cases and presents it in articles. When writing this chapter I used some statistical data regarding homicide-suicides which I obtained from the General Inspectorate of The Romanian Police, the parquet near the High Court of Cassation and Justice, the General Directorate of Bucharest Police (Homicide Unit) and the parquets near Court Houses from 25 counties in Romania. In order to write this book I also got important information from Mărgineni Penitentiary, Rahova Penitentiary of Maximum Security, Jilava Hospital Penitentiary, Galați Penitentiary, Ploiești Penitentiary and Jilava Penitentiary. Where necessary, I used statistical data published in the annual reports from The Romanian National Institute of Statistics, from the Mina Minovici National Institute of Forensic Medicine or from the parquet near the High Court of Cassation and Justice from Romania. I interviewed aggressors and analyzed the penal files of the people who committed homicide against their intimate partners.

The conclusions written in the seven chapters represent, in fact, some proposals for preventing homicide-suicides taking into consideration the socio-economic conditions in Romania. Some of the proposals are general and can be included in programs of preventing homicides in general. Most of the proposals are, though, specific to every type of homicide-suicide. I can say that even if all homicide-suicides have some common elements, there are also particularities specific only to some types of homicide-suicide. These particularities are connected to the ways of committing homicide, the aggressors' profile, the relationship between aggressors and victims and the risk factors identified for every type of homicide-suicide.

This book offers information found in empirical research made for a subject that is little covered in Europe and not at all tackled in Eastern Europe. This is the reason why I hope it will manage to bring necessary information for understanding the factors that determine the committing of homicide-suicides in the European space. It will also emphasize elements that are specific to homicide-suicides from the South-East of Europe. The book is aimed at both researchers from the criminology, sociology, psychology, forensic medicine and criminalistic domains, trainers from the judicial domain (criminalist experts, detectives, prosecutors, judges, forensic doctors), and professionals from media and communications (TV journalists, online and written press).

Acknowledgments

First of all I want to thank the Romanian Ministry of Education, CNCS – UEFISCDI for the financial support given to the author for the project PNI-II-RU-PD-2012-3-0414 Homicide – Suicide in Romania: Incidence, Patterns and Risk Factors. Without this financial support I could not have conducted the research regarding homicide-suicides in Romania. Moreover, the results could not have been disseminated at the level of the international academic community through a book that is published through an internationally regarded publishing house.

During my research regarding homicide-suicides, I was helped and supported by some professional people from various fields. They helped me overcome most difficulties that I encountered in different phases of the project. Some of these professional people were constant collaborators with my past research projects. Others were people I met for the first time while investigating homicide-suicides. Among the specialists who constantly supported me to make my documentation in good terms and conditions were three police officers with experience in the domain of investigations regarding homicides. These professionals helped me identify the concrete ways of writing the Homicide-suicides in Romania (2002–2013) database and they made time to answer all my questions when we talked about the particularities of homicide-suicides. I am talking about chief commissioner Radu Gavriş, Head of Bucharest Homicide Unit, Chief Commissioner Iulian Bocu, Head of Bucharest Homicide Unit, and Chief Commissioner Florin Bălăceanu from the Directorate of Criminal Investigation (the General Inspectorate of Romanian Police). I thank them and all police officers who helped me extract from their files the data regarding homicide-suicides in every county of Romania. I am grateful for the special way in which they supported the making of a research project focused on a type of homicide that is so difficult to cover.

An important phase of my research was in the penitentiary system from Romania. The interviews with perpetrators who committed intimate partner homicide and the analysis of their penal files contributed to identifying some risk factors specific to intimate partner homicides. These activities were supported by many specialists who work in the penitentiary system in Romania. I thank the National Administration of Penitentiaries from Romania and the management of Mărgineni Penitentiary of Maximum Security, Rahova Penitentiary of Maximum Security, Ploiesti Penitentiary, Jilava Hospital Penitentiary, Galaţi Penitentiary and Jilava Bucharest Penitentiary for providing the best conditions for my investigations and activity in these units. I am giving my special thanks to Mrs. Cristina Pripp, a psychologist who advised me during my investigations. She also helped me go over all the steps of legal and ethical procedures and make the documents necessary for respecting the rules that govern all investigations made with prisoners. I also thank Mrs. Cristina Pripp for the support given in identifying the penitentiaries which had, in their custody, people convicted for committing homicide against their intimate partners.

I am very grateful to all the staff from the six penitentiaries that contributed to the achievement of my research. I thank all specialists from the Services of Intervention and Psycho-Social Assistance, the people from Services of Prison Security and Penitentiary Regime who helped me conduct my interviews safely and in a proper atmosphere for my research objectives. My research in penitentiaries involved also the study of penal files for the people who agreed to take part to interviews. The staff from the Services of Personal Records had an important role in these activities. First of all, I filled in the documents necessary to access the data from the penal files and I had the prisoners' approval to consult the files. Then, the staff from the Services of Personal Records helped me identify the important elements from the penal files (sometimes from hundreds of pages and tens of documents found in an order that was difficult to comprehend). They also helped me understand the logic of the documents from the penal files. I thank all of them for their patience and for all the explanations that they gave me every time I needed.

An important role in making my investigations in penitentiaries was played by chief commissioner Camelia Steliana Herea, deputy director of the Intervention and Psycho-Social Assistance Department from Mărgineni Penitentiary. She helped me find the best way to conduct interviews with perpetrators who committed homicide against their wives. I thank Mrs. Herea for the professionalism and generosity that she offered me during my work in Mărgineni Penitentiary. Working as a psychologist, Mrs. Herea shared her experience of interviews with people who committed homicide against their wives and she suggested having the interviews before checking the data regarding the way in which they committed the homicides. This strategy allowed me to conduct the interviews without having a preconception about the person to whom I was talking and I was accepted more easily by my interlocutors. This experience of my cooperation with Mrs. Camelia Herea was completed also by the collaboration with other specialists from the penitentiaries where I made the interviews.

The research work in Rahova Penitentiary of Maximum Security and in Jilava Bucharest Hospital Penitentiary gave me the opportunity to meet two other experienced psychologists, Chief Commissioner Nicoleta Doser and Chief

Commissioner Daniela Nagy. I give all my special thanks to these two ladies who shared their experience with me and supported me during my research.

The parquet near the High Court of Cassation and Justice and 25 other parquets in Romania contributed to the achievement of the Homicide-suicides in Romania database. They gave me statistical data regarding the homicide-suicide cases committed in the competency area of parquets from Romania. This is how I validated the information regarding homicide-suicides and the confidence level of data registered in the database grew. I thank all the prosecutors, court clerks who were directly involved in the identification of files of homicide-suicide cases.

My special thanks also go to the specialists who helped me finish this book. I want to also thank Professor Valentina Marinescu for the advice given to me during my research regarding homicide-suicides and during the writing of this book. I thank Mihaela Onică who had the patience to translate this book into English and who accepted working at a fast pace and thus constrained to give up much of her family time.

I also have much gratitude for Doctor Andrew Fox from the University of Huddersfield (United Kingdom) who was patient enough to read and make all the observations and modifications needed for increasing the quality of the text written in English. I thank him for all his suggestions and for all the work he did during the writing of every chapter of this book.

Last, but not least, I want to thank the excellent editorial staff from Peter Lang Publishing House, especially Ute Winkelkötter from the GmbH Hamburg office who supported me during the editing process and helped me choose the best variant for publishing this book.

List of Tables and Figures

Part I Homicide-Suicides in an Eastern European Country: Romania

1. Homicide-Suicides in Romania: Incidence, Risk Factors and Particularities

Situated in the South-East of Europe, Romania is a country which for the last 25 years has faced a transition period from the communist regime (that ended with the Revolution in December, 1989) towards a democratic society. The transition from dictatorship to democracy was still marked by social, economic and political events which were sometimes associated with an increase in interpersonal acts of violence. In order to better understand the context of the cases of homicide-suicide in Romania, I consider it necessary to have a description of the evolution of criminality in Romania in the last 25 years and especially of the criminality for the period 2002–2013 from which I identified the cases of homicide-suicide. I will present some information regarding the criminality rate, the murder rate and the suicide rate in Romania. The murder rate was calculated as being the number of murder felonies registered in the statistics of the General Inspectorate of Romanian Police for 100,000 inhabitants. The information regarding the population from Romania was the one published by the National Institute of Statistics in the Tempo online database and in the Statistic Annuary of Romania. In Romania, only felonies committed on purpose were included in the murder felonies. We excluded: manslaughter, attempted murder, battery causing death and robbery ending with the death of the victim, all these felonies being included in the categories corresponding to the statistics of the Romanian police.

Homicides and Suicides in Romania

The analysis made from the data regarding criminality and included in the official reports of the General Inspectorate of Police, the Public Ministry or Ministry of Justice, showed an increase of the criminality rate starting in 1990 (414 crimes per 100,000 inhabitants) until 1998 (1765 crimes per 100,000 inhabitants) (Balica 2008: 174, Balica and Descarpes 2011). After 1998, the tendency of the criminality rate in Romania decreased until 2005 (961 crimes per 100,000 inhabitants) (Balica and Descarpes 2011). If we analyze the period 2002–2013 separately, we can notice a decrease in the criminality rate in the period 2002–2005 (from 1390 crimes per 100,000 to 961 crimes per 100,000 inhabitants). The year 2006 was the year when the criminality rate started increasing again, the tendency of increase in criminality was maintained until the end of the analyzed period of time (2013 – 1,462 crimes per 100,000 inhabitants) and even until now (2014 – 1,799 crimes per 100,000 inhabitants) (according to the statistical data of the General Inspectorate of Romanian Police 2006–2014).

In this context, the murder rate increased only in the first years after the revolution, when the murder rate grew from 3.4 murders per 100,000 inhabitants (1990) to 3.6 murders per 100,000 inhabitants (1993) (Balica 2008). After 1994, the murder rate decreased. This decreasing tendency of the murder rate was maintained for the period 2002–2013. Between 2002 and 2013, the average murder rate was 2.02 murders per 100,000 inhabitants. The murder rate was, in the first part of the period 2002–2005, higher than the average of the analyzed period (2.5 – 2.1 murder rate per 100,000 inhabitants). After 2006 and until 2013, the values of the murder rate were under the average of the period (the murder rate varied from 2 to 1.6 per 100,000 inhabitants). The year 2008 was an exception and the murder rate in that year was 2.2 per 100,000 inhabitants. All these rates were calculated starting from the statistical data regarding murder offered by the General Inspectorate of Romanian Police and the data regarding the population of Romania from the National Institute of Statistics.

The analysis of data regarding suicides committed in Romania can be made only for the period 1996–2013. This time, for the calculation of the suicide rate I used data regarding suicides registered in the annual reports of activity of the National Institute of Forensic Medicine Mina Minovici. The suicide rate had an increasing tendency between 1996 and 2000 from 13 suicides per 100,000 inhabitants in 1996 to 17.7 suicides per 100,000 inhabitants in 2000. We registered high values for the suicide rate in 2002 and 2003 (16 suicides per 100,000 inhabitants). The period 2004–2013 was marked by a decreasing tendency of the suicide rate, the average rate for this period being 13.2 suicides per 100,000 inhabitants. We also registered values that were higher than the average in 2005 (13.4), 2006 (14.7), 2009 (13.7) and 2010 (14.2).

Homicide-Suicides in Romania

The international studies regarding homicide-suicides showed that this type of violence is rare, but the impact on the community is much bigger than an act of murder or of suicide. Until now, studies regarding homicide-suicides have been made in the USA (Adler 1999, Bridges et al. 2011), Australia (Easteal 1994, Milroy et al. 1995), Hong Kong (Chan 2007), and Ghana (Adinkrah 2014) and in some European countries. For the European space, studies were made in countries from the West, Center and North of Europe as well as for countries from the South-East of Europe. The studies made in West, Center and North were rigorous and could promote information regarding the rates of homicide-suicides. Moreover, the researchers from the Netherlands, England and Wales, Finland, Germany, Switzerland, Poland and Spain managed to create a common database regarding homicide-suicides, the European Homicide-suicide Study (EHSS), and to make some comparative analysis for some indicators (Liem and Oberwittler 2012). The studies from the South-East of Europe (Greece, Turkey and Croatia) were quite rare and few of them could promote information regarding the homicide-suicide rate. Only one study from Greece estimated the homicide-suicide rate for the period 1998–2005 as being 0.07 per 100,000 inhabitants (Vougiouklakis and Tsiligianni 2006), while studies from Turkey and Croatia were limited only to describing some cases from the forensic perspective. A study in Konya province in Turkey identified ten homicide-suicides with 12 victims between 2000 and 2007 (Dogan et al. 2010), while a study in south-western Croatia identified 17 homicide-suicides with 19 victims in the period 1986–2009 (Cengija et al. 2012).

The rates of homicide-suicides varied in the European countries between 0.05 – 0.22 per 100,000 inhabitants, with high rates of homicide-suicide being registered in Denmark between 1959 and 1960, 0.22 per 100,000 inhabitants (West 1965) and Finland between 1987 and 1988, 0.20 per 100,000 inhabitants (Saleva et al. 2007).

Smaller values for homicide-suicide rates were registered in Spain (2002–2004 – 0.038 annual mean homicide-suicides) and Poland (1999–2006 – annual mean 0.444) (Liem and Oberwittler, 2012). In the context in which the values of murder rates from Romania were similar to murder rates registered in some European countries for which the homicide-suicide rates were also calculated, I could not help wondering whether there are similarities between the homicide-suicide rates. For example, Poland and Romania were situated by some authors in the group of Central and Eastern European countries and they had in the period 2006–2008 similar intentional completed homicide rates (Romania average rate 2.03 and Poland average rate 1.67) (Marshall and Summers 2012: 49–50). Moreover, among the 15 countries included by Marshall and Summers in the cluster of Central and Eastern European countries, only Poland had homicide-suicide rates calculated until making the present study. This was also one of the reasons why I tried to make a comparison between the two countries: the fact that they are both from the same group of countries and the similarities between the murder rates and the existence of data regarding the homicide-suicide rates. Beyond these reasons, I was interested to see if, through the homicide-suicide rates, Romania is getting closer to the group of Central and Eastern European countries or to the groups of the Western, Northern countries or to the groups of countries from the Baltic or Mediterranean area for which there are data regarding homicide-suicides.

Before presenting the results of the research made in Romania, I will describe the methodology for making the Homicide-Suicides in Romania (2002–2013) database. I will emphasize the sources of the data included in the database and the difficulties and limits of a research regarding homicide-suicides in Romania.

Research Methods and Data Sources

The present paper is the result of the analysis of data regarding the cases of homicide-suicide committed among Romanians in the period 2002–2013. The information regarding the cases of homicide-suicide committed in Romania was extracted from the *Homicide-Suicides in Romania* database made in a post-PhD project of the author supported by a grant of the Romanian Ministry of Education, CNCS – UEFISCDI, project PNI-II-RU-PD-2012-3-0414 Homicide-Suicide in Romania: Incidence, Patterns and Risk Factors.

In Romania, there has not been, until the aforementioned project, any database that contains information regarding this type of violence. The Homicide-Suicides in Romania database is the first electronic format database which includes all cases of homicide-suicide identified in Romania between 2002 and 2013. In order to make the database I used three data sources: data registered by police, data from the penal files of parquets and data regarding the cases of homicide-suicide identified in the online media from Romania. In order to have a proper image of the analyzed data I will shortly present the way in which information regarding homicide-suicides was picked from the three sources, and the way in which the Homicide-Suicides in Romania (2002–2013) database was made and finished in September 2015.

The Homicide-Suicides in Romania (2002–2013) Database

The operational definition used in order to include a case of homicide-suicide in the database was: homicide-suicides represent the murder acts committed on purpose followed by the aggressor's suicide in a period of time which did not exceed one week (Liem et al. 2009).

In the case where there were more victims from the extended family, I registered the case as being familicide-suicide. When there were more victims and one of them did not have any family relation with the aggressor, the registration of the homicide-suicide case was made according to the relationship between the aggressor and the victim who was the closest to the aggressor (for example, when the aggressor murdered two people – the wife and the wife's lady friend – homicide-suicide was registered as being intimate partner homicide-suicide).

Sources of information regarding the cases of homicide-suicide

Police

My intention to make a database regarding the cases of homicide-suicide proved hard to implement for Romania. Even from the beginning, I faced a series of difficulties. The first of which was the lack of a database regarding murder/suicide from which I could have extracted only data regarding homicide-suicides. Moreover, I had to deal with the lack of some statistical indicators included in the police and parquet statistics and with the lack of some digital archives of newspapers for the analyzed period. In these conditions I tried every time to identify alternatives which could allow me make an analysis of information regarding the cases of homicide-suicide in Romania.

The first difficulty identified in my work of identifying the cases of homicide-suicide was the one generated by a lack of a database regarding murders in Romania, as some European countries have (e.g. the Netherlands, Finland and Sweden have the database included in the European Homicide Monitor – Liem et al. 2013) or the USA.

Secondly, the databases regarding criminality in Romania (found at the General Inspectorate of Romanian Police and the parquet near the High Court of Cassation and Justice) did not contain clear information regarding homicide-suicides. The lack of homicide-suicides from these databases was explained by the fact that statistics include information regarding felonies as they are formulated in the articles from the Romanian Penal Code. For example, in the Romanian Penal Code, more felonies are mentioned for murder according to the relationship between victim and perpetrator or to the way of committing the deed (intentionally or unintentionally, attempted murder, battery causing death) or according to the association with other felonies (rape with the death of the victim or robbery with the death of the victim), but for homicide-suicides there is no article in the Penal Code.

In the case of homicide-suicides, policemen and prosecutors investigate the case as being a murder act with two or more victims. All investigations are made according to the necessary procedures in the case of murder foreseen in the Romanian Penal Code: article 174 – murder, article 175 – qualified murder (against the wife or a close relative), and article 176 – degree murder. If the penal investigation proves that one of the persons found at the crime scene was the aggressor and the other(s) the victim, prosecutors decide not to start the penal tracking based on article 10, paragraph G from the Code of Penal Procedure (until February 1, 2013) or article 16, paragraph F from the New Code of Penal Procedure (after February 1, 2013). These cases of homicide-suicide for which they decide not to start the penal tracking are registered in the statistics of police and parquets in a category, where they also include other situations specified by the two above mentioned articles.

More precisely, article 10, paragraph G from the Code of Penal Procedure includes in the same category: the cases for which "amnesty, prescription or death of the offender occurred or, depending on the case, the cancellation of the legal entity when this is the offender" (the Old Code of Penal Procedure, April 30, 1997 – February 1, 2013) or the cases for which "amnesty, prescription or death of the suspect or of the offender as a physical person occurred or the radiation of the suspect or of the offender as a legal entity was demanded." (The New Code of Penal Procedure, February 1, 2013)

In these conditions, the practical solution to make a database was to try to identify the first official source where information regarding homicide-suicides was included. I found out that the officers from Homicide Division and Criminal Investigations include information regarding homicide-suicides in the registers of their units. Consequently, these units had the possibility to transmit some information regarding the homicide-suicide cases which could have helped in identifying other sources (e.g. the penal files from the custody of parquets in Romania).

In order to have a proper picture of the way in which the data was managed and in order to identify concrete ways regarding the identification of data about homicide-suicides, I made a pilot study for Bucharest. I chose this city for some methodological reasons: Bucharest is the capital of Romania, it has the highest number of inhabitants (2,148,098 persons in January 1, 2013) (National Institute of Statistics 2015), there is the only Homicide Unit in Romania working with officers who only instrument murder cases and it was the city where the author could conduct research without being constrained by time or by economical resources (she was working and living in this city).

With the support of police officers from the Homicide Unit in Bucharest, I identified all the homicide-suicide cases registered between 2002 and 2013 in Bucharest (N=21 cases, attempts included). Discussing with the police officers, I found out what types of information could be extracted from the police units which investigate the homicide-suicide cases. A grid of indicators was made to send to all Services of Criminal Investigations in Romania (these units investigate the murder cases in all the counties in Romania). The grid of indicators was made according both to the indicators that I wanted to have in the database and to the limitations generated by the way in which the registers were made in the Services of Criminal Investigations, clarified by discussions with police officers. Finally, the grid contained the following indicators: identification data regarding the case file (number of registration at the police unit and number of registration at the county parquet), date and hour of committing the murder, place of committing the murder, data about the victim (name, occupation and age), data about the perpetrator (name, occupation and age), the relationship between the victim and the aggressor, the type of homicide-suicide (homicide-suicide, attempted homicide-suicide, homicide–attempted suicide), weapons used for murder and suicide and motive of homicide-suicides.

After the grid was validated in the pilot study in Bucharest, it was transmitted to the General Inspectorate of Romanian Police and the Directorate of Criminal Investigations, which coordinates all Services of Criminal Investigations for Romania (the officers from this service deal with all penal felonies, homicide-suicides cases included) kindly requesting transmission to the researcher of the information regarding homicide-suicides registered in the counties from Romania and contained in the grid. The researcher promised to ensure the confidentiality of information regarding the victim and the aggressor, according to national regulations and professional deontology. After a period of time necessary for picking up information regarding homicide-suicides from the registers of police units, the Directorate of Criminal Investigations transmitted the data from the country to the researcher. The data transmitted by the services from the country allowed me to identify N=132 homicide-suicide cases for which the police data mentioned that murders were committed and followed by the aggressor's suicide (not including the period of time from murder to suicide). The police units gave information about homicide-suicides committed between 2005 and 2013. Only Bucharest Homicide Division and several units of police could give information about homicide-suicides committed between 2002 and 2013.

For the 132 homicide-suicides identified in the registers of the Services of Criminal Investigations, the registration data of files from the parquets in the country was also mentioned. This information allowed the passage to the next step, the formulation of a solicitation to the parquets in the country for transmitting some information regarding homicide-suicides from the files in their custody.

Parquets

In the first phase of my research, in order to identify the institutions which could offer data regarding homicide-suicides in Romania, I sent a solicitation to the parquet near the High Court of Cassation and Justice to ask for data about homicide-suicides. This institution provided us only the number of the closed files according to article 10, letter G from the Code of Penal Procedure which also included the number of homicide-suicides next to other types of files (see section

Police above). It was suggested contacting every parquet from Romania which had the penal files of the homicide-suicide closed cases according to article 10, letter G. This was also the reason why I asked the services of Criminal Investigations to give us the number of the penal file as it was registered at the police unit and at the territorial parquet (the two numbers are different).

Moreover, the pilot study helped me identify the documents included in the penal files which contain most of the information about the homicide-suicide cases. Based on these findings, I formulated a request for the parquets in Romania to give us copies of some documents from the homicide-suicides files, documents which helped me complete the information for the database.

The homicide-suicide cases identified at the Homicide Division from Bucharest could be analyzed in a special way as I had access to all documents from 16 penal files (from the total of 21) archived by the Bucharest Parquet. Several files (5 files) could not be consulted as they were damaged by the floods that affected the archive. The 16 files were consulted and the necessary information was selected and included in the database. The possibility to consult the files entirely allowed me to become more familiar with the way in which the cases were instrumented by all institutions and also gave me information about the history of the relationship between victims and aggressor as a consequence of the way in which the prosecutors' investigations were structured. The experience of consulting the homicide-suicide files from the Bucharest Parquet allowed the proper structuring of the collaboration with the other parquets which asked for additional information regarding the way in which I wanted to receive the information about the homicide-suicide cases.

After finishing the pilot study in Bucharest, I expanded the research at the level of parquets from the entire country. In Romania, the parquets function near law courts, courthouses and appeal courts. Given the specific hierarchy of the justice system in Romania, I decided to contact all the parquets subordinate to courthouses (42 courthouses in Romania). The name of the felony, the name of the victim and the registration number of the penal file were the elements that were included in the official address towards the parquets near the courthouses (N=42 parquets). Each of these parquets received the list with the name and registration number of the files identified by the police in the county where every parquet was functioning. I also asked the parquets to send a copy of the file which had information regarding the victim and the aggressor, the crime and the solution given in the file of each and every case. The prosecutors sent copies of the existing documents in 110 homicide-suicides cases, copies of resolutions of not starting the penal tracking, ordonnances of declining the competence and indictments (for homicide-suicide attempts). One parquet only sent a synthesis of the documents found in the homicide-suicide files, a synthesis which briefly contained the information solicited and discussed with the prosecutor delegated to collaborate with the researcher. In general, all the documents sent by the parquets contained detailed information about: how the case was identified (a call to 112 was made, the police were called by the relatives, neighbors or witnesses), information from the reports of policemen who arrived at the crime scene, information from the reports of coroners (coroners who made the first examinations and the ones who made the autopsies), information from witnesses and the results of the investigations of police and prosecutors. All the information was analyzed, part of it being registered in the chart of the homicide-suicide case (see The Registration Paper of Homicide-Suicide case). Based on the information received from parquets, I checked whether the homicide-suicide cases corresponded to the definition used for homicide-suicides or if they were out of the ordinary. At the same time, I also identified attempted homicide-suicides or homicide-attempted suicides. All the information received from parquets was conflated with the data received from the police. Where there were differences (age, occupation or type of homicide-suicides) between the two institutions, I decided that the information from parquets to be introduced in the database was correct. The documents from the parquets contained information received from more institutions and information resulted from the investigation made in a period of time longer than the police reports. It is true that these reports were closer to the crime moment, but they were made only based on information picked from the crime place and from the witnesses' hearings.

Internet – online media, social media, YouTube and blogs

Studies about homicide-suicides made at the international level also used newspapers as a main source of information. Most of the researchers had access to the electronic archives of newspapers from where they extracted information regarding the covered cases of homicide-suicides (Liem and Koenraadt 2007, Shon and Roberts 2010) while in other countries, some content analyses of the press were made manually with the help of several students (Roma et al. 2012, Adinkrah 2014). In some countries, special programs of qualitative data analysis such as NVivo were used (Harper and Voight, 2007), which made the researchers' work much easier. My attempt to use newspapers as a source for the database regarding homicide-suicides in Romania encountered some obstacles. The first difficulty identified for the research in Romania was the fact that the newspapers did not have archives in an electronic format and we needed a lot of time and a lot of human resources in order to consult the printed archives. The research regarding homicide-suicides in Romania was a post-doctoral project, therefore it had to be limited to the activities run by only one researcher who did not have a research team that could have helped analyze the written press. On the other side, for the analyzed period of time (2002–2013) some newspapers had digital archives and others did not. At the same time, the newspapers that had archives did not have archives for the entire period of time selected by me. Consequently, the analyzed corpus was on the edge of being limited only to the periods of time for which I had the archives and it might not have offered information about many cases of homicide-suicide.

In these conditions, I decided to use the Google search method and keywords to identify all the media articles published in the online environment about the cases of homicide-suicide committed in Romania. The Google search method was used for more studies, most of them using the Google search in order to identify media articles (articles, web-sites etc.) in English (Asal and Harword 2008, Westerlund et al. 2012, McClure 2014). In the present research I used the Google Chrome.ro engine also in Romanian in order to identify the media articles about the cases of homicide-suicide. When I talk about a media article I am referring to any kind of media product posted in the online environment in Romanian: online press articles, news, reportages, materials posted on YouTube, posts on personal blogs or blogs of personalities/journalists, posts on socializing networks (Facebook, Twitter) and articles posted on television websites.

In the first phase I used keywords which referred to the violent act in general: "he killed and then killed himself". This was the phrase in the Romanian language which could be used as an equivalent for the homicide-suicide term. At the beginning of the research (2013), the term homicide-suicide (in Romanian "omor-sinucidere") did not exist in the Romanian language and it was not included in the language of Romanian specialists until the completion of this book (January 2016).

The next keywords used in order to identify the cases of homicide-suicide were "he killed his wife/girlfriend and then killed himself", "he killed his child and then killed himself" and "he killed his mother/father and then killed himself". In order to validate the results further, I decided to attach to the above mentioned expressions the year when the act of violence was committed (2002–2013). The searches were even more precisely formulated after I obtained information about the cases of homicide-suicide. For every case identified in the media, I searched all the media articles published in the online environment at the moment of the searches. In order to identify as many articles as possible, I extracted from the already identified articles keywords which referred to the case: name of the aggressor/victim, city (village) where the homicide-suicide was committed, modus operandi (name of the aggressor associated with the weapon), and the occupation of the perpetrator (for example the cases committed by policemen were easy to find with the help of keywords "the policeman killed and then killed himself"). All these elements were used in the initial phase of the research (2013) before having information about the cases of homicide-suicide received from the police units and parquets. As information about homicide-suicides came from these institutions (2014), the searches from the online environment were adapted to the new information. Information regarding the cases identified by police was introduced and reintroduced in the searches and new media articles were found about these cases.

My interest in identifying all the media articles published in the online environment about the cases of homicide-suicide was motivated by the desire to 1) have a database with precise information about homicide-suicides from more sources (official and unofficial); and 2) make an analysis of the way in which journalists from the online media tackle this subject.

The Google search method made possible the identification of some information which was not found in the documents received from parquets or in the documentation to which I had access with the help of police. Journalists brought attention to information regarding the victim and the aggressor that I did not have access to from the other two sources. I found in the media articles and information about the history of the relationship, about the victim and the aggressor, information about the aggressor's threats towards the people from his group of friends, about the occupational status or about the pendulation periods between the two countries (Romania and the emigration country) searching for a job.

Moreover, I identified media articles which made the initial investigations wider. The modification of the research directions was generated by the identification of some cases of homicide-suicide committed by Romanian citizens working abroad (in the European space, Canada and the USA). The online newspapers from Romania also brought to the public's attention the cases of homicide-suicide which occurred in other countries. The cases of Romanians who killed their wives/current girlfriends or former partners were tackled quite well, the Romanian journalists being interested in covering information about Romanian emigrants. The number of cases of homicide-suicide committed abroad was substantial and this is why I considered it necessary to also include this aspect in the analysis of homicide-suicide cases in Romania. This is why the searches from the online environment were made with the help of some keywords regarding the countries to which Romanians had emigrated. More exactly, I used keywords such as "a Romanian man from Italy killed his wife and then killed himself", and after that I changed the name of the country. The information about the homicide-suicide cases between the Romanian emigrants was also searched in other languages (English, French, and Italian) in order to have a complete overview of the cases. All the information extracted from the media articles was completed and checked with the help of information from police and parquets whenever that was possible. The results of the case analysis in which Romanian emigrants were involved, had already been brought to the attention of the academic environment by an article published in the European Journal of Criminology (Balica and Stöckl 2016).

Homicide-suicides in Romania database

After all the data from the three sources were gathered, 177 cases of homicide-suicide were included in the database. As in the international studies in the homicide-suicide sphere only included the acts of murder followed by the aggressor's suicide in a period of time that was not longer than a week (Liem et al. 2009), I decided to exclude from the database those cases of suicide that occurred in a period of time longer than a week (5 cases) and the cases that were registered for the year 2014 (3 cases). The cases of attempted homicide-suicide (7 cases) were excluded and also the cases of homicide-attempted suicide (18) and attempted homicide-attempted suicide (12 cases). In the end, 132 cases of homicide-suicide that met all the criteria of selection used also in other studies regarding homicide-suicides, remained. The present book presents the results of the analysis made at the level of these 132 homicide-suicides cases. Due to the fact that up to now, few studies were made regarding the cases of attempted homicide-suicides (N=37), I decided to also analyze the information regarding these acts of violence in a separate section at the end of this chapter.

Sources of Homicide-suicide cases included in the database

As I have said before, the final number of homicide-suicides identified with the help of the three sources used over the research was N=132. Most of the cases included in the database had at least one official source (77.3 per cent) and only one quarter of these had only media articles as a source (22.7 per cent) (see Table 1.1). The cases identified only in the media articles were included in the database because an analysis of primary definers for these cases showed that journalists used official sources of information (see Chapters 5, 6, and 7).

Table 1.1 Sources of information used for the Homicide-suicides in Romania database

Sources of information used for the cases of homicide-suicide	Frequency	Percentage
Online articles, police and parquet	38	28.8
Online media	30	22.7
Police	12	9.1
Parquet	1	0.8
Police and Parquet	44	33.3
Online media and police	7	5.3
Total	132	100

Dimensions and indicators included in the database

The Registration Paper of Homicide-Suicide cases

The Registration Paper of Homicide-Suicide cases was structured using six key elements: 1) Data regarding homicide; 2) Data regarding suicide; 3) Data regarding the perpetrator of the act of violence; 4) Data regarding the victims (direct victims, indirect victims and survivors); 5) Data regarding institutions involved in solving the case and 6) Data regarding case coverage.

1. In the Data regarding homicide section, variables regarding murder were included: way of committing the act, place, motivation, period of time between murder and suicide, methods of committing the violent acts, weapons used, place of the victims' death, type of victim's wounds, number of strikes, number of victims, witnesses.
2. In the Data regarding suicide section, variables regarding suicide were included: way of committing the act, place, motivation, methods of committing the violent acts, weapons used, place of the aggressor's death, type of aggressor's wounds, messages left by aggressor, number of strikes.
3. The section regarding the perpetrator of the act of violence was structured so that it could pick up some information regarding: age, level of education, criminal background, occupation, whether he worked abroad or not; the aggressor's mental state, alcohol/drug abuse, citizenship, marital status.
4. In the section regarding the victims I included variables such as direct victims, indirect victims and survivors: age, level of education, occupation, victim and aggressor's relationship, whether they worked abroad, health state, alcohol/drug abuse, citizenship, marital status, history of abuse.

5. Due to the fact that I intend to have interviews with specialists that conducted homicide-suicide cases, I included in the case paper a section regarding the institutions involved in solving the case and the name of persons responsible for the case. Thus, I picked up information regarding institutions (police sections, parquets, SMURD units or forensic medicine laboratories) and professionals that conducted the case.
6. The Romanian journalists constantly bring the cases of serious violence to the population's attention, especially murder and homicide-suicide. In order to increase the media's audience, the journalists select some cases and often break the law regarding image rights. To have the scientific arguments necessary for making a proposal to modify the way of presenting these acts of violence, I decided to include in the structure of the case paper a section inserting data regarding case coverage. This section has data regarding: the period of time during which the case was covered, the distribution of articles on days, the type of presented information (about the perpetrator, victims, murder, suicide, institutions, others), the type of images included in the articles and the journalists who wrote about the homicide-suicide cases.

All the data from the Registration Papers were inserted into an SPSS database so that they could be more easily handled according to the research objectives.

Rate of homicide-suicides in Romania

The finalizing of the database regarding the cases of homicide-suicide committed in Romania for the 2002–2013 period, also allowed the calculation of the homicide-suicide rate with more precision than in the study made at the end of 2014 with the help of data received from the police, Bucharest Parquet and online newspapers (Balica and Stöckl 2016). The data given by the parquets from the country brought new information, which allowed a more precise identification of the homicide-suicide cases and eliminated the attempt cases.

The homicide-suicide rates were calculated starting with the number of homicide-suicides registered in the database at the end of 2015 and with the statistical data regarding Romania's population according to the statistical database Tempo-online of the National Institute of Statistics for the 2002–2013 period. The results for 2015 emphasized some modifications of the values for the rates calculated at the end of 2014, the modifications being more visible for the last part of the analyzed period (2009–2013). Given the fact that the data introduced in the analysis at the end of 2015 was also extracted from the documents received from parquets, the values presented for the period of 2009–2013 diminished compared to the ones calculated in the Balica and Stöckl (2016) study.

The results of the analysis of the homicide-suicide rate show that the values registered for 2002–2013 varied between 0.005–0.103 per 100,000 inhabitants, while the previous study mentioned values between 0.005–0.146 per 100,000 inhabitants (Balica and Stöckl 2016). The tendency of evolution of the homicide-suicide rate was the same in both studies, with higher values being registered after 2007. In the following I will limit myself to describing the data results of the last investigations.

According to the most recent investigations, the average rate for the analyzed period was 0.05 per 100,000 inhabitants. In the first part of the period, 2002–2006, the average rate of homicide-suicide was 0.02 per 100,000 inhabitants. Starting with 2007, the values of rates grew significantly (except for the year 2010), and the average rate for the 2007–2013 period was 0.07 per 100,000 inhabitants (see Table 1.2).

The results of the present study can be only partially compared with the results of the studies made in other European countries. The studies for the other European countries were made for a different period of time (1980–2006) compared to the study from Romania (2002–2013). There are though, some periods of time that coincide and for which we can make some statements regarding the level of the homicide-suicide rates. If we take into consideration the time period 2002–2006, we can notice that, Romania registered the smallest values of the homicide-suicide rates from the European space.

Table 1.2 Rates of homicide-suicides (N=132)

Year	Number of homicide-suicides	Rate of homicide-suicides
2002	3	0.014
2003	3	0.014
2004	1	0.005
2005	10	0.046
2006	4	0.019
2007	11	0.051
2008	16	0.074
2009	18	0.084
2010	7	0.033
2011	19	0.089
2012	18	0.084
2013	22	0.103

The values registered in Romania were even smaller than the homicide-suicide rates from Poland (1999–2006 the homicide-suicide rates were 0.035–0.053) and Spain (2004–2006 the homicide-suicide rates were 0.037–0.039); these countries were famous for the small number of homicide-suicides (Liem and Oberwittler 2012: 206).

After 2007, the situation changed, the values of the homicide-suicide rates for 2007–2013 were higher (annual mean 2007–2013 – 0.07). The rates from Romania came closer to the rates mentioned in the Liem and Oberwittler (2012) study for England and Wales (0.071 annual mean), Germany (0.093) and Switzerland (0.091). This statement must be seen with reluctance as the time periods for which the the homicide-suicide rates were calculated in England and Wales (1988–1992), Germany (1996–2005) and Switzerland (1980–2004) were different from the time periods of the homicide-suicide rates in Romania (2002–2013).

The country where homicide-suicides were committed

The analysis of data showed that most homicide-suicides happened in Romania (90.2 per cent) while approximately 10 per cent were committed in other countries (Italy – 7, Spain – 2, the USA – 2, Switzerland – 1 and Greece – 1). Although there were 13 cases committed abroad, only 2 aggressors (of all 132) and one victim were of a citizenship other than Romanian.

Rural versus urban

Romania is a country where the population is distributed almost equally between the rural and urban area. The percentage of the population from the urban area was, for the analyzed period, slightly higher than the one from the rural area (the average percentage of the population from the urban area was 54 per cent).

The distribution of homicide-suicide cases according to the environment where they were committed showed that the differences between the number of cases committed in the urban and rural area are very small. 47.7 per cent of homicide-suicides were committed in the urban area and 43.2 per cent were committed in the rural area (for 12 cases I did not have information regarding the environment).

Emigrants versus non-emigrants

The analysis of the information from the documents sent by parquets allowed us to obtain some information regarding the emigration of victims or of aggressors. One quarter of the registered cases had at least one person (aggressor or victim) who emigrated for a period of time, according to our information (N=33 cases, 25 per cent). Most of the information confirmed the status of emigrant for 17 aggressors and 20 victims. Therefore, only in 4 cases both the victim and the aggressor were emigrants. These persons emigrated especially in the European space (only three were emigrants in the USA). In general, I am talking about emigrants who were leaving and coming back for short periods of time in order to have a job (only 4 persons left for longer periods of time – 3 in the USA and one in Switzerland). In other words, most of the emigrants had temporary and circulatory emigration. The analysis of data regarding the cases of homicide-suicide committed between Romanian emigrants or against a Romanian emigrant was published by Balica and Stöckl in a recent study in the European Journal of Criminology (2016).

The rest of the homicide-suicides occurred between persons about whom I did not have information of being emigrants until the moment of the violent act.

Types of homicide-suicide

Most homicide-suicide cases occurred between persons who were relatives (97 per cent). Only in four cases of homicide-suicide, the victims were acquaintances and not relatives of the aggressor (bosses, neighbors).

Table 1.3 Types of homicide-suicide

Types of homicide-suicide	**Frequency**	**Percentage**
Intimate partner homicide-suicides	88	66.7
Filicide paternal-suicides	12	9.1
Filicide maternal-suicides	5	3.8
Patricide-suicides	9	6.8
Familicide-suicides	5	3.8
Kinicide-suicides	9	6.8
Others	4	3

Intimate partner homicide-suicides are the type of homicide-suicide that are most frequent over the analyzed period and represent 66.7 per cent of the total of cases. Filicide-suicides (paternal and maternal) (12.9 per cent), kinicide-suicides (6.8 per cent) and patricide-suicides (6.8 per cent) were other types of homicide-suicide committed by Romanian people. The number of familicide-suicides was quite small (3.8 per cent) (see Table 1.3).

Aggressors' characteristics

Most of the aggressors (94.7 per cent) were men and only a few women committed homicide-suicides (5.3 per cent). Most of the aggressors were between 40–64 years old (45.4 per cent), while the aggressors who were between 26–39 years old represented almost a third (36.3 per cent). The percentage of aggressors aged over 65 (6.8 per cent) was almost similar to the aggressors aged from 18 to 25 (5.3 per cent). Most of the aggressors were Romanian people (97.7 per cent) and only 2 aggressors had a different nationality (Italians who murdered Romanian citizens and then committed suicide).

Two thirds of the aggressors (58.1 per cent) were intimate partners of the victim, and two fifths (39.7 per cent) were relatives of the victims (the aggressor was the father of the victim – 16 per cent; the aggressor was the mother of the victim – 3.8 per cent, son/daughter of the victim – 5.7 per cent, other relatives 10.2 per cent).

Although I used three sources of information, I had data about the level of education only for 19.7 per cent of the aggressors. Among those for whom I had information, 14 aggressors had a high level of education (13 had a university education and 1 had post-university studies), 9 aggressors had an average level of education (high-school) and 3 had a low level of education (1 primary school and 2 secondary school).

The information regarding the occupational status was available to a larger extent (76.5 per cent) than the data regarding the level of education (19.7 per cent). Almost half of the aggressors had a low occupational status (41.6 per cent), while only 7.5 per cent had an average occupational status and 9.1 per cent a high occupational status. 14.3 per cent of the aggressors did not have a job at the moment of committing the act of violence. Among the cases of homicide-suicide committed in Romania, 20 cases (15 per cent) were identified as being committed by aggressors who worked in police or military units and security and protection services. The police warrant officers and officers (some of them being retired) committed 9 homicide-suicides, army warrant officers and officers committed 5 homicide-suicides and security agents committed 6 cases of homicide-suicide.

Regarding the country where the aggressors were working, almost two thirds of them were working in Romania (59.1 per cent). Approximately 14 per cent of the aggressors were working abroad and only 6.1 per cent did not have a job at the moment of committing the act of violence. Out of the 18 aggressors who were working abroad, the majority had a job in the European Union (15) and only 3 were working in the USA. Almost half of the aggressors were working in Italy (8) and this situation needs additional investigations in order to identify the factors which led to the committing of violent acts associated with the status of emigrants in Italy. It is true that in 2011 approximately 997,000 Romanians were registered in the official Italian statistics (Centro Studi e Ricerche 2012) but, at the same time, a high number of emigrants was also registered in the Spanish statistics – 769,608 Romanian emigrants at the end of 2013 (Instituto Nacional de Estadistica 2014). Moreover, the number of homicide-suicide cases committed by Romanians who were working in Spain was only 2 cases. Although the communities of Romanians from other countries are much smaller, we had homicide-suicide cases committed by Romanian emigrants from Switzerland, Austria, Germany, Cyprus and Israel (one case for every country). Therefore, there are also other factors except the size of the community that lead to committing homicide-suicide and these factors must be identified at a micro-social and individual level. For a fifth (21.2 per cent) of the aggressors I did not have information regarding the country where they were working.

22 per cent of the aggressors drank alcohol before committing the homicide-suicides and 7.6 per cent used drugs. The information regarding the state of health of the aggressors was seldom recorded by the official sources used in this study. According to my data, 14.4 per cent had psychological disorders (depression) and 2.3 per cent other disorders. Only a small number of aggressors (6.8 per cent) had a criminal history.

Victims' characteristics

The number of victims registered for the 132 homicide-suicides was 160 people. Most of the cases had only one victim (82.6 per cent), but there were also cases with more victims (19 cases with 2 victims, 3 cases with 3 victims and one case with 4 victims). Only three victims had different nationality to Romanian (Spanish, Greek and Polish).

Most of the victims were women (81.8 per cent), the percentage of men is smaller in the case of homicide-suicides (18.1 per cent). A third of the victims were between 26–39 years old (34 per cent). Important percentages were registered for the victims aged between 40 and 64 (26.2 per cent) and for minor victims (20.5 per cent). Young people aged between 18 and 25 and victims aged over 65 represented approximately 10 per cent of the total each.

The number of victims killed in an urban environment (56 per cent) was significantly bigger than the number of victims killed in a rural environment (44 per cent). The information regarding the level of education was quite limited, being presented only for 33 victims (20 per cent). Among these, 7 had no education, 7 had a low level of education (primary and secondary school), 6 of them were high-school graduates and 13 university graduates.

The sources consulted for making the database contained information about the occupation of 107 victims (67 per cent). Among these, most had a low occupational level (82.2 per cent). The victims with an average occupational level (5.6 per cent) and the ones with a high occupational status (12.1 per cent) represented almost a fifth of the cases. Among the registered victims, 22 were emigrants. Most of them worked in the European Union space (21) and only one was an emigrant in the USA. Italy was the country where half of the emigrant victims had worked (11). The rest of the victims worked in Spain (3), Germany (2), and the UK (2) the USA (1), Greece (1), and Switzerland (1). According to the data, 14 victims had consumed alcohol and 9 had used drugs before being killed. I had information only about three victims who were supposed to be mentally ill and about five who were known to have other diseases.

Data regarding homicide-suicides

The homicide-suicides registered in Romania were committed both in the urban and rural environments. The differences between the number of murders (urban – 47.7 per cent, rural – 43.2) and of suicides (urban – 47 per cent, rural – 43.9 per cent) committed in the urban and rural environments were very small. In 30 cases (22.7 per cent) of homicide and 21 suicides (16.6 per cent), the presence of witnesses was found. This led to the calling of the police and qualifying the cases as being homicide-suicides and not double homicides. The members of the victims' families (homicides – 13.6 per cent; suicides 8.3 per cent) were present to a larger extent than the members of the aggressors' families (homicides – 6.8 per cent; suicides – 5.3) or neighbors (homicides – 2.3 per cent; suicides – 3 per cent).

As I considered that, in order to prevent the committing of a homicide-suicide, it is important to know the period of time when homicide-suicides were committed, I decided to include this information in the database. For a better limitation of the time period, I split the 24 hours of a day in 4 sections of time, 6 hours each (6 am–12 am, 12.01 pm–6 pm, 6.01 pm–10 pm, and 10.01 pm–5.59 am). Homicides and suicides were committed especially during the night (6 pm–6 am). The period of time when a bigger number of homicide-suicides were committed was the one between 6 pm and 6 am (homicides – 57.5 per cent, suicides – 44.7 per cent).

The period of time with the highest risk for committing a murder followed by suicide was the one between 10 pm and 6 am (homicides – 32.5 per cent; suicides – 27.3 per cent). I did not notice significant differences between the two periods of time during the day regarding the number of homicide-suicides. During the morning, between 6 am and 12 pm, 21.9 per cent of murders and 19.7 per cent of suicides were committed. During the day, between 12 pm and 6 pm, 19.7 per cent homicides and 18.9 suicides were committed. Therefore, during the evening and night there is a bigger risk of committing these acts of violence than during the day.

The place of committing the homicide-suicide was a place which was known and accessible to the aggressors. I am talking about the common house of the victim and of the aggressor (including household) (homicides – 55.2; suicides – 48.5), the victim's house (homicides – 15.1; suicides – 3.8) and the aggressor's house (homicides – 5.3; suicides – 3.8). I considered it important to find out whether there is a certain type of homicide-suicide which is committed especially in the common place of the victim and the aggressor and this is why I decided to analyze the relationship between the type of homicide-suicide and the place of committing the homicide-suicide. As already seen in the section *Types of homicide-suicides*, most of the homicide-suicides were intimate partner homicide-suicides. If we connect this information regarding the type of homicide-suicide and the one regarding the place where the violent act was committed, we can notice that only half of the intimate partner homicide-suicides were committed in the common place of the two partners. The rest of intimate partner homicide-suicides were committed in the victim's house, in other places or in the aggressor's house. On the other hand, if we take into consideration the fact that most homicide-suicides were committed by relatives, we can notice that there is a relation between the type of relationship between the victim and the aggressor and the place of committing the homicide-suicide. The fact that most of the victims and the aggressors were members of the same family (close or extended family) explains why most homicide-suicides were committed in the common place of the victim and of the aggressor (in the victim and aggressor's house 51 per cent) or in places that are known and easily accessible to the aggressor (15 per cent in the victim's house, 5 per cent in the aggressor's house, 4 per cent outside the house, but in the household).

Motivation

The motivation of committing homicide-suicides was identified for 74 per cent of the cases. For the cases for which I had information regarding the acts that determined the violent action, three large categories of cases were emphasized; they were motivated by: 1) conflicts, 2) jealousy associated with infidelity and 3) the partner's refusal to accept separation/divorce.

Most of the homicide-suicides were motivated by frequent conflicts associated with various problems which appeared during the relationship between victims and aggressors (31.6 per cent). The financial problems generated by the economic crisis that affected the families that made bank loans or borrowed money from moneylenders led to more and more conflicts in the families and to 11 cases of homicide-suicide (11.2 per cent of the total cases for which I had information regarding motivation). Conflicts between partners associated with alcohol consumption were mentioned for 7 cases of homicide-suicide motivated by conflicts. Frequent domestic violence was found in 16.3 per cent of the cases (16 cases). Although some violent acts from some couples were signaled to the police and justice (4 cases) and restraining orders were obtained (1 case), they ended with the death of the victims and the suicide of the aggressors. Some of the violent acts were generated by financial problems (bank loans or loans from moneylenders, difficulties with splitting inheritances or family assets after the divorce) or by problems about the way in which the household chores were fulfilled or not, but there were also cases whose motivations were jealousy or infidelity (proven infidelity, but most of the times only the suspicion of infidelity).

A third of the homicide-suicides were generated by jealousy and suspicion of infidelity (27.5 per cent). Another important group of homicide-suicides was committed after the victims expressed their desire to be separated from or to divorce the partner. The percentage of homicide-suicides committed between partners in a separation/divorce process was of 28.5 per cent. The decision of the woman to divorce or to leave her partner and to have another one or the decision to move abroad in order to find a job generated a violent reaction from the partners who were left behind. In most of the cases, the woman was the victim of the abandoned partner, but there were also situations where the desire of the man to extract revenge on his partner and to punish her ended with the murder of the children (3 cases).

The desire for revenge was the one which led to cases of homicide-suicide committed against parents (2 cases) or against female partners (2 cases) because their families did not accept, for various reasons, the relationship of the aggressor with the chosen partner. The parents' refusal to accept a relationship which their son wanted to have with a divorced woman who also had a child from a previous marriage, or the parents' refusal to accept their son's relationship with a Roma woman eventually led to some intimate partner homicide-suicides. In other cases, the parents' refusal to accept their sons' relationships with the chosen women led to either the murder of the entire family that refused to accept the woman, or to the murder of one of the parents.

A special category of homicide-suicide is that of cases motivated by psychological exhaustion of the aggressors (6 cases) due to their direct involvement in the care of some family members who were incurably ill (psychiatric illnesses, cancer or paralyzed persons) and that of cases committed by persons who were mentally ill (depression) (5 cases).

Modus Operandi

In order to commit homicide-suicides, the aggressors from Romania used more types of weapons, the most used being in fact the most accessible. In Romania, firearms can be used only by people who have a gun permit and who have a professional status that allows ownership: dignitaries, policemen, diplomats, magistrates, military people and hunters (Law 295 from June 28, 2004 regarding the regime of weapons and munition). Therefore, I was expecting that firearms would be less frequently used, or not used at all, in the committing of homicide-suicides. The data obtained from the research showed that firearms were used in one of 5 homicide-suicides (19.7 per cent). The aggressors who used firearms were police officers/warrant officers, military people, security agents or persons who had a hunting weapon permit. All of them had a legal gun permit.

The analysis of the types of weapons used for committing homicides and suicides emphasized the fact that, the most used weapons were knives (homicides – 57.6 per cent; suicides – 39.4 per cent). Strangling with cords, cables or ropes was one of the most used ways to commit homicide (22 per cent). Striking with legs and arms (13.6 per cent) and hitting with an ax or with other blunt objects (9.8 per cent) were other ways of committing homicide. The perpetrators' suicides were committed with knives (39.4 per cent), through hanging (38.6 per cent) and with firearms (16 per cent) (see Table 1.4).

Table 1.4 Modus operandi of the homicide-suicides

Weapons used	**Total**	
	Homicide	**Suicide**
Firearms	26 (19.7)	21 (16)
Knife	76 (57.6)	52 (39.4)
Ax	12 (9)	-
Hitting with an object	13 (9.8)	-

Weapons used	Total	
	Homicide	Suicide
Hammer	1 (0.7)	
Striking with legs and arms	18 (13.6)	-
Choking	29 (22)	-
Hanging	4 (3)	51 (38.6)
Jumping in front of a train/car	1 (0.7)	5 (3.8)
Jumping from heights	1 (0.7)	13 (9.8)
Poisoning	1 (0.7)	5 (3.8)

The aggressor's message

After committing the homicide or even before committing the homicide, some perpetrators transmitted/left messages for family members, friends or colleagues. More than a third of the aggressors left at least one message for people who knew them (36.4 per cent). Most of the aggressors left hand written messages (60.4 per cent) and only seven of them sent text messages on mobile phones (16.4 per cent). The messages sent on the phone were addressed either to the family, or to friends and colleagues who were informed about the homicide-suicides. A message of this type sounded like this: "Call the police, I am dead, the door is open". Some of the aggressors spoke on the phone with family members in order to announce to them that they had committed a murder and that they would kill themselves or in order to associate their gesture with the act of revenge against their partner who kept refusing to come back home (5 cases). In some situations, the threats made by aggressors on the phone were associated with the hand written messages of the aggressor before killing himself. This was the case of a father who hung his two-year-old child in order to extract revenge on his wife who refused to come back to the country. After calling and threatening to kill her child, the aggressor left a message that said this:

> I killed your child, now I'm killing myself. Farewell, you didn't know how to cherish our lives, we died for your love, you didn't send any money, and you thought that we can survive with air. You can stay with … That man with whom you hooked up, we forgot you. I curse you not to have a life of happiness for as long as you live, I curse you, and I loved you clearly, I'm sorry, now you will see also what pain is like. Farewell, I loved you deeply!

Some messages explained why they had chosen to commit homicide-suicides and they were asking their relatives to take care of the family children. This was also the case of an aggressor overwhelmed by the debts that he had to moneylenders, who killed his wife and then, before killing himself, asked for the relatives' forgiveness. He explained why he committed the murder and asked them to take care of their daughter. At the same time, a part of the message was addressed to the daughter who was asked to listen to her grandparents and relatives.

Some messages were trying to explain the violent acts, others to make some people feel guilty or to give indications about the perpetrator of the homicide. A Romanian who had emigrated to Switzerland for 31 years came back to Romania after a professional failure. Before committing familicide-suicide, he left a note to explain his gesture: "At my age of 52, I failed in everything, but I'm still hoping to succeed in this last gesture of mine. I don't want to leave my family alone. I'm trying to take them with me."

After murdering his wife and son, another aggressor left a note on the body of every victim. With these messages, the aggressor blamed the two homicides and his suicide on a particular person: "All of this is because of D.P., the secretary of T City Hall who can come and bury us now because 40 hectares of land and two houses with no papers will become his."

A mother exhausted by the effort that she had made for 29 years in order to take care of her ill daughter, decided to appeal to a center for people with mental disorders. After the institutions of assistance for the people with mental disorders from Bucharest refused to hospitalize her daughter, the mother threatened several times that she would murder her and then kill herself. Before committing filicide-suicide, she left a hand written note:

> Please forget about me, I live on this earth for nothing, I can't stand to hear screaming, yelling, mountains of poop and piss. We are going to Hell, there is only the crematory left for us. 2 nails missing, the authorities did not want to hospitalize. What can I do? That's it, it's enough; we are leaving. Don't cry because you have no reason to cry for, be happy that you got rid of two crazy women. Farewell.

Another mother murdered her children and then committed suicide because the relationship with her husband was not accepted by his family. It was about a relationship between a young Romanian woman (Orthodox Christian) and a Turkish man (Muslim). Unsatisfied with the way in which she and her children were treated, but also with the problems generated by interfamilial conflicts, the young woman murdered her daughters and then committed suicide. After killing the little girls, the mother left a note:

> How can we stop hurting very good people on this earth? I had an extraordinary family, a great village, some gorgeous children like angels, but I could never enjoy them. Ofer felt that something was happening, maybe the other ones felt it also, but nobody could stop it. If you did not love me, why didn't you tell Ofer? He loved me. But you, Turkish

people, do you love your children and grandchildren? Why aren't you showing this to them? How much time do you want to spend with our children? No knife cuts well. I'm leaving now. Nobody is coming. Are you fighting for the inheritance? Why?

Other aggressors spoke on the phone with friends or colleagues (4 cases). An aggressor wrote on the victim's body with a red marker "Facebook kills! See you in the other land". The notes and messages left by aggressors were used by investigators as clues for closing the cases as the aggressors were already deceased and could not start the penal following.

Attempted Homicide-suicides

The Homicide-suicides in Romania database also includes information regarding attempted homicide-suicides (N=35). When I am talking about attempted homicide-suicides I am referring to the cases of attempted homicide-suicides, homicide-attempted suicides and attempted homicide-attempted suicides. The cases of attempted homicide-suicides were the cases that had as survivors the persons who were attacked with the intention of being killed by a person who killed himself after committing the deed. The cases of homicide-attempted suicides were the ones that had as survivors the persons who, after committing murder, decided to kill themselves but the act of attempted suicide did not lead to their death. In the specialty literature, homicide-attempted suicides are known to be homicide-(para) suicides (Liem, 2009 2010). What I considered attempted homicide-attempted suicides were the cases that had as survivors both the attacked person with the intention of being killed and the aggressor who wanted to kill and then to commit suicide. I used the term *attempted homicide-suicides* in this subchapter in order to refer to all these three subtypes.

The information regarding these cases had as sources: police units, parquets and the media. For ten cases I had as information sources only articles from the online media, for the rest of the cases the information from the media was conflated with the data from the police registers and from the penal files found in the custody of parquets. The data from the police was used in 24 cases (68.6 per cent), the information from the penal files from parquets was used for 19 cases (54.2 per cent), and the ones from the media for 14 cases (40 per cent). For 21 cases I used two sources of information and for one case three sources of information.

The fact that I used three sources of data in order to make the database allowed me to have more information regarding these cases and to make the distinction between three sub-types: attempted homicide-suicides (5 cases, 14.3 per cent), homicide-attempted suicides (18 cases, 51.4 per cent) and attempted homicide-attempted suicides (12 cases, 34.3 per cent). All the cases of attempted homicide-suicides were committed between 2006 and 2013 (see Table 1.5). We can notice the fact that the number of attempted homicide-suicides was high starting with 2010, a situation which was repeated in 2012. The number of attempted homicide-suicides for 2010 was higher than the number of homicide-suicides (7) and represented 64.7 per cent of the total of homicide-suicides committed during this year (including attempted).

Table 1.5 Attempted homicide-suicides

Year	Frequency	Percentage
2006	1	2.9
2007	1	2.9
2009	2	5.7
2010	11	31.4
2011	4	11.4
2012	10	28.6
2013	6	17.1

The situation was slightly different for 2012 because the number of attempts was smaller than the number of cases ended with the death of the victim and the suicide of the aggressor. That year, 28 cases were registered and 10 were attempted homicide-suicides (35.7 per cent).

All the cases were committed in Romania by Romanian citizens. The great majority of attempted homicide-suicides were committed between Romanians that were not emigrants (27 cases; 77 per cent), but there were also cases of homicide-suicide committed by Romanian emigrants (8 cases; 23 per cent). More than half of the cases were committed in the urban environment (60 per cent).

Types of attempted homicide-suicides

The number of the violent acts between intimate partners was also high for attempts. Approximately 63 per cent of the attempts were intimate partner homicide-suicides (23 cases). This situation is similar to the results of other studies regarding homicide-parasuicides that identified more attempts in the case of intimate partner homicide-suicides (Bourget et al. 2000, Hanzlick and Koponen 1994, Liem 2010).

For the other types of homicide-suicide, fewer cases were registered in Romania: attempted patricide-suicides (6 cases), attempted filicide-suicides (4) and attempted kinicide-suicides (2). All attempted homicide-suicides, regardless of the identified subtype (attempted homicide-suicides, attempted homicide-attempted suicides or homicide-attempted suicides) happened between family members.

What is interesting is the fact that 3 of the attempted filicide-suicides were paternal filicide-attempted suicides and only one case was attempted maternal filicide-attempted suicide. In Romania, filicide-suicide and attempted filicide-suicide tends to be committed in a high percentage by fathers. This affirmation must be seen with caution because the number of cases was quite small, although the analysis was done over 12 years (2002–2013).

The fact that fathers commit more attempted filicide-suicides is in agreement with some studies that demonstrated the prevalence of father aggressors in relation to the mothers who commit filicide-suicides (Liem et al. 2009). The results of my study seem to contradict the results of the studies regarding attempted filicide-suicides. Until now, few studies regarding the attempted filicide-suicides were made. There is an interest in this type of filicide-suicide, and the study made in the Netherlands starting with the comparative analysis of filicide and of attempted filicide-suicides brought new elements regarding the cases committed in the period 1953–2004 (Liem et al. 2010). The results of the analysis from the Netherlands showed the fact that there were no differences between the number of attempted filicide-suicides committed by fathers and mothers, but only differences regarding the age of the aggressors (the aggressors for the cases of attempted filicide-suicide are older than aggressors who commit filicides) (Liem et al. 2010).

The aggressor's characteristics

Among all the aggressors, only one was a female. The age of the aggressors was mostly between 26–39 years (14 aggressors) and between 40–64 yeas (14 aggressors). Only three aggressors were aged between 18–25 years and 4 aggressors were over 65. I had information about the level of education only for 40 per cent of the cases (13 cases). In most of these cases, the aggressors had an average educational level (high-school – 6 aggressors) and only four of them had university studies. The occupational status was according to the level of education. Thus, among the aggressors there were people with high occupational status (a businesswoman, an accountant and two police officers), but also persons with an average occupational status (4 persons: security agent, taxi driver, footballer) or persons with a low occupational status (21 persons: workers, daily workers, farmers, pensioners). Two thirds of the aggressors were working in Romania (20 aggressors, 57.1), and 12 per cent were working in the European space (1 in Italy, 1 in Spain, 1 in Greece and 1 in Israel). 40 per cent of the aggressors had consumed alcohol or drugs before committing the attempted homicide-suicides

(12 had consumed alcohol and two drugs). For 11 aggressors I had information that they were mentally ill (31.4 per cent). Only four aggressors were registered with penal records.

Among the aggressors with a criminal history, there was also a man who had committed an attempted homicide 12 years before. I will briefly present the information regarding this case.

Case A: Homicide-parasuicide committed by a recidivist

H. C. decided to kill his former girlfriend three days after the victim and B.N. (the present partner) announced to him that they were together. Initially married to B.N., the victim decided to divorce him in 2003. Although they were divorced, the victim continued the relationship with her former husband and had a child with him. They decided together to settle in Austria for a period of 4 years. In this time, the victim came back to in Romania quite often. In 2005, the victim announced to her former husband (B.N.) that she had had a relationship with another man (H.C.) for a year and a half. The 2005 winter holidays made the meeting between the three possible so that they could discuss the relationship between the victim and H.C. The discussions happened in a civilized way, the former husband (B.N.) managed to convince the present partner (H.C.) to end their relationship. Three days after the discussion between the three people, H.C. murdered the victim after breaking into her house through a window. He stabbed her with a knife and then he injured himself (self-inflicted injuries). After injuring himself, H.C. called his brother and told him what he had done. Then, he left the victim's house and came back home (he lived in the same building with the victim). The brother called the emergency service 112 and some relatives. The relatives went to the victim's and aggressor's house. H.C. was saved by doctors who noticed that the wounds around the heart and the kidneys were relatively superficial. The investigations of the police showed that, one night before committing the murder, H.C. had told his father about his desire to kill his former girlfriend because "she had done too many things to him". Moreover, H.C. had a criminal record where more minor felonies committed in Italy and an attempted murder committed in 1994 (at the age of 24) were mentioned. For the attempted murder committed against a young man after fighting in a club, H.C. was rehabilitated according to the Romanian legislation ten years after committing the crime. The person who testified for the rehabilitation of H.C. was his girlfriend who he killed 12 years later. In both murder cases the aggressor premeditated his acts. In the case of the attempted murder from 1994, the aggressor took his weapons (a knife and a tranquillizer spray) and went to look for his victim the second day after the conflict. In the case of the 2006 murder, the aggressor tried to enter the victim's house all day long after the victim's partner had left home. When the victim refused to let him in the house, he broke into her house (with a knife on him) through a window. The forensic psychiatric expert showed the fact that H.C. had personality disorders of the antisocial type, marked by mental instability and impulsive tendencies. The psychiatrists noticed that the aggressor had discernment when he committed the murder. H.C. admitted that he was guilty. The aggressor was not married, did not have any children, he had a low educational level (8 years of school – primary and secondary school) and he did not have a job. (Aggressor with a criminal history, 31 years old)

Victims' characteristics

Attempted homicide-suicides had 38 victims and all of them were Romanian citizens. Most of the cases had only one victim (32 cases, 91.5 per cent). Three out of every four victims were women (76.3 per cent) and only one victim in four was a man (9 cases, 23.7 per cent). The age of the victims of attempted homicide-suicides was lower than in the case of homicide-suicides ending with the death of the victims and of the aggressors. More than half of the victims of attempted homicide-suicides were up to 39 years of age (22 cases), and a third of the victims were up to 25 years of age (11 cases). The low age of victims was associated with homicide-attempted suicides (7 cases) and attempted homicides-attempted suicides (3 cases) and less with attempted homicide-suicides (1 case). In other words, out of the 11 cases of attempted homicide-suicide where the victims were younger than 25, 4 victims and 10 aggressors survived. If we analyze all the cases of attempted homicide-suicide, out of the 38 victims and 35 aggressors involved in the violence acts, 17 victims and 30 aggressors survived. The analysis of data regarding the attempts of homicide-suicide emphasized the fact that 25 per cent of the attempted homicide-suicides had close persons of the victims and of the aggressors as witnesses (members of the victim's family (1 case), members of the aggressors' family (2 cases) or neighbors (6 cases)).

Moreover, some of the cases of homicide-suicide which had witnesses were categorized as attempted homicide-suicides due to the presence of witnesses who alerted the 112 emergency special services. In Romania, the emergency number for calling the police in case of violence is 112. The police came with SMURD (doctors with special training for emergency), forensics and a coroner. The doctors' intervention in the period of time necessary for saving the lives of the injured persons thus reduced the number of homicide-suicides that ended with the death of the victims and of the aggressors. On the other hand, we must say that there were more factors that led to the saving of lives: the presence of witnesses and the doctors' intervention also correlated with the length of the period of time necessary for the arrival of intervention teams and with the complexity of wounds. In order to show the witnesses' role, I synthesized in the table below the way in which they came to the victims and aggressors' help. I considered it useful to present this information in order to emphasize the witnesses' role in the evolution of the violent act, even if they could not interfere or stop the violent act in the first phases (see Table 1.6). The fact that the intervention of witnesses who were or were not at the crime scene led to the saving of some lives, shows that, if the persons found near the ones who risk becoming victims (people who are frequently exposed to violence acts from their partners, family members or people who face certain crisis generated by financial reasons or professional failure etc.) are involved in supervising the respective persons.

Table 1.6 Information about attempted homicide-suicides

Type of homicide-suicide	**Information about violence**
Homicide-attempted suicide	After killing his wife, the aggressor went out in the street. Then he killed himself. The relatives who were in the area when he killed his wife called the police (112) and an ambulance.
Homicide-attempted suicide	The aggressor killed his wife in the street, during daytime. Immediately after he hit her, he cut his throat. The persons who were in the area at that time called for an ambulance and the police.
Homicide-attempted suicide	After killing his girlfriend, the aggressor took some pills. As it was the victim's birthday, her friends were worried that she did not answer the phone so they came to her house. When they found both the victim and the aggressor, they called for an ambulance and the aggressor was taken to the hospital. The aggressor had another attempted suicide in prison but he survived.
Attempted Homicide-suicide	The injured victim (the aggressor's girlfriend) called her brother for help. After shooting her twice with a gun, the aggressor left and jumped in front of a train.
Attempted Homicide-suicide	The victim (64 years old) was hit by her husband and went into a coma. The aggressor thought that she died so he killed himself (by hanging). The victim was saved by her son who called the police and an ambulance.
Attempted Homicide-attempted suicide	A mother (the aggressor) and her 7-year-old child (the victim) took sleeping pills. They were found by a friend worried that she did not hear from them.

Type of homicide-suicide	Information about violence
Homicide-attempted suicide	The victim went out in the street after being cut with a knife by the aggressor. The doctors were unable to save her. After hitting her, the aggressor cut himself with the knife, but was saved by the doctors called by the neighbors.
Homicide-attempted suicide	In the day of the conflict the aggressor took drugs, had a fight with his mother and the neighbors called the police. When the police arrived, the woman was dead and the aggressor's hands and legs were covered with wounds. The police had to immobilize him to prevent him committing suicide.
Homicide-attempted suicide	After killing his wife, he committed suicide by cutting himself with a knife. The neighbors called the police and the ambulance. He survived thanks to the quick intervention of the police and the doctors.
Homicide-attempted suicide	After killing his former wife, he stabbed himself in the heart. The relatives called the ambulance.
Homicide-attempted suicide	The aggressor (an 80-year-old man) killed his brother-in-law and then he went to the kitchen to turn on the gas. Meanwhile, his wife called the ambulance for the injured brother-in-law. His son who found him in the kitchen saved the aggressor.

The information regarding the level of education and the occupational status of the victims was quite limited. I had information about the level of education only for 7 of the 38 victims (2 had no studies at all, 2 were high-school graduates, one was a secondary school graduate and 2 were university graduates). The occupational status could be identified for more than 55 per cent of the total of victims (21). 45 per cent of the victims (17) had a low occupational status (workers, housewives, pensioners), approximately 5 per cent (2) had an average occupational status (a nurse and a pharmacy assistant) and 5 per cent (2) had a high occupational status (a school teacher and a kindergarten teacher).

History of abuse

As I have said before, most of the cases of attempted homicide-suicides occurred between intimate partners (23 cases). Through the investigations I tried to identify more information regarding the history of the relationship between the people involved in attempted homicide-suicides in order to notice if homicide-suicides represented the final moment of violent acts repeated during the relationship. Because of this, the grid used to analyze the cases also included variables regarding: the duration of the relationship, the status of the relationship at the moment of murder (married couple, separated, divorced), the interval between marriage/separation/divorce and the moment of the crime, presence/absence of violent acts during the relationship and presence/absence of death threats.

Although I used three information sources, there was little data regarding the history of the relationships. The official documents from the penal files (resolutions, prosecutors' orders and other documents from penal files) did not refer to the elements that I proposed myself to analyze. Therefore, I had information regarding the duration of the relationships for 9 cases. There were relationships that lasted between one year and one year and a half (3 cases), relationships that lasted three years (1 case), and between 11–12 years (3 cases). Only two cases had a relationship that lasted longer than 15 years: one case in which the relationship was 16 years old and one case where the relationship was 31 years old.

The case of the aggressor who, after 16 years of living with his wife, committed homicide-attempted suicide was the result of the action of more individual risk factors associated with jealousy and infidelity suspicion from the aggressor, domestic violence, the victim's desire to separate and death threats against his wife.

Case B: Attempted intimate partner homicide-parasuicides after 16 years of relationship

C.D. and C.N. had a 7-year relationship when the wife C.D. was hit for the first time, at least this is how the facts were recorded by the police officers after talking with the victim. The verbal and physical conflicts were associated with the aggressor's frequent alcohol consumption. Unsatisfied with the fact that her husband was not contributing financially to the household expenses and the expenses for their two young children any more, the wife kept reproaching him so he became violent (he was destroying objects from the house and he was even beating her). In August 2012, the husband asked his wife to leave his house until the end of August, because he found out that she was cheating on him with another man. Moreover, he told his wife that if she did not leave the house, he would kill her. For fear of being killed, the wife left the house on September 1. Seven days after her departure, C.N. went to her new house (armed with a bat) and asked the (non-existent) wife's lover to get out of the house so that they could talk. The wife called the police who interfered (gave him a finc) and pushed him away from the woman's new house. The husband kept phoning his wife and asking her to come back to him. The victim refused constantly so the aggressor became verbally violent. The wife asked for the second time for the help of the police, but the aggressor did not end his threats. The death threats continued and more and more people from his group of friends were informed by him that he wanted to kill her and then kill himself.

Approximately one month after their separation, the witnesses became aware that the husband really wanted to kill her and they tried to discuss with him and stop him. The day when he decided to kill her, the aggressor was more insistent and kept asking his wife to come back home. In the first part of the day, he phoned her and asked her to come back home. The wife refused. The aggressor did not stop and decided to follow her until he met her. Around noon, he met her at a shop and asked her to come back to him. The wife refused him again. Because the wife was working evening shifts, the aggressor decided to wait for her when she was coming back from work and kill her. He expressed this decision in front of a family friend who also tried to make him change his mind. At midnight, when the woman was coming back from work, the aggressor waited for her in the bus station and followed her until she was alone and then he attacked her with a penknife several times.

The victim managed to escape only with a few wounds because she fought the aggressor and a car was passing by. After the car stopped, the driver helped the victim call an ambulance. The aggressor ran from the crime scene and hid himself. Meanwhile, he hurt himself with a penknife, the wound was quite deep. The police officers found him, although he tried to hide for a longer period of time. During the investigations, the aggressor did not admit that he had tried to kill his wife and he said that he did not remember what had happened. Both people survived, and the aggressor was condemned for attempted murder. (Male, 40 years)

For these 9 cases I also had information regarding the status of the relationship at the moment of the crime. Only three of them were still married, while the other 6 were already separated (2), in a divorce process (1) or divorced (3). The violent act occurred in a short period of time from the moment of separation between the two partners. In two cases, the homicide-suicides happened three days from the moment of the victim's decision to separate, in two cases the homicide-suicides happened a month after the separation and in one case, the violent act happened after three months. In seven cases, frequent acts of domestic violence were committed for which the victims called either the police or their relatives. Only two victims were threatened with death according to the information that I had.

Data regarding attempted homicide-suicides

The difference between the number of attempted homicide-suicides committed in the urban environment and the ones committed in the rural environment was quite significant. Most of the attempted homicide-suicides were committed in the urban environment (20 cases, 57.1 per cent). The analysis of the relation between the type of attempted homicide-suicide and the environment where it was committed emphasized the fact that more cases of attempted intimate homicide-suicides were committed in the urban environment (15 cases) than in the rural environment (6 cases).

The presence of witnesses was an important element in the evolution of homicide-suicides, the role of the witnesses being emphasized in the section regarding the victims of attempted homicide-suicides (see the above section). Another important element of the analysis was the moment of the day when the attempted homicide-suicides happened, and we all know that the violent acts committed during the day can be more easily identified/noticed by witnesses to the fast intervention of services and they have a bigger chance to not end with the death of the victim or of the aggressor. A third of the attempted homicide-suicides were committed during the night (28.6 per cent were committed between 22.00 – 5.59). The rest of the attempted homicide-suicides were committed between 6.00 in the morning and 10 pm. The time periods with most of the attempted homicide-suicides were in the morning (28.6 per cent were committed between 6.00 and 12.00) and during the night.

Attempted suicides were committed in a relatively short period of time after the committing of the murder. The information that I managed to extract from the used sources allowed me to identify the distance between murder and suicide for two thirds of the analyzed cases of attempted homicide-suicides (I did not have information regarding the distance between murder and suicide for 10 cases). More than half of the cases for which I had information (21 cases, 60 per cent) were committed within one hour of the murder. The reduced gravity of the self-induced injuries, the presence of witnesses and the rapidity of the intervention of emergency medical services were the factors that made these cases attempted homicide-suicides. In approximately one out of ten cases (11.4 per cent), the suicide happened in a period of time that varied between 1 and 8 hours.

Two thirds of the attempted homicide-suicides were committed in the victim's or aggressor's house (65.7 per cent). One third of them were committed in the common house (34.3 per cent), while 17.1 per cent were committed in the aggressor's house and 14.2 per cent in the victim's house. A significant number of attempted homicide-suicides were committed outside the victim's or aggressor's house, but in the space of their household (20 per cent were committed in the courtyard of the house).

Motivation

The murders and attempted murders committed by the perpetrators of attempted homicide-suicides were preceded by frequent conflicts (3 cases), old conflicts (3 cases) or spontaneous conflicts (4 cases) generated by current problems that victims and aggressors were facing (frequent domestic violence associated with alcohol consumption, dissatisfactions generated by the victims' attempts to limit the alcohol consumption, misunderstandings between aggressors and their life partners, or misunderstandings between mothers-in-law and sons-in-law, etc.) Jealousy (5 cases), the suspicion of infidelity (4 cases) and the desire of the victim to separate or to divorce the aggressor (8 cases) were other reasons that caused the murders. The aggressors' revenge on the victims who either wanted to leave them and to find other partners, or did not fulfil the aggressors' solicitations (for example a victim refused to iron the aggressor's trousers) was signaled in four cases. Two murders were motivated by the mental exhaustion of the aggressors who were taking care of ill parents. In only one case, the victim was physically harmed because she interfered when the aggressor was trying to kill himself.

Case C: Homicide-parasuicide involving a consumer of psychoactive substances

Young man D. had a year-and-a-half relationship with his girlfriend before committing homicide-parasuicide. Because of jealousy, their relationship was tense and marked by many verbal conflicts and break-ups. Every time they made up was only because the young man kept insisting. 3 months before the homicide-parasuicide, the two broke up again. Trying to make up again with his girlfriend, the young man became more aggressive and one day, after realizing that the victim was alone, he took her by force in his car. All this happened after he put his hand on her mouth so that she could not scream and after he took her phone so that she could not let anyone know that she had been taken by force. The relationship continued even though the young man kept abusing her verbally in front of other persons, especially when he was consuming alcohol. After a month, another conflict with his girlfriend happened. This time, the young man also had a suicide attempt (alcohol consumption associated with medicine and psychoactive substances) confirmed by the doctors from the hospital where he was submitted. Approximately a month after this suicide attempt, the young couple had another fight. This time the fight started from the messages that the young woman had received on the telephone. The two were on drugs and their conflict ended this time with the death of the girl and the attempted suicide of the young man. In a first phase, the young survivor said that he remembered how they started fighting because of the messages she was receiving. They shoved each other and after that he did not remember what had happened between them. Then, the young man said that he wanted to kill himself and the girl tried to stop him, and this is why he stabbed her to death. The forensic psychiatric expert said that D had a personality disorder of the instable-impulsive type and that he had discernment at the crime moment. (Male, 22 years old)

The suicides had various motivations. Most of them were committed by the aggressors who were full of remorse after realizing that they had killed their life partners, children or relatives (9 cases). Two aggressors killed themselves for fear of the sanctions of the murder they had committed, one aggressor killed himself because of the financial problems that he had after taking a loan, and one aggressor killed himself because he had problems at his job. In three cases there were more complex situations. Two aggressors killed themselves after consuming drugs (psychoactive substances), for one of them the consumption of psychoactive substances was associated with an older suicide attempt. Another aggressor who committed an attempted homicide-suicide already had in his background three suicide attempts. According to my information, in two cases of attempted homicide-suicide, the aggressors had threatened the victims to kill them and then they would commit suicide.

Modus operandi

Two thirds of the attempted homicide-suicides were committed with a knife (67.5 per cent of homicides and 59.6 per cent of suicides). The objects that were on hand for the aggressors (iron bar, wooden bat) were used for seriously injuring six victims (15 per cent) and for the committing of suicide of three aggressors (8.1 per cent). Hanging was one of the most frequent ways to commit suicide (24.3 per cent). Firearms were used only in one attempted homicide-suicide (see Table 1.7).

Table 1.7 Modus operandi of the attempted homicide-suicides

Used weapons	Total	
	Homicide	**Suicide**
Firearms	2 (5)	1 (2.7)
Knife	27 (67.5)	22 (59.6)
Ax	1 (2.5)	-
Hitting with an object	6 (15)	3 (8.1)
Striking with legs and arms	3 (7.5)	-
Hanging	1 (2.5)	9 (24.3)
Poisoning	-	2 (5.4)

The aggressor's messages

Before committing the violent acts, some aggressors left messages for their relatives. In the case of attempted homicide-suicides, only three aggressors left messages for the survivors. One of them left a written message, another one left a message on the phone and another one spoke on the phone with the family members. In most of the cases (91.4 per cent) there were no written or sent messages for other members of the family.

The prevention of the homicide-suicide act in Romania

The analysis of data regarding the acts of murder followed by suicide and committed by Romanian citizens in the period 2002–2013 emphasized a series of elements that were common to all European countries where studies had been made which had particularities specific to Romania. The rate of homicide-suicides in Romania evolved in a similar way with the rate of homicide-suicides in Europe. The homicide-suicides committed between Romanian emigrants present common features for all the acts of homicide-suicide. Among these common features we can mention: committing especially types of intimate partner homicide-suicide and filicides-suicide, committing HS immediately after the separation with the aggressor and relational history affected by the domestic violence prior to the act of homicide-suicide. On the other hand, there are also some features that are specific to homicide-suicides between Romanian emigrants: the victims and aggressors' younger age than in other types of homicide-suicides or the smaller duration of the relationship between the victim and the aggressor. In this context, the prevention of the homicide-suicide acts must be focused both on diminishing the action of risk factors specific to all homicide-suicides and on giving a special attention to the factors specific to the Romanian space.

1. The external temporary and circulatory migration generated by the low economic level and the lack of jobs seems to be one of the factors which contributed to the dissolution of intrafamilial relations and to the evolution of family conflicts to lethal acts of violence with really serious consequences for the family (Balica and Stöckl 2016). The small number of cases of homicide-suicide between the Romanian emigrants limits our conclusions. This is why we consider it necessary to expand the research regarding the violent acts between Romanian emigrants/immigrants in order to more accurately identify the risk factors specific to this group.

The research confirmed the need to develop a strategy of preventing violence between Romanian people and between Romanian emigrants, a strategy which was also proposed in previous studies (Balica and Stöckl 2016). The fact that the homicide-suicides between emigrants were committed both in Romania and in the countries where they were working, shows that we need measures of preventing violence between Romanian emigrants in the countries where there are communities of Romanian emigrants. Therefore, prevention measures must be taken in Romania and also in host countries.

The development of an institutional network of support for victims of domestic violence in the countries with large communities of Romanian immigrants, but also in Romania could lead to diminishing the risk of committing homicide-suicide. The awareness of the population from the host countries towards the problems/acts of violence which Romanian immigrants are subject to and the act of informing the Romanian immigrants about some ways of intervention in the host countries in emergency situations/problems regarding domestic violence should be priority objectives of the prevention programs. Creating opportunities of integration/adaptation for Romanian immigrants in the host country like foreign language courses, informing the people about rights and obligations, institutions and services for the victims of domestic violence/human trafficking are all ways of intervention which could be efficiently used in preventing the acts of violence between Romanian emigrants. The present research and the international studies that treated the subject of domestic violence between Romanian immigrants (Vives-Cases et al. 2014) emphasized a series of factors which contributed to the victimization of Romanian immigrant/emigrant women. I consider it necessary to initiate prevention activities whose audience should be the emigrant/immigrant women from Romania or from the countries they had emigrated to. In this way, I consider it necessary to develop the following activities: a) initiating information campaigns regarding the rights of victims of violence; b) initiating some information campaigns regarding the institutions in Romania which offer services of assistance and counseling to the victims of domestic violence; c) information campaigns regarding the rights and institutions which offer assistance services to the victims from the host countries to which the Romanian emigrants went; d) the development of some projects of international collaboration meant to initiate assistance activities for the victims of Romanian origin from the countries where there are communities of Romanian emigrants.

2. Homicide-suicide is committed between intimate partners most of the time, as shown by international studies. Research regarding homicide-suicides in Romania emphasized the same particularity. Therefore, we must give special attention to preventing the violent acts between intimate partners and, especially the violent acts that tend to become murder acts. As seen throughout this research, there is a series of elements that are signaled before the acts of homicide-suicide are committed. These acts are preceded by other acts of physical violence that frequently occur between partners and they are also associated most of the time with death threats or other suicide attempts.

The development of a proper tool to measure the risk of committing a serious violent act would allow the identification of cases that require the preventive intervention of police or of other institutions meant to act for diminishing the risk of committing a homicide-suicide. There are tools of this type in other countries and they are successfully used in Europe and North America (e.g. in the USA the Danger Assessment/Danger Assessment for Immigrant Woman, Messner et al. 2013). The creation of such a tool adapted to the risk factors specific to our country and the development of an international collaboration to allow the testing of a tool for certain types of immigrants from the European space would lead to the efficiency of the actions meant to reduce the number of homicide-suicides committed both between and by Romanians from the European space and between and by Romanians in Romania.

The development of the types of services offered to the victims of domestic violence/violence between intimate partners could contribute to the prevention of violent acts prior to homicide-suicide. The creation of a bigger number of shelters for women and informing women about these shelters and also informing women from the rural environment about the services offered to the victims of violence would be just a step in intervention.

The aggressors still remain a category of people who do not benefit from services of assistance and counseling adapted to the identified needs as a consequence of their involvement in actions of violence. Protecting the victims is an important element, but we also have to make activities meant to give counseling that is adapted to the aggressors' particularities (counseling and treatment for alcoholism, drug addiction, and anger management).

Special attention should be given to people with suicide attempts in their background. The family doctors who have these persons in their care or specialty doctors who treat them should direct them towards the psychological programs which could help go over the eventual breakdowns and suicide attempts. People with mental illnesses seem to be exposed, to a larger extent, to the risk of becoming aggressors. The people who were diagnosed with depression and other mental disorders who interrupt their treatment present the risk that, in some situations of great stress, they will direct their aggression towards their family members. A deep analysis of the data regarding the health state of the aggressors from the Homicide in Romania database could lead to the creation of a better procedure concerning the treatment of persons with mental disorders and maintaining them in the community. A periodic evaluation of the patients known for their mental disorders and the psychological testing of some persons could lead to identifying some moments of crisis and to the intervention in advance through proper therapies.

3. The maternal filicide and the paternal filicide represent the second type of homicide-suicide with a bigger number of cases in Romania. In order to avoid such violent acts, we should pay more attention to the families known for acts of violence between parents or to the families with a parent who has moved abroad. For these families, I consider that social services should visit children at their homes and identify the eventual risks of children's victimization. Their intervention in the tough situations in which the remaining parent no longer has resources could prevent the acts of homicide-suicide of this type.

4. The homicide-suicides committed against old people or between old people need more attention from the communities which they belong to, from the social services and doctors. These violent acts were the result of some life stories marked by acts of domestic violence which ended with the death of the victim. There is also another category of homicide-suicide associated with older people. I am talking about homicide-suicides committed by the ones who take care of old sick people (members of their families) for a long period of time and who do not find another solution for the daily difficulties they deal with, but murder and then suicide. The development of a service system proper to old people could prevent the violent acts. All these counseling, intervention and assistance activities could be developed only if the necessary human and material resources are available.

5. Beyond the financial resources necessary for the building of some institutional networks proper for the fast intervention in the case of committing the acts of violence, we need financial resources for forming the personnel that could

interfere, counsel and assist the persons with a risk of involvement in violent activities or with a victimization risk. We need training courses for the police officers who have contact with the cases of domestic violence and for the officers from the county prevention services. We also need training for social workers so they can recognize and identify the risks associated with some types of violence that can become lethal, and their intervention in time to prevent the committing of homicide-suicide. The formation of some social workers who could offer proper services for the aged people from the urban and rural environment is necessary, as is the formation of a network of professionals that could identify the families or persons with a risk of victimization from an early stage: policemen, social assistants, teachers, doctors. Their formation and transformation in resources for the communities where they run their activity.

6. The development of some assistance programs for aged people, families with members abroad and persons with mental disorders who do not have the necessary resources (economic, physical, but also psychological) in order to get over the crisis they were dealing with. The audience should be informed of these assistance programs for groups with a victimization risk. Informing the audience regarding the risk to which they expose themselves by living in conditions where they are victims of repeated violence and not taking actions earlier.

Including a special section in *The National Strategy Controlling and Preventing Violence in the Family* regarding the ways of preventing the domestic violence between and against women and children from the families of temporary emigrants. A proper development of the assistance and intervention system in order to prevent the violent acts with a lethal risk needs both a development of studies regarding the health state of the population of Romania, and evaluation studies of programs and intervention methods used in the field of preventing the acts of domestic violence. The multiplication of the research centered on identifying the risk factors specific to some acts of violence (family violence, violence against aged people, violence of persons with mental disorders) must be accompanied by research activities meant to evaluate the present treatments and intervention methods associated to these types of violence with a higher risk of homicide-suicide.

2. Intimate Partner Femicides versus Intimate Partner Femicide-Suicides in Romania

Before giving reasons for the need for the comparative analysis made in this chapter, I consider necessary to clarify the meaning of some terms used. In order to describe the deliberate homicide of an intimate partner (husband/wife, former husband/wife, boyfriend/girlfriend, former boyfriend/girlfriend, concubine, former concubine) the specialty literature used the terms intimate partner homicide (Liem and Nieuwbeerta 2010, Liem and Roberts 2009) and intimate partner femicide (Mathews et al. 2008). When the term 'intimate partner homicide' was used, the perpetrator might have been the male or female partner. In the case in which the term intimate femicide was used, then it was certainly a homicide committed by a man against a woman who is or was in a relationship with that man.

Conversely, in order to refer to the deliberate homicide of an intimate partner and the suicide of the perpetrator, the terms 'intimate partner homicide-suicide' or 'intimate femicide-suicide' were used. These terms are not identical in content. Intimate partner homicide-suicide includes the homicide committed both by a man and by a woman against their intimate partner and then the aggressor's suicide. The terms 'intimate partner femicide-suicide' (Adinkrah 2014) and 'intimate femicide-suicide' refer only to the homicide committed by a partner against a woman who is (or was) in an intimate relationship with the perpetrator; after which the perpetrator commits suicide (Mathews et al. 2008, Koziol-McLaine 2006, Dawson 2005).

My investigations in the three last years showed that the number of intimate partner homicide-suicides is higher than that of other types of homicide-suicide. Intimate partner homicide-suicides represent 66.7 per cent of the total of homicide-suicides registered for 2002–2013. Moreover, all perpetrators of intimate partner homicide-suicides were men. Therefore, the most proper term to describe homicides committed by male perpetrators against their intimate partners followed by the suicide of the aggressor is that of intimate femicide-suicide. In this book I will use the term 'intimate partner femicide' in order to designate the homicide committed by a male perpetrator against a woman who was or had been in an intimate relationship with the aggressor. The term intimate partner femicide-suicide will be used for homicides committed by a male perpetrator against a present or former intimate partner followed by the suicide of the aggressor.

The debates regarding the association of homicide-suicides with homicides or suicides generated an increase in researchers' interest to make studies meant to emphasize the belonging of homicide-suicides either to homicides or to suicides. In the last five years, researchers have made comparative studies between homicide-suicides, homicides and suicides (Liem and Niewbeerta 2010, Logan et al. 2008) and studies which compared intimate partner homicides (femicides) with intimate partner homicides (femicides) followed by suicide or attempted suicides (Liem and Roberts 2009, Mathews et al. 2008, Dawson 2005). These studies identified factors that are common to homicides and homicide-suicides, and they also showed some elements that differentiate them. As the number of comparative studies is still quite small, and the results are limited to used samples, I decided to analyze the particularities of intimate partner femicides versus intimate partner femicide-suicides committed in Romania.

Unlike previous research, my study compares two samples of perpetrators who committed violent acts against their intimate partners; 40 intimate partner femicides and 40 intimate partner femicide-suicides. I decided to make this analysis in order to highlight the common factors and the factors specific to every type of violence.

Methodology

In the first phase of the study, I built two samples of perpetrators who committed intimate partner femicide (IPF) and intimate partner femicide-suicide (IPFS) and whose profile was relatively similar. At the same time, I tried to gather as much information regarding the two types of perpetrators in order to identify the specific risk factors and compare the results of my study with the results of other studies. The design of my analysis was structured according to some dimensions for which I could identify concrete data for both samples during my investigations. The analysis of the two types of perpetrators was limited by the type of information registered in the Homicide-suicides in Romania database (for the perpetrators of intimate partner femicide-suicides). I had in this database a series of indicators and variables regarding: homicide, suicide, aggressors, victims and coverage of the cases. The sources used for this database allowed the compilation of some information regarding some indicators from the database. I did not have information for some indicators because this information was not mentioned by the sources used (police, parquet and online media). For example, I had little information about the level of education, duration of the relationship between perpetrator and victim, history of violence or the perpetrators' health state. The lack of this information also occurred, to a small extent, in the case of the IPF sample. The researcher's access to the penal file of IPF perpetrators allowed me to pick up the aforementioned information only if this was written, or if the perpetrators wanted it to be mentioned during the interviews.

The comparative analysis of the two samples of perpetrators also involved making some additional investigations and analyses next to those used in the writing of the Homicide-suicides in the Romania database. In fact, in order to analyze the two samples, I needed to first gather information about them and then I had to analyze it. The information regarding the intimate partner femicide-suicide sample was extracted from the Homicide-suicides database. For the intimate partner femicide sample I had to make a database for which I made a specific methodology. I will present below the way in which I gathered data regarding the two samples of perpetrators.

Sample Intimate Partner Femicide-Suicides (IPFS)

The data regarding the sample of intimate partner femicide-suicide perpetrators was extracted from the Homicide-suicides in Romania (2002–2013) database. As I mentioned in the previous chapter, in order to make the Homicide-suicides in Romania database, I used three sources; online media, data from the police and data from parquets regarding homicide-suicides (see Chapter 1, *Methodology* section). From this database, I selected 40 male perpetrators who committed homicide against their partners and then committed suicide. I included in this sample only intimate partner femicide-suicides ending with the death of the victim and of the aggressor. Attempted femicide-suicides were excluded. I tried to choose perpetrators with the same socio-demographical characteristics as the aggressors from the sample of intimate partner femicide (sex, age, emigrant/non-emigrant, rural/urban). From the Homicide-suicides database I took the data regarding the 40 perpetrators as they were registered in the database (data regarding homicide, suicide, perpetrator and victim). I excluded, though, the indicators regarding the coverage of the cases (period of time, frequency of appearance, primary definers, etc.).

Sample Intimate Partner Femicide (IPF)

For the sample of perpetrators involved in intimate partner femicides I made a database which was structured so that it could allow a comparative analysis of the two samples. More exactly, I structured the database starting from the same dimensions (except the ones regarding suicide and the coverage of the case). Unlike the IPFS sample in the case of perpetrators of intimate partner femicides I had the advantage that information could be highlighted about the violent act directly by the perpetrator. Moreover, with the aggressor's agreement, I could also use other information sources which contained data regarding perpetrators and which I could not obtain in the case of IPFS (e.g. the data regarding health state, alcohol or drug consumption, level of education). In this context, I decided to use for the IPF sample three data sources which could ensure most of the necessary information. The methodology of picking up this information was made after I contacted the National Administration of Penitentiaries and I discussed the ways of obtaining some data regarding the perpetrators convicted for intimate partner femicide. Both international and Romanian legislation protect the rights of the people who are in the custody of penitentiaries, and the National Administration of Penitentiaries has a specific methodology of collecting research which involves convicts. This is why I had to make, in the first phase, a set of information which could be discussed with the representatives of the National Administration of Penitentiaries. This set of information contained data regarding the objectives of my research, the methodology, the investigated population, the ethical involvements and legal frame of the research, the protection measures for convicts (protecting data regarding identity, confidentiality of identification data, informing subjects about the objectives of the research). I attached to the set of information, the research tools that I wanted to use: the interview guide and the analysis grid of penal files (list with indicators that I wanted to pick up from files) found in the custody of penitentiaries. In the set of information, I created a separate section with documents in which every subject could give his approval (or not) to participate in my research: the Informed Approval and Acceptance Form.

After talking about the generalities of the methodology with the representatives of the Directorate of Psycho-Social Intervention from the National Administration of Penitentiaries, the set of information (with all the previously mentioned sections) was debated by the Ethic Commission from the Institute of Sociology. After the Ethic Commission and the representatives of the National Administration of Penitentiaries validated the methodology of the investigations necessary for making the database about the 40 IPF perpetrators, I got to the next phase; identifying IPF perpetrators in the penitentiary system. For better organization of my research, I discussed with the representatives of the National Administration of Penitentiaries that indicated to me several penitentiaries where there were more people convicted for homicide. After identifying some penitentiaries where I could make my investigations, I contacted them all and informed them about my research. I sent the set of information regarding the research and I continued my collaboration with every representative of every penitentiary. Finally, in order to collect data about the sample of 40 IPF perpetrators I collaborated with six penitentiaries: Mărgineni Penitentiary, Rahova Penitentiary, Jilava Bucharest Hospital Penitentiary, Ploiesti Penitentiary, Galaţi Penitentiary and Jilava Penitentiary.

During my investigations, I had more difficulties with identifying subjects for the sample of IPF perpetrators. These difficulties were, first of all, generated by way of organization of the penitentiaries (according to the types of detention regimes). Secondly, I faced difficulties because of the way of registering convicts (according to the Penal Code article taken into consideration when they were sanctioned). Another difficulty was how the staff from the Service of Psycho-Social Intervention had previously informed convicts about my research.

In Romania, according to Law 254/2013 regarding the regime of executing imprisonment punishments, article l 1 (a–d), there are four types of detention regimes: maximum security regime, closed regime, semi open and open regime. The penitentiaries in Romania are organized in special detention sections for every type of regime. In some penitentiaries there are sections for all detention regimes, in other penitentiaries there are sections only for some types of detention. Hence the difficulty to reach people who were convicted of homicide. Some penitentiaries had all types of detention regime and I had a larger chance to identify a sufficient number of perpetrators for my research. The penitentiaries which had only some types of detention had in their custody only certain types of convicts. For example, if there were only sections with an open or semi-open regime, the convicts could have been people convicted for homicide, but in their last period of detention.

Another difficulty was generated by the fact that, in the last two years, there were legal modifications which affected the Penal Code. Thus, starting with February 1, 2014, a New Penal Code proposed some modifications for homicides. Penitentiaries included in their databases both people convicted for homicide according to the Old Penal Code (article 174–176) and people convicted according to the New Penal Code (article 188–189 and article 199 paragraph 1). The situation was quite complex also due to the fact that the Old Penal Code had different sanctions for more types of homicide: homicide (art. 174), qualified homicide (art. 175) and aggravated homicide (art. 176). IPF perpetrators could be found in the penitentiary databases (made in such a way as to allow the quick identification of a felony according to the Penal Code) after the selection of the people convicted for qualified homicide and degree homicide (the homicide of intimate partners could be found in both categories according to the way in which it was committed). In order to find only IPF perpetrators, we had to check every list of sanctions for qualified homicide and degree homicide and identify the type of victim. This is because, in both types of homicide, the victims could have been wives, relatives or other types of persons.

Consequently, it was quite difficult to identify possible subjects for my research and I needed significant involvement from the staff of the penitentiaries. These staff had direct access to the penitentiary databases and extracted the list of persons who corresponded to the selection criteria stipulated in the research (men over 18 years old at the crime moment, persons who committed intimate partner femicide, Romanian citizens). After that, the lists were sent to the staff from the Service of Psycho-Social Intervention. Psychologists discussed with every convict and informed them about the research I was to make in the respective penitentiary. The convicts were asked to express their wish to participate or not. All these activities were made before my arrival in the penitentiary.

The period in which I had to collect my research in the penitentiary was settled in such a way so that I did not disturb the activities. Together with the person designated by the management of the penitentiary, I was discussing the work program and I was organizing meetings with the eligible persons. Only convicts who had previously accepted participation in the meeting with me were taken out from the detention sections every day. The meetings took place in specially organized offices (offices of staff or clubs for educational activities) where we had all the confidentiality and security conditions (the security personnel was present quite close to me according to how dangerous the convict was). In the first phase of every meeting, I informed convicts about the research I wanted to make. Then I explained the objectives and answered their questions. After being informed about the research and about the way in which I was protecting their identification data, I asked for their written approval to participate in the research. I also asked them to allow me to access the data from the penitentiary databases and from the penal files from the custody of penitentiaries. After receiving written approval, my next step was to collect information for every case. Every meeting was made of one part of information and expression of approval (or disapproval) and one part in which I had the interview with the convict.

The semi-structured interviews included questions regarding the family to which they belonged until they became of age, the relational background of perpetrators, history of violence, level of education, profession and job, health state, relation with the victim, day of the crime, motivation of homicide and relationship with the family after being convicted for homicide. With the questions regarding the relational background, I tried to find out if this type of perpetrator had one or more intimate relationships during their life and why they chose to commit homicide against the last partner. I picked up information about the first marriage (when he got married for the first time, who influenced the choice of the partner, how long the relationship lasted, why they broke up) and about the following marriages (duration of relationships, their parents' and friends' opinion about their relationships). I also tried to identify the economic level of his original family and of the family the perpetrator had made, to identify the presence of some periods of family crises generated by the low economic level of some regions and some periods of time (e.g. the period of economic crisis).

Migration inside the country (from poor areas to more developed urban areas) and external migration were other two important elements that were included in my research. The analysis of data regarding intimate partner femicide-suicide showed that the partners' emigration in order to find a job led to some discrepancies in the family which favored the committing of intimate partner femicide-suicide (Balica and Stöckl 2016). Due to this, I considered necessary to analyze the role of internal and external migration in committing intimate partner femicide. In addition, during the interview, I asked questions regarding the presence of intimate partner violence during their relations with the intimate partners.

After every interview, the information from penal file and from the database of the penitentiary was analyzed. The information from these two sources was conflated with information from my interview and at the end I kept only the data that coincided with those from the penal file and the penitentiary database. All information regarding the socio-demographic data, modus operandi, information regarding the victim and the health state collected from the penal file, the database and the interview was included in the Registration Paper of Homicide for the case.

Dimensions and indicators included in the IPF database

The Registration Paper of Homicide cases was structured on three criteria: 1) Data regarding homicide; 2) Data regarding the agent of the act of violence and 3) Data regarding the victims (direct victims, indirect victims and survivors).

1. In the data regarding homicide, variables regarding murder were included: way of committing the act, place, motivation, period of time between homicide and suicide, modus operandi, weapons used, place of the victim's death, type of victim's wounds, number of strikes, number of victims and witnesses.

2. The section regarding the perpetrator of the act of violence was structured so that it could allow me to pick up some information regarding: age, level of education, criminal background, occupation, whether he worked abroad or not; the aggressor's mental state, alcohol/drug abuse, citizenship and marital status.

3. In the section regarding victims I included variables such as: age, level of education, occupation, victim and aggressor's relationship, whether she worked

abroad, health state, alcohol/drug abuse, citizenship, marital status and history of abuse.

The information about the two samples of perpetrators was included in SPSS database.

The structure of the intimate femicide-suicide and intimate femicide samples

The IPFS and IPF samples were structured in such a way as to be similar according to some variables: sex of the perpetrator (male), environment where the homicide was committed (rural/urban), the emigrant or non-emigrant status of the perpetrator and distribution according to the age of the perpetrator (26–39 years old and 40–68 years old). As I showed in the section regarding the methodology used to gather information regarding the IPF sample, there were more factors which influenced the selection of perpetrators who committed IPF. My attempt to select aggressors who corresponded to the selection criteria was quite difficult to put into practice. This was because few of the hundreds of convicts interviewed in the six penitentiaries that I visited met the selection criteria, and even fewer accepted to take part in my research. Some of them gave up during the interview, for others I did not have access to the penal files (they did not agree to have penal files consulted), and others found the excuse that they were not Romanian native speakers (they were Magyar) and refused to participate in an interview in Romanian. I eliminated all these cases for which I did not have access to three data sources or whose interviews were incomplete. At the end, the two samples had similar structures (see Table 2.1).

Table 2.1 Socio-demographic features of perpetrators from IPFS and IPF samples

	Intimate Partner Femicide-Suicides (N=40)	**Intimate Partner Femicides (N=40)**
Male	40	40
Urban	19	19
Rural	21	21
Emigrants	12	11
Non-emigrants	28	29
Age 26–39 years	13	14
40–68 years	27	26

I will try to emphasize some elements specific to intimate partner femicides starting from these two samples of perpetrators.

Characteristics of perpetrators of IPF and IPFS

The analysis of the two samples of perpetrators showed the fact that the information regarding the level of education of the two categories of perpetrators could not be compared. Although I had information sources for every sample, the information about the IPFS sample did not exist for 82.5 per cent of the total. Due to this fact, statements about education are limited to IPF. Approximately a third of the IPF perpetrators had a low educational level (secondary school – 30 per cent), and two thirds had a medium level of education (58.2 per cent). Only one IPF perpetrator had a superior level of education. Alcohol consumption was confirmed by the forensic experts for 25 IPF perpetrators (58.1 per cent) and 14 IPFS perpetrators (35 per cent). Only one IPF and one IPFS perpetrator had consumed drugs.

The information regarding health state was less recorded in the case of perpetrators from the IPFS sample. For more than half of the perpetrators (26 cases, 65 per cent) data about the health state was not recorded. Investigators (policemen and prosecutors) concentrated on detecting the proof that identified the offender and they were not interested in finding out about the health state of the aggressor, who had already committed suicide. Only three of the perpetrators, for which data regarding health state were recorded, did not have mental illnesses. The situation of data regarding the health state of IPF perpetrators was different. The fact that the aggressor allowed me to consult the penal file and to extract information regarding his health state contributed to the completion of the database with this information. Moreover, during the investigation, some forensic examinations regarding the health state of perpetrators were made. Their results were recorded in the penal file to which I had access. All these contributed to obtaining a large sum of data about the health state of the IPF sample. According to the information that was at my disposal, 13 IPF perpetrators (32.5 per cent) were diagnosed with mental illnesses and 7 IPF perpetrators (16.3 per cent) with other types of diseases (ischemic heart disease, spinal tumor, diabetes, angina pectoris, and arthritis). Among the mental illnesses recorded in the official reports, we can find organic personality disorder (2), borderline personality disorder (3), depressive disorder (4), polymorphic personality disorder (2), paranoid schizophrenia, disharmonic personality and epilepsy.

Criminal antecedents

Some perpetrators also had other acts of violence in their records. Only a small number of perpetrators from the IPFS sample had penal records (3). On the other hand, the number of IPF perpetrators with penal records was much bigger (17 perpetrators, 39.5 per cent). Some of them committed less serious felonies (thefts, fraud, trespassing, threatening, abuse, beating and other violent acts) and others committed serious felonies such as attempted homicide against their children or against other people from their group of friends (2 cases) or homicide (2 cases).

During interviews, the perpetrators with homicide or attempted homicide in their records tried to blame others for the committed acts of violence. Even if I told them that it was not an interrogation, the perpetrators were trying, in fact, not to be sanctioned for the homicide committed against their wife (the second homicide in their criminal career) with a bigger punishment because they were at their second homicide. N.M. was one of the perpetrators with serious violent acts in their records. He was sentenced to 8 years for attempted filicide. Although the perpetrator played the main role in committing attempted filicide, he does not take responsibility for his action and blames the mother (the wife against whom he committed homicide 12 years after the attempted homicide against his child).

> At some time in 1997 I went to jail because of her. They gave me about 8 years of jail for attempted homicide! About the baby; she dropped the baby from the crib. I took the deed on me and because of this I lost my life. I thought that, if they put her into jail, they will take the children and put them in an orphanage. So I took 8 years of jail for her. She was drunk, after all I admitted the deed so she doesn't go to jail. Yes, I went to jail for 5 years and two months. (IPF, 39 years old, high school, mason)

Victims' characteristics

The information regarding victims was registered to a smaller extent by the institutions involved in investigating IPF and IPFS. In fact, the police and prosecutors' investigations are focused more on the analysis of the aggressor and of the modus operandi and less on the analysis of data regarding victims. The data about the victim's health state are also important for the investigators, in the case where the perpetrator tries to have his punishment diminished by invoking the fragility of the victim's health state.

Due to this there was little data about the level of education and the alcohol consumption of IPFS victims and about the health state of the victims from the two samples. In these conditions, the data regarding the level of education of IPF victims show that one third of victims (33.6 per cent) had a low educational level. The percentage of victims with an average level of education (high school

23.3 per cent; secondary school + vocational school 14 per cent) was a little higher than the percentage of victims with a low educational level. The information about the IPFS sample was missing for 39 cases so we cannot make any statements about this sample.

Alcohol consumption was mentioned in 37.2 per cent of IPF. The data regarding IPFS were limited to only 6 cases (5 victims had consumed alcohol and one victim had used drugs). The victims' health state was too little explored by investigators. For the IPFS cases we have no data and for the IPF cases we have information that 5 victims suffered from chronic diseases.

The analysis of data regarding the age of the victims from the two samples shows that there are some differences. The number of IPFS victims aged between 40 and 65 (52.5 per cent) is higher than the number of IPF victims (37.5 per cent). On the other hand, in the case of IPF victims aged between 26 and 39, we have a higher number of victims (47.5 per cent) than in the case of the IPFS sample (35 per cent).

Characteristics of IPF and IPFS

Place where IPF and IPFS were committed

Intimate partner femicides and intimate partner femicide-suicides were committed especially in spaces that were accessible to perpetrators, but hardly accessible to other persons who could have potentially saved the victims' lives. When I mention that IPF were committed in accessible places for perpetrators, I am talking about the victim's or the aggressor's home, or the perpetrator and victim's common home.

The number of IPF committed in an accessible place for the perpetrators (76.7 per cent) was higher than that of IPFS sample (63.5 per cent). The number of intimate partner femicides committed in the perpetrator's house (11.6 per cent) was also higher than the number of intimate partner femicide-suicides committed in the perpetrator's house (2.5 per cent).

Modus operandi

The analysis of modus operandi for the two samples showed that approximately a third of the cases included in the two samples were committed with a knife (IPF – 34.9 per cent and IPFS – 37.5 per cent). The number of IPF committed by hitting with an object (18.6 per cent) or by beating (hitting with hands and legs 18.6 per cent) was higher than that of IPFS committed by hitting with an object (5 per cent) or by beating (5 per cent). Conversely, IPFS committed by strangling (7 cases, 17.5 per cent) were more numerous than those included in the IPF sample

(3 cases, 7 per cent). Another particularity of the IPFS cases was the fact that 10 of the homicides were committed by shooting (25 per cent), while we did not have any case of IPF committed by shooting.

The distribution of IPF and IPFS cases according to the period of time in which they were committed was almost identical. Most of the cases were committed during the night, between 10 pm and 5.59 am (IPF – 27.9 per cent, IPFS – 32.5 per cent). The presence of witnesses (relatives of the victim and of the aggressor or neighbors) was mentioned only for one out of five cases of IPF and one out of four cases of IPFS.

Motivation of IPF and IPFS

The analysis of reasons which generated the IPF and IPFS cases shows that jealousy and suspicion of infidelity were the most frequently mentioned in the official reports (IPF – 37.5; IPFS – 35 per cent). Infidelity was mentioned only in four cases of IPF and two cases of IPFS. Divorce and the victims' decision to leave the aggressors were the reasons which determined a higher number of IPF (11 cases, 27.5) compared to IPFS (6 cases, 15 per cent). Familial conflicts generated by daily problems (IPF – 10 per cent; IPFS – 15 per cent) or by the alcohol consumption of the victim (IPF – 15 per cent) or of the aggressor (IPF – 1 case; IPFS – 1 case) were other types of reasons identified during my analysis.

Interviews made with perpetrators from the IPF sample allowed me to explore the perpetrators' arguments for the decision to commit homicide against their partners.

Jealousy and infidelity

As I mentioned before, jealousy and suspicion of infidelity represented the reason for approximately a third of IPF and IPFS. Most IPF perpetrators had, during their lives, more intimate relationships (marriage, concubines or intimate relations of several months). For some cases, the separation from the intimate partner was determined by the perpetrator's jealousy and infidelity suspicion towards all the intimate partners that they had. At the same time, jealousy and infidelity suspicion are present in the lives of perpetrators with a different level of education. Among perpetrators who admitted they were jealous and had information (verified or not), regarding the partner's infidelity, I met both perpetrators with a low educational level (primary or secondary school) and perpetrators with a high educational level who grew up in intellectual families with a life and education standard specific to the middle class.

Case A: IPF Perpetrator with traditional mentality regarding intimate relations and jealousy

An interesting case is that of a perpetrator who, during the interview, described the drama that he lived with his first life partner, who seemed to have had a major contribution to the onset of his jealousy. His parents chose his wife and decided that he had to get married immediately after finishing military service. Although the two parents were intellectual and lived in the capital of Romania, they had a traditional mentality which you would rather find in the Romanian rural environment and in families with a low educational level. According to tradition, young men could get married after finishing the mandatory military service which had to be done when boys became of age (18 years old). Compulsory military service ended on January 1, 2007, when Romania became a member of the European Union (Law 395/December 16, 2005). It was not the fact that his parents decided to marry him that marked the young man, but the fact that his parents did not trust and did not listen to him when he complained about his wife. The lack of his wife's virginity seemed to have been the source of his distrust in his life partner. Moreover, this was a quite strong reason for a man with a traditional mentality, and this mentality was dominant in men during the '80s–'90s. The wife's virginity was a rule and those who were breaking it had to bear a public odium because their husbands would reveal in front of the community, immediately after the wedding, whether the wife was a virgin or not (it was a tradition that, at the end of weddings, the husband should show the bride's night gown as a proof of her purity). I made these specifications in order to better understand the context in which this young man developed his mistrust of women. Lied to by his first partner and constrained by parents to remain married to this woman (divorce was also a stigma for those who were married), the young man became an isolated and jealous man, always suspecting his partner of infidelity.

> So, in general, I apologize, they kept telling me that she was a good girl, a virgin. I thought they were right. I'm young, let's give it a chance. I was working, I had a good salary, and she kept telling me that she had everything, that she was the best, she was a virgin, and she hadn't been a virgin. So why are you telling me that she was when she wasn't? Look, she was with that man and that man, it's not true, you are just imagining. Now I'm telling you from my far away past. She was lying, she was taught by an aunt to do this when she had to sleep with me (I apologize again). They didn't trust my words. No, it had been her and then another one. But I had no right to judge her, but what upset me was the fact that she said she had been a virgin. Everybody was throwing this in my face, look, you are distant, and you are that and that and look at this girl. Then I said it wasn't true, I had a burst. And I wasn't believed for a long time. I went on this way of life with some jealousy,

with distrust and skepticism. (IPF, 42 years old, high school + technical school, telecommunication technician, urban)

After four years of marriage, the perpetrator divorced and he had more short relationships over 19 years. In 2009, he met another partner online and they decided to live together. Step by step, he found out that she was an alcoholic and after several months he found out that his partner had more bank loans that she could pay. There were discussions about the payment of these loans, but the element that determined the violent reaction of the perpetrator was his partner's infidelity.

And they joined and after that I found out that she had had an affair with a person in jail, after which I found out that she had met a former partner and had started a relationship with him and after that I said, wait a minute, I invested feelings in this relationship, let's end this as everything is useless. I had an attempt, I packed her bags and at the second attempt, in fact at the third attempt. But, I repeat, the first time I packed her bags I was still in love with her, I admit. She didn't want to go and when the action happened, I packed her bags and I told her please go and I had the talk but it is not written there, in the file that the scandal started. (IPF, 42 years old, high school + technical school, telecommunication technician)

Beyond the perpetrator's declarations during the interview, the papers from the penal file recorded declarations of witnesses and former partners. According to them, the perpetrator was violent more times during the relationship with the wife he killed. His violence was generated by his jealousy. The violent acts that killed the last partner were preceded by other violent acts which the coroners said were one week old. Former partners and witnesses mentioned that the perpetrator was a violent person who had been aggressive towards most of the identified partners.

I had little information regarding the relational history of IPFS perpetrators and this was because both partners died. For some IPFS cases, though, I found information regarding some manifestations of jealousy of IPFS perpetrators that were registered in the witnesses' declarations and included in the resolutions and documents from the penal file of IPFS cases.

Case B: Romanian emigrant IPFS Perpetrator – jealousy and infidelity suspicion

I will present as an example, the case of C.I, a 38-year-old man, who was on his second marriage with a woman 11 years younger than him. C.I. had been working in Sweden for some time in order to be able to support his new family that he had with the victim (a 3-year-old and a 4-year-old). During the investigations, more witnesses (the victim's parents) mentioned to the prosecutor that the victim had been physically abused and death threatened by C.I. The perpetrator was jealous and he suspected that she was cheating on him with a man she had met online. His former partner gave us the same information about the violent behavior of C.I. The perpetrator's former concubine declared that he was jealous and he also wanted to beat her when they were together. Moreover, the former concubine also mentioned two attempted suicides that the perpetrator had when she told him she would leave him. His jealousy and infidelity suspicion determined C.I. to be even more aggressive in the relationship with his second partner. C.I.'s aggression was well known also among the policemen from the town. The victim made a complaint to the police and asked for police intervention, but she withdrew her complaint a short time after that. When the perpetrator left for a period of time, the victim was less exposed to physical violence and the aggressor was satisfied just to threaten her on the phone. After his last threat, the woman even tried to convince a friend to go home with her because she was afraid to go home alone. The friend's refusal to accompany the victim was one of the factors that determined the committing of the homicide without witnesses who could have interfered and rescued her (the homicide was committed in the presence of the two 3 and 4-year-old children). His decision to commit homicide came a short time after the perpetrator had a phone conversation in the presence of witnesses. The victim forgot by mistake to hang up the phone and the jealous perpetrator heard the victim talk with the witnesses. On the same day, the perpetrator threatened that "he will come back home in the country, he will gas her, take her clothes off and he will write with a marker on her body". Four days after this threat, C.I. strangled his wife to death. Policemen found the victim's body half naked and covered with Swedish crowns. As he had promised, the perpetrator wrote a message with a black marker on his wife's body: "On the other world adios, wash your hair with them and we'll see each other". The perpetrator committed suicide a short time after he killed his wife, throwing himself from a tall building.

Both cases emphasize the mechanism of the evolution of relationships affected by jealousy and infidelity suspicion. I am talking about perpetrators who had more relationships (at least two) during their lives and who sometimes had children from previous relations. Unlike the first partners who were able to leave these aggressors, the following partners did not have this possibility any more. Jealousy, infidelity suspicion associated with their desire to be separated from the violent perpetrator (to which we can add in some cases the emigrant status of the husband and wife who maintained the infidelity suspicion) determined the end of the relation as the perpetrator wanted, through IPF or IPFS. The only difference which we can identify between the two cases is the presence of attempted suicide and of death threats mentioned by witnesses in the case of IPFS.

The woman's wish to be separated/divorced

The prosecutors' resolutions for the IPFS cases also mentioned some information regarding the connection between women's separation/divorce and the perpetrators' decision to make their wives come back to them. Witnesses, in most of the cases relatives or family friends, told prosecutors about the separation and negotiation periods between the two, about the wife's coming back or about her strong decision to leave the abusive partner.

As other researchers interested in the cases of homicide-suicide mentioned, it is difficult to restore the information about the relations which ended with homicide-suicide (Liem 2010). Due to this, some researchers tried to analyze the cases of homicide-parasuicide in order to examine more thoroughly some aspects regarding similarities and differences between homicide-suicides and homicide or suicide (Liem 2010, Hillbrand 2001). Starting from the idea that there are some similarities between homicide-suicides and homicide-parasuicides, I considered that I could bring to the discussion information obtained during my investigations regarding intimate partner femicide-suicide. During my investigations made in penitentiaries, I had the opportunity to meet a perpetrator who survived the intimate partner femicide-suicide. Although I am talking about only one, his interview confirms the information from other studies regarding the symbiotic relationship between the perpetrator and the victim of homicide-suicide (Berman 1996, Liem 2010).

Intimate Partner Femicide – Suicide

After committing homicide against his wife in the street, he cut his throat with a knife. The homicide was committed near a bar where there were more neighbors. They called an ambulance and tried to save the victim and the perpetrator. The victim could not be saved, but the aggressor was saved by doctors. After being on trial, he was convicted and sentenced to 18 years in prison. The interview made with this perpetrator emphasized some aspects regarding the way in which he took the decision to commit both the homicide and the suicide. Although she was not his first wife, the relationship with the victim seemed to be a special one from the start. At least, this is what the perpetrator claims. His desire for them to die together was expressed even from the beginning. The perpetrator's speech is ambivalent, though. On one side, it emphasizes his desire to commit suicide immediately after committing the homicide in order to fulfill the wish from the beginning of the relationship. The aggressor highlights the fact that he did not commit suicide for fear of the police or of prison. On the other side, he expresses his dissatisfaction that judges did not want to apply article 320 from the Code of Penal Procedure.

According to article 320, if the aggressor admits his act, he can receive a punishment reduced by one third.

> "I wanted to die also! I decided this from the beginning. When I married her, I told her: When you die, I want to die with you at the same time!". And now I wanted to die also, not because of the penitentiary, no, in jail, not because of that, I wanted to die with her! But look, I didn't die, and I suffered in here, and I will suffer from now on, I'm not sorry, I have to do my duty! I did it myself, I'm not sorry! I'm doing my duty, I have no problems with anybody, I have no problems with policemen. Well, I want to do my duty, to be sure that this is what I did and what I had to do! It was my fault here, I didn't have to do this, but if it happened, it happened! But these judges; they judged us very harshly! I asked for 320, he didn't give it to me, he took me from the crime scene! I didn't go anywhere and I cut my throat there! And he took me from there and he told me: "No, you were judged!", whatever, this is what is written in the file, "You were judged!". Well, not necessarily 320, my jealousy didn't go away, nothing, but nothing, absolutely nothing went away! Only that, he gave me 18 years inside, 18 years also in Bucharest and this how I came back with 18 years! This is how much is left! What can I do? (Attempted intimate partner femicide-suicide, 48 years old)

His decision to commit homicide came, as in many cases of homicide-suicide, when he found out that his wife wanted to leave him. Moreover, many intimate partner homicides happened after the partners informed the aggressors that they wanted to separate. The news that she was having a relationship with another man determined his decision to leave Italy where he was working and come to Romania to convince her to come back to him.

> This was it! I loved her very much and I'm sorry she's dead, but, I don't know, I can't have another one! It wasn't for the money, I was upset that she hung up on me then, and she ran away from home and I wanted to see what the problem was when she told me that she was having another man! Then I finished everything, I didn't need a job anymore, I left that owner and I was gone! I told him "I'm going to Romania!". And I came home and I committed this deed! I didn't have to do what I did! Maybe if I hadn't come home, may be if I hadn't had the money to come home, I can't realize. My owner gave me money and I came home! If I hadn't had, maybe none of this would have happened. I also had a boy and a girl there, a girl of hers and a boy of mine, there in Italy! I found good jobs for them there, the girl in a restaurant and the boy a pizza maker, whatever, he was making pizzas! The boy told me: "Don't go home, leave them alone!". But look, I left, I came home and I did this. (Attempted intimate partner femicide-suicide, 48 years old)

Intimate Partner Femicide

As I was saying, the wife's wish to separate is one of the reasons why a perpetrator decides to commit homicide against his partner. The interviews with the 40 perpetrators who committed homicide against their wives showed that most of them had more relationships (marriages) during their lives. Their wives had more relationships as well. Most of them had children from other relationships (both husbands and wives), but they decided to have another one and raise their children together. Although they accepted that their wives had a background with more concubinages/marriages and even children from other relationships, perpetrators could not accept the fact that they were cheated on or abandoned by their partners.

> So I earned this money, and I was sending it home, I loved this concubine of mine very much! More than the first one! More! I had two children with the first one, I didn't have any children with this one, whatever, this one had 4 children of her own.
> I: Was she married before?
> R: Yes! And, whatever, I took her how she was! Then the children got bigger, I took 2 children to school in my village, the other two were older. They all left, whatever! This wasn't a problem, but all this money that I was earning, I didn't know what the problem was with it, I was sending it home, and she was spending it with other people, with someone else.
> I: With other men?
> R: Yes! With another man! And my parents told me: "Hey, Petrică, look what the problem is ...", I didn't believe them! My brothers told me also, I said, "Hey, will you leave me alone to have my own life?". I didn't believe anyone! This happened until one day when I got home. She hung up on me and she wasn't answering anymore. She said: "Hey, I found myself another man and you should leave me alone!". Just like this. I got home, my house was empty, everything was gone, doors, everything, everything. I made up with her again in the past, it was the same, I took her from the same man also and I made up with her. I loved her very much, what can I say, I loved her enormously! After that it happened like this, she said some words to me, she said "Hey, I have another man, from now on you'll mind your own business, I went out with him every day!". I was going out there, I was going to the cafeteria there, to the restaurant there, this is how it's called in the village, cafeteria, and I was drinking a cup of coffee and I was expecting her to come and buy bread and to talk to her, maybe I'll bring her home! Not a chance, it was getting worse! It wasn't a problem about this, I wasn't interested in the money, I wasn't interested in anything, I wanted to live with her again! This was the problem. And I don't know how it happened, she told me some words, some problems with her first husband, that he wanted to cut her, cut her with the screwdriver, she kicked him with her leg, whatever, things like this. I said: "I will never do this! (IPF, 48 years old)

The idea of losing his partner seems to dominate the perpetrator's mind and he does anything in order to bring her back. He tries to talk to her, to threaten or "scare" her. This perpetrator's tone is also ambivalent. As his story is getting closer and closer to the crime moment, he tries hard to say that he did not mean to commit homicide and it was just an accident. On the other hand, we find out during his interview that he was trying to meet her every day (he was following and waiting for her where he knew she might be) and that "he made himself a knife" which he sharpened.

> I loved her deeply, what more can I say? During this, another idea came into my head, I said: "Hey, if I scare her, she has to come back to me, it can't be different!" And I made myself a knife which I had left home for cutting pigs. I took that knife, I sharpened it, I said, when I go, if another man comes in front of me, I'll cut that one instead of her, I'll only scare her to come to me, it can't be otherwise!". But it wasn't like this. Just the opposite, I didn't see any blood on her, I didn't see anything, and I cut her, I mean I dropped my knife into her, then I was confused, how to say, I lost my conscience, because I didn't know that I, after she fell, I saw the knife in my hand. I said: "Come on, I killed her, I cut her!". Then I came to my senses, but I didn't see any blood, I didn't see anything. And I felt so sorry, and I'm still sorry, I didn't have to do this, I was stupid! (IPF, 48 years old)

What is interesting with perpetrators who commit homicide against their partners is that they do not discuss their intention with other people. Those who decide to commit homicide are socially isolated people and the lack of contact with other people with whom they could talk about their separation seems to play an important role in the evolution of conflict towards homicide.

> I couldn't talk to anyone, I didn't talk to anyone, whatever, maybe I could communicate with someone so that, I don't know "Hey, don't do this!". I didn't communicate with anyone! I was sad and I was walking, I was upset! I didn't eat anything for a whole week! I kept going to the cafeteria and I was coming back. I was drinking a coffee, I was coming back! My house was empty without TV, without anything! I got to sleep then I woke up, come on, could I sleep? I kept saying: "I have to bring her home!". And this was my deed. (IPF, 48 years old)

Some of the perpetrators pass the responsibility of homicide over to their wife. In some cases, we find out that the wife was accepted as a partner after the former partner had thrown her in the street and had beaten her. The current partner (in fact, the one who committed homicide) thinks he is a hero who saved her from a violent former partner.

> I talked to her downtown, there, we sat on a bench there in Brăila and we talked. I said: "If you are a good woman, I'll take you home with me right now. She was thrown out by her husband. I didn't take advantage of things like this, I said: "If you are a good woman, it doesn't matter to me! You don't have to struggle too much, you don't have to work like this at my place, I work too!". (IPF, 48 years old)

The perpetrator is the one who usually goes to work (sometimes abroad) and solves economic problems for the family, while the wife is the one who receives money from the husband. The difficult periods that the emigrant perpetrators face abroad in order to have a job seem to contribute to the failure of the relationship despite all efforts that the aggressor brings to the discussion. The shortcomings and difficulties of emigration are used by the aggressors in order to emphasize their positive qualities and to support their decision to punish the abandoning partner.

> I had a good period, I don't say I didn't have a good period, I did! But after I left home, maybe I neglected some things. Maybe if I hadn't left home… we didn't have any money. This poverty… I earned 3 million and a half, I didn't earn at that time 3 million and a half. How can I live like this with so many children, 4 children? I had to go immediately! And I left home only because of poverty. I was sending them money, I was sending all my money home. I had for myself only 100 euros for food, I didn't have to pay for sleeping, whatever, for the phone, because I was sleeping there. But everywhere I went, I managed like this, I was sending her my money. If I received 50 euros from here and 50 euros from there, I sent it all home.

> If you were going like this from one country to another and you didn't know anyone, you could sleep in the bushes, but where else? You can't sleep in the middle of the city because the police are coming! Oh yeah, I slept, I slept for months like this! Especially in Italy, they were chasing us, and in Turkey! Yes, I slept in Italy for more than a month, because I was going in town, I found myself a job and I didn't have anywhere to sleep! The owner kept telling us: "Hey, do you have any place to sleep?", and we were saying "We live at the margin of the city!". And he said: "Hey, you'll live there as much as you can, until I look for a place to live for you!". He found us a place to live, but for 450 euros for 3 people and he was paying us 20 euros a day! We didn't have any choice then! Then it was … He found a job for us, he gave us food, this 20 euros a day, working with vegetables, at the market. We were moving the vegetables, we were picking them, we were selling them.
> I: What year did you get to Italy?
> P: Well, in the last years, before, how should I tell you, in the '90s and in '96–'97 like that. '96 yeah. Oh no, not in '96 in 2006, 2006 yes! 2006–2007 that's it. (IPF, 48 years old)

In other cases, the perpetrator supports his decision to commit homicide with the fact that she separated him from the child. If, for some of them, the separation from the partner does not mean much, the separation from the child is crucial.

> And of course she cursed me, I cursed her, she spoke bad words, I run wild myself and I hit her. That's what happened. I would have never thought that I'd become like this because of a woman! Like there were no more women on earth! But I also sent her to her mother! She went to her mother and stayed for 5 weeks! I went to the boy because I missed my boy. Yeah! I missed my son. (IPF, 39 years old, high school, mason)

In their attempt not to assume the responsibility of the homicide, the perpetrators bring to our attention incidents from the history of the relationship with the victim or information about the wife's health state. Moreover, the perpetrator's intention only to "slap" her ended with the death of the victim because the latter had a depreciated health state. While the wife's neglect of the child appears quite rarely as an argument to motivate the aggressive act, the victim's health state is used more often as a fact that led to the partner's death. The message that the perpetrator wants to send is that he did not want to commit homicide, he just wanted to "punish" her.

> I had also a son, there were 3 days left until his baptism, he was little, and she, she wasn't quite drinking at that time, she turned herself in the bed and she suffocated him. She breastfed him and she suffocated him. The baby was very little. And since then she started drinking. But she was ill… Because I didn't commit the homicide. I hit her, I beat her. I hit her with the back of my hand, I wanted to hit her shoulder and I hit her in the eye and she hurt her head, I don't know how. She had epilepsy, children's disease, she had heart problems, diabetes, and dry cirrhosis of the liver, and other 2 diseases, I don't remember their names. I took her to the county hospital. That's why I didn't commit the deed. That's why I'm staying here. I'm guilty because I didn't have to hit her, but I hit her angrily. I hit her twice with the back of my hand. One here, in the back, and one in the shoulder. And I accidentally hit her eye, but I didn't hit her with revenge so I could kill her. (IPF, 39 years old, high school, mason)

IPF and IPFS generated by the woman's desire to be separated from an abusive husband are not specific only to Romania. Studies made in other European countries and in countries from other parts of the world (Showalter et al. 1980, Campbell 1992, Wilson and Daly 1992, Dobash and Dobash 2011, Adams 2007, Brookman 2011) also showed that IPF and IPFS are motivated by the perpetrator's fear of losing control over his wife. Perpetrators think their wife is their property and they feel they could control her even after she decided to divorce. (Dobash and Dobash 2011, Brookman 2011). Moreover, some authors emphasized the fact that there is a sum of factors which combine and act in the cases of IPF perpetrators: domestic violence during the relationship, jealousy, infidelity suspicion and the victim's desire to separate (Adams 2007, Dobash and Dobash 2011). Starting from these results, I decided to include in my research a section regarding the history of violence from the IPF and IPFS relationships. The results of the study showed that there were some similarities between previous studies and the results of my research.

History of violence

Previous studies regarding intimate partner homicide and intimate partner homicide-suicide emphasized the fact that the victims of the two types of homicide had been abused by perpetrators during their relationships. Intimate partner violence was thus signaled both in the case of intimate partner homicide and in the case of intimate partner homicide-suicides (Liem and Roberts 2009, Lindqvist and Gustafsson 1995, Malphurs and Cohen 2002, Morton et al. 1998, Palermo 1994, Stack 1997). Among the questions that I had asked myself when I was organizing my research, there was also the one regarding the presence of domestic violence during the relationship between perpetrators and victims. Interviews with IPF perpetrators showed, to a small extent, the presence of violent acts before the homicide. Perpetrators avoided admitting that they had physically, sexually or emotionally abused their partners so that these violent acts would not be added to their acts of violence in the penal files. Their fear was also generated by the fact that, during interviews, according to the penitentiary regulation, either the psychologist or a security agent was near me and the perpetrator (when the convict was supposed to present a bigger danger for me).

This lack of information regarding the violent background was due to information from the penal files and interrogations. Among the included documents, the penal files had also interrogations with witnesses (former partners, family members, neighbors, friends or colleagues). These witnesses brought a lot of information regarding the violent acts to which they or the killed victims were exposed. The analysis of all data that I gathered about IPF cases showed that domestic violence cases were signaled in 17 cases (42.5 per cent). For the IPFS cases, the information regarding the violent acts prior to homicides was given by the witnesses who were interrogated during the judiciary investigation. Their declarations were also stipulated in the interrogations made for the cases of intimate partner femicide-suicides that I had access to. Thus, I had information about the presence of violent acts only for 10 cases of the analyzed sample.

In the case of IPFS as well, three death threats addressed to victims or relatives were mentioned and in two cases, the perpetrators threatened to commit suicide. The violent acts were committed by perpetrators who were married to the victims at the moment of the crime (IPF – 44.2 per cent; IPFS – 30 per cent). The number of IPF committed after the victim got separated from the perpetrator (11 victims; 26.6 per cent) was higher than that of IPFS committed after the separation of the two partners (7 victims; 17.5 per cent). IPFS committed after the two partners' separation happened in a period of time that was smaller than one month (5 out of 7 cases).

Beyond the data registered in the official documents, during the interviews with IPF perpetrators there were also some mentions of violent acts.

> The first one, I admit, she took my money twice, I admit I wasn't very good myself, I had my faults, but I don't understand how I ended like this, so I had been violent before with the first and with the other woman that I had lived with. Because she hid money from me I had these bursts but only when I was motivated, an intelligent person would walk

away if he found out that his partner was having an affair, I didn't have to be violent or jealous. (38 years old, rural, worker, criminal antecedents)

What is interesting is the fact that some perpetrators, although they admit that they had hit them ("I slapped her several times, but not to beat her"), the intention and intensity of strikes did not mean the victim's homicide. The witnesses are the ones who confirmed that they were violent and were aggressive towards their wives, and these witnesses wanted revenge themselves.

They took me into consideration when they called me at parquet, a nephew gave a statement, a boy of my sister. He declared that I was beating her more times and I had another woman and I wanted to live with another woman. This is what they told me at the parquet: "Hey, you beat her deliberately!". I didn't know what that meant, this was my first time in jail, I never received a fine in my life. "Hey, you beat her so you can live with the other one!" I turned blue, I couldn't speak anymore! How could I, well, I loved her, she was my wife. I have children with her, how can I beat her like this? I hit her several times with my hand, but I didn't want to beat her, I loved her, she was my wife! I didn't treat her badly. I cared about the baby, I was coming home, I was always bringing something, a bag of something, something sweet, juice, this was when I was coming home from work, I was bringing food. I was telling her, she was also going to the shop, she was buying, we weren't eating only beans and potatoes. We had these at home, because this is how you live in the countryside, we had them in the attic, in the basement, but I was buying from the shop also. But she wasn't, then, not with this state. (IPH, 39 years old)

Although they avoided giving information about their acts of domestic violence, there were also perpetrators who told proudly about how they punished their wives to embarrass them, that they were drinking (at least this is what they claimed). In this case, physical violence meets psychological violence and the victim ends by being killed after being exposed to the family and community odium. Moreover, the perpetrator admits that "I hit her twice in the head, I drove her crazy!".

I cut her hair, when she went to the bar, I shaved her head. I told her "So that you see what I can do to you! Instead of beating you, who knows how I can hurt you, I'm shaving your head." She started talking bad words. I say "But am I talking bad words to you so that you talk bad words to me? Come on, now I am really going to shave you!" and I shaved her head. When mum saw her she asked "But what's wrong my dear, why are you wearing that hat? It's warm outside!" I took off her hat "I shaved her head!"

Mum: "Does this mean that she was having an affair? Did you catch her with anyone?"
I say: "Oh no!"
Mum: "But what did she do? What mistake did she make? You realize you disfigured her."
I say: "Nah, I didn't disfigure her, I cut her hair because she had lice."
Mum: "Well why didn't you cut your hair too? It means that you have lice too."

> I say: "No mum, look this and this. I told her. The woman likes to drink." (42 years old, worker)

The prosecutors' resolutions also bring important information about the violent behavior of IPF and IPFS perpetrators. We have clues about the violence of IPFS perpetrators only from the witnesses who gave declarations during investigations made by prosecutors. The documents written by prosecutors contain information regarding the violent acts to which the wives of IPFS perpetrators were exposed. Due to investigations made by prosecutors, I found out that, in the case of some IPFS, there were more acts of social, economical or psychological violence before committing the IPFS. Some IPFS perpetrators tried to control their wives by socially isolating them and making them financially dependent on the husbands (the victims were not allowed to work). When the victims refused to respect the perpetrators' requirements, the perpetrators tried to control their wives by limiting their access to financial resources (blocking credit/debit cards). The following step of sanctions applied by perpetrators was the wife's homicide and then their suicide. In other cases, the prosecutor's investigations emphasized a history of physical violence that lasted for long periods of time.

Case C: IPFS after 10 years of relation marked by frequent domestic violence

The relation between A.B. and V.B. was a tense one even from the beginning. The two partners were known by family and community to be alcohol consumers, who were frequently quarrelling. Most witnesses said that the wife was frequently beaten by her husband, the family and friends were witnesses of the violent acts between the two. The relatives who had seen the violent acts tried to interfere and end the conflicts between them and sometimes they even called the police. Even the policemen from the village knew about the violence applied to the woman and they interfered several times in order to end the conflict. The perpetrator had been married twice before meeting his present partner. Both former wives declared that they left him because he was violent and he was beating them. His third wife had also the intention of leaving him. From the discussions with the witnesses, we found out that the victim was complaining about the physical violence of the perpetrator. She wanted to leave him, but she was waiting to be retired (she had to receive her retirement decision in only a short period of time) in order to become financially independent. After more episodes of physical violence during the relationship that lasted for more than 10 years, the third wife was killed around Easter. After a new episode of violence, the victim wanted to leave the aggressor, but the latter managed to make her stay another night with him. The perpetrator took advantage of the victim's coming back and the relatives' lack of involvement in ending the conflict and killed her with a sharp object. The aggressor managed to hide the victim's death and relatives saw him consuming alcohol in this period. Several days after that, the relatives found both of them dead in the house.

The information regarding domestic violence applied to victims of IPF and IPFS shows the importance of intervention in order to prevent the evolution of violence and its ending with the victim's homicide and the aggressor's suicide or not. Domestic violence associated with other risk factors can lead to IPF or IPFS. One of the risk factors that appeared during investigations was the perpetrators' or victims' alcohol consumption.

Alcohol consumption

One out of five IPF perpetrators said that their wives were alcoholics (9 cases, 22.5 per cent) and due to this they were not taking care of their children and they were not doing their daily chores. The forensic experts confirmed the presence of alcohol in the victims' blood for a third of IPF (16 cases, 37.2 per cent). Moreover, there were witnesses who said that the perpetrators were getting their victims drunk and then beating them (2 cases). On the other hand, as shown in the section about perpetrators, 25 perpetrators (58.1 per cent) had consumed alcohol when they committed homicide. All the data emphasizes the fact that alcohol can be one of the situational factors in starting physical aggression with lethal consequences. The homicide committed by N.V. brings the importance of partners' alcoholism to the discussion.

Case D: Intimate partner femicide motivated by the wife's alcohol consumption

After graduating from a technical faculty, N.V. got married for the first time when he was 22 and the relationship lasted less than one year. His wife, who had graduated from a Mathematics and IT faculty, left him (after the revolution in December 1989) and went to the UK with a journalist. After that, the perpetrator had a four-year relationship with a colleague who he married. His second wife left him and went to Italy, but the divorce between the two was pronounced only after the perpetrator killed his third partner with whom he had a relationship for another four years. His last partner had an average educational level (high school graduate), she had also a child from a previous marriage and she was an alcoholic according to the aggressor. During this last relationship, the child of the two partners died and this contributed to the degradation of the health state of the alcoholic wife.

> It was love at first sight. The bad thing was, God damn it, I don't know how I could choose an alcoholic woman. But love forgives many things, this was my fault also. When we love somebody very much, we have the tendency not to see a lot of things. And I forgave, well, how to say... I was drinking two beers; she was drinking one. I said it didn't matter. After a while I rented my apartment in Bucharest and I went to the countryside together with my mum. This is where problems started. I discovered she was hiding liquor inside the house although we had liquor in our house. Well, I started to find those small brandy bottles, hidden who knows where. This is a clear sign. You don't have to be a doctor to realize this is alcoholism. I was worried, but instead of taking measures ... From this point of view it seems a little unfair to me. Why did she have to be an alcoholic person? If she weren't an alcoholic woman... I haven't met a calmer and nicer person in my life, how to say, you could stay with her 24 hours and not get bored. She was simply my completion. This is what hurts me and preoccupies me even now. This is a frustration, instead of taking measures: that's it, we're going to rehab. (IPF, pensioner for health problems, 42 years old)

The wife's alcoholism was noticed also by the aggressor's mother who contributed also to raising the tension in the family, especially because the perpetrator had moved with his wife and mother into the same house in the countryside. The perpetrator's mother had quite an important role in his life and she used to comment on her son's relationships. The aggressor also mentioned his mum's contribution to the evolution of the situation towards homicide: "Well, I suppose that my mother noticed her drinking and started nagging her. How can you satisfy them both? I think the pressure was pretty big. You can hold yourself, but unconsciously." In this context, the aggressor talked about what had happened the day of the crime, insisting on two elements: the wife's alcohol consumption and the fact that she threatened him first with a knife. These were the reasons which determined that the perpetrator should punish her. Disciplining the alcoholic wife ended with the death of the victim, but, as the aggressor says, the intention was only to punish her because she dared threaten him with a knife.

> After that, I don't understand why, because I hit her hard. I know I hit her hard. She turned and I don't know why, now I said I would kick her behind (you will see in the file, you can see in the forensic report). I don't know what I was thinking about... I said "hey, now you will sleep only on your tummy for this ... now that you took the knife you'll see!". And the first two were on her buttocks. I don't know why... I never hit my children, I never hit anyone, so look. This is why I am saying, I broke my principles, how to say. See, I broke my principles for 10 seconds and now I am the one to pay. (IPF, pensioner for health problems 42 years old)

In reality, the so-called sanctioning of the wife's alcohol consumption is just a technique to pass the homicide responsibility onto the victim. Motivating the homicide act through sanctioning the wife's alcohol consumption appeared only in the case of IPF. In the case of IPFS, I did not have a single aggressor who committed IPFS and passed the homicide responsibility onto the wife who was consuming alcohol. In the case of IPFS, perpetrators blamed their partners who cheat on them, abandon them, but there is no information about the woman's alcohol consumption. However, there were cases of homicide-suicide committed against some relatives (mothers or sons) who were trying to limit the alcohol or drug consumption of the perpetrators (by hiding alcohol bottles or refusing to give them money).

Emigration – a risk factor for IPF and IPFS

The economic emigration of Romanian people in the European or non-European space generated some problems at the level of emigrant families. Beyond raising the economic level and solving some financial problems for some families, emigration led to the appearance of some issues which affected the role distribution inside the family. The fact that only one partner left abroad generated modifications of both the role of the one who remained with the children and of the emigrant's role (Balica and Stöckl 2016, Anghel and Horváth 2009). Emigrant women took over the man's traditional role of family breadwinner, while the husband who remained home was forced to take over the role of the absent mother (to cook, to do the laundry, to take care of the family's children). In the case where the man was the one who left, the woman took over some of the man's tasks (Irimescu and Lupu 2006). In both situations, children were the ones to suffer because one or both parents were away. Moreover, one of them was transformed into an object of revenge by a husband against his wife. The woman was suspected of infidelity or she may have wanted to divorce her husband because she was tired of working for an abusive man. I can give as an example the results of the analysis of homicide-suicide cases in Romania. On this occasion, I found three cases of fathers who committed homicide against their children in order to punish the emigrant mothers who wanted a separation. The cases of filicide-suicide generated by the perpetrators' wish to sanction emigrant women will be discussed in Chapter 4. What I want to mention now is the fact that, among IPF and IPFS, there were cases of perpetrators and victims who were emigrants at the moment of homicide or in their last years of life. In the sample of 40 IPF perpetrators, I had 11 cases in which emigrant people were involved. Regarding IPFS, I identified 26 IPFS committed between Romanian emigrants in the period

2002–2013. Only in four cases of IPFS, victims and perpetrators were working abroad together. In most of the IPFS only one partner was away. And although the differences are not big, women were the ones who emigrated (17 perpetrators and 20 victims). Studies regarding the consequences of migration at the level of emigrant families emphasized the fact that women's migration led to the growing of jealous feelings and infidelity suspicions (Girigan 2011, Anghel and Horváth 2009, Vlase 2011, Lupu 2006, Torre 2013). Moreover, the results of the study regarding the role of emigration in committing homicide-suicides in Romania showed that jealousy and infidelity suspicion were the reasons for 50 per cent of IPFS between Romanian emigrants (Balica and Stöckl 2016). In this context, I tried to identify the role of emigration in the evolution of relationships between intimate partners involved in the cases of IPF and IPFS.

Intimate Partner Femicide-Suicides

IPFS committed by Romanian emigrants represented 19.7 per cent of the total of homicide-suicides registered in the Homicide-suicides in Romania in 2002–2013 database. Approximately a third of IPFS were motivated by jealousy (36.4 per cent), while 12.1 per cent were motivated by infidelity suspicions. Divorce or the victim's wish to be separated from her partner was mentioned in a quarter of IPFS between emigrants (24.2 per cent). Five IPFS (3.8 per cent) were generated by the women's departure to Germany, Italy and Spain. After analyzing the indictments of the 40 IPFS included in the present research, we can notice that, in the case of IPFS between emigrants, there is a sum of factors which led to the end of the relationship with a homicide of the woman and a suicide of the perpetrator. On one side, the declarations of the witnesses interrogated by prosecutors or policemen confirmed the jealousy and infidelity suspicion of the partners who remained in Romania. Moreover, there are in these cases also proof of the domestic violence which the woman was subjected to. The physical and psychological violence (death threats addressed to children, relatives or even the partner) were mentioned in most of the cases in which the woman was an emigrant. These types of violence appear even in the cases in which both partners were emigrants.

Case E: Intimate Partner Femicide Suicide between partners who emigrated to Italy

M.P. killed his wife a short time after he was released from prison. He had been sentenced to six years of prison for attempted homicide against his manager. While he was in prison, his wife worked in Italy for 3 years. After being released from prison, the perpetrator left for Italy as well. More conflicts happened there because of financial difficulties and the perpetrator's jealousy. The situation got worse when the wife threatened to divorce him. Witnesses said that the victim was psychologically abused by the perpetrator "he was terrorizing her; he was telling her that he would hang himself... when he was in Italy he threatened to kill them all". The two partners stayed together in Italy for almost a month and then they came back to Romania. When they got back in the country, the wife mentioned divorce again and this made the perpetrator mad. Their son told the investigators that his father did not want to divorce and said "instead of divorcing her, he would rather kill her and commit suicide". The son also said that, in fact, his father suspected his mother of having another relationship: "when they came back to Romania, mum was very determined to divorce, which made my dad really mad. All this time, dad thought that mum had someone else in Italy". After a conflict which happened one day before the IPFS, the perpetrator threatened again to kill her. The following evening, after some drinking, things got worse and the perpetrator took a knife and stabbed her with it several times. Although the victim tried to escape and ran into the street asking for help, she could not be saved. After committing the homicide, the perpetrator phoned his son and let him know that he had killed his wife and that he wanted to commit suicide. Police found the perpetrator hung in his courtyard.

The presented case is not a singular one. By presenting it, I wanted to emphasize the fact that emigrant women are exposed, to a greater extent, to the risk of being abused by their partners. Their vulnerability is just as big if they have temporarily gone to work abroad. The violent partner has the possibility to get in contact with the victim and abuse her even if she goes to another country to work. Even if more people around the victim knew about the acts of violence or they were threatened at their turn, nobody tried to contact the police and ask for specialty help in order to solve the situation.

The victim and relatives' lack of information regarding the ways of intervention in the case of domestic violence accessible in Romania or Italy (the country where the victim emigrated looking for a job) maintained the victim's vulnerability in both countries. However, the victim was killed when she came back to Romania because the aggressor realized that the wife wanted and could divorce him here, in the country. What seemed only a threat in Italy could become reality in Romania. Unfortunately, although the victim was in her native country and could have had access to protection (even by dialing the emergency number 112), everything ended with the death of both partners.

Intimate Partner Femicide

The interviews with the prisoners condemned for homicide brought new elements about the husbands' idea of controlling their wives, even after their relationship got worse because of his infidelity. The emigration of both partners in order to find a job created different situations for the emigrant spouses. Some of them had the possibility to work and live in the same town, maintaining the family relations. But others had to work in different cities that were at great distances from another, and even though they were in the same country, they were almost as separated as if one of them had stayed home. In these situations, jealousy and infidelity suspicion of some partners became even more prominent.

Another situation that was emphasized during interviews was the one of the unfaithful husband who emigrated to the same city as his wife. He is the type of unfaithful husband who swings between two relationships and does not want to give up either of them. The disloyal partner thinks he is allowed to have two relationships at the same time, and his wife must accept this situation. In the end, the jealousy of the unfaithful partner and the impossibility to accept the fact that his wife can have another relationship with another man leads to the homicide of the wife.

Case F: Emigrant IPF perpetrator motivated by jealousy and infidelity

N.M. was married twice, his last wife killed by him in Spain. One month after divorcing his first wife, he got married to his second wife. His decision to marry her so soon was motivated by the fact that: "She was my first girlfriend, she was my first love …". Their relationship seemed to have been calm enough, the husband was the one who went to work in Spain for two years. After two years, he came back to Romania and handed in his retirement file (he had been a warrant officer for more than 21 years). After that, they decided to go together to work in Spain. Each of them found a job there. The wife was a housekeeper and she lived in the house of the woman she was taking care of. The husband, a truck driver, met in the meantime a Spanish girl with whom he had an affair although his wife knew about this affair. Fascinated by the fact that a woman with such a financial status was interested in him, the man tried to keep both women.

> I was with both of them. I continued my relationship with the mistress. My wife was telling me: come on, what are you doing? You can either let her go and stay with me or let me go and stay with her. And I told her: I don't want to let either of you go. The truth is I was leading a good life with the Spanish girl. I had other advantages, she had 2 restaurants, she had four apartments at the Mediterranean Sea that were rented. She had also

> two shops at her parents' in the countryside. She had a lot. So she didn't stop me from anything. Anything I needed, money, anything.

The wife who was cheated on kept discussing this subject with her husband and she kept asking him to choose between the two. Her husband's indecision made her to be more radical and she threatened that she would find another man too. The man was a little confused by her reaction, but he did not believe that the wife would have a relationship with another man. At least this is what he declared, because in reality, he killed her only two weeks after she told him she would find another partner.

> Everything started from here, if you don't break up with the Spanish lady, I will do what you are doing. What's wrong? Are you crazy? You haven't done anything wrong for so many years and now you start to… I thought it was a joke. But she's not the one to joke about that.

The perpetrator continued his relationship with the mistress, keeping however the keys to the apartment where his wife lived. One day, after spending the night with his mistress, he decided to visit his wife. The fact that he found her with a man in her house, made him attack both of them with a knife. The man was hurt, but he survived. However the woman was killed.

> And I left in the morning, I had the keys to the door. I had the keys from where she was working, let's go to her. And I went there where my wife was working. I got the elevator, I entered the house and I went there where she was sleeping. And when I saw her, I saw her in bed with a gentleman. Everything started from here. I say like this: any man who finds his wife in bed with another one, loses his memory, he loses everything and is able to do anything.

First of all, the analysis of IPF and IPFS cases committed between Romanian emigrants emphasizes the need to make studies focused on identifying the incidence and risk factors specific to these violent acts at the level of Romanian emigrants. Studies regarding violent acts between immigrants from the European space are quite few, but they offer some guidelines regarding the vulnerability of immigrant women compared to non-immigrant women (Carmen Vives Cases et al. 2008/2013, Balica and Stöckl 2016). Identifying the incidence of IPF committed between Romanian emigrants could allow the design of a new intervention direction for the institutions from Romania. This direction would be one of preventing the acts of domestic violence and of IPF/IPFS given that the official data show a number of Romanian emigrants in the European space higher than 2.3 million people (EUROSTAT 2012).

Conclusions

The analysis of data regarding the two samples emphasized some similarities between perpetrators, especially about the motivation of IPF and IPFS (jealousy and infidelity suspicion were motivations for 37.5 per cent of IPF and 35 per cent of IPFS) and the period of time in which the violent acts were committed (most of the IPF and IPFS were committed between 10 pm – 5.59 am). Beyond these similarities, during my analysis I identified some elements that make the IPF perpetrators different from the IPFS ones. The particularities of the two categories of perpetrators come from the socio-demographic features of the perpetrators, from the data regarding the acts of violence and the victims' features. Regarding perpetrators, I notice the presence of a criminal background to a larger extent in the case of IPF (39.5 per cent) than in the case of IPFS (7.5 per cent). Mental illnesses were more often for the IPF sample (32.5 per cent) than for the IPFS sample (7.5 per cent). We could notice significant differences in the case of alcohol consumption at the moment of homicide (IPF – 58.1 per cent; IPFS – 35 per cent).

Modus operandi of IPF differs from the modus operandi of IPFS. IPF were committed especially through hitting with arms and legs or with objects, and IPFS were committed with firearms or by strangling the victim. IPF were committed in the house of the aggressor (11.6 per cent) to a larger extent than IPFS (2.5 per cent). The woman's wish to leave the perpetrator was a more important reason for committing IPF (27.5 per cent) than for committing IPFS (15 per cent). IPF victims (most of them aged between 26 and 39) are younger than IPFS victims (most of them aged between 40 and 65).

The results of this analysis complete some information regarding the motivations and mechanisms which determine IPF and IPFS. At the same time, they bring to discussion some elements which make them similar or different. The fact that I only analyzed data about these two samples limits these results. What is interesting is the fact that some of the differences identified between the two samples of perpetrators were also emphasized by other researches from the European space. Future comparative researches made with bigger samples will be the ones to confirm or infirm the particularities of IPF and IPFS.

3. Intimate Femicide – Suicides. A Comparative Analysis of Eastern and Western European Countries

The results of research regarding homicide-suicides in Europe showed that intimate partner homicide-suicides represent more than 50 per cent of the total (Balica and Stöckl 2016, Liem and Oberwittler 2012, Panczak et al. 2013, Gregory 2012, Pereira et al. 2010, Mathews et al. 2008). In some European countries, such as Spain, intimate partner homicide-suicides represent 80 per cent of homicide-suicides (Liem and Oberwittler 2012). Almost all victims of intimate partner homicide-suicides were women (Balica and Stöckl 2016, Panczak et al. 2013). The comparative analysis of data regarding homicide-suicides in seven European countries (1990–2005) made during the project European Homicide-Suicide Study (EHSS) showed that most perpetrators of intimate partner homicide-suicides were men (Liem and Oberwittler 2012). According to the EHSS, all intimate partner homicide-suicides were committed by men in Finland, while only 6 per cent of offenders were women in Switzerland (Id. 207). The research that I made in Romania for the period 2002–2013, showed that intimate partner homicide-suicides are approximately 70 per cent of homicide-suicides. All victims of intimate partner homicide-suicides identified in Romania for the analyzed period were women. This is why I decided to focus my attention on intimate partner femicide-suicides in Romania. Due to the fact that I wanted to identify the particularities of intimate partner femicide-suicides in Romania, I tried to approach this type of violence from a comparative perspective and to bring to discussion the results of research from other European countries.

Methodology

As I already mentioned in the previous chapter (see Chapter 2), the term "intimate partner femicide-suicide" is used in order to designate the homicide committed by an intimate partner (man) against his partner, followed by the suicide of the offender. Starting from this definition of intimate partner femicide-suicide, I extracted from the Homicide-suicides in Romania (2002–2013) database all the cases of intimate partner femicide-suicides registered in Romania (N=88). Attempted intimate partner femicide-suicides were excluded.

The data about intimate partner femicide-suicides from the European countries were extracted from scientific publications (articles, research reports, PHD theses) written by European researchers in English or French. Some articles were published online and they were found with the help of some keywords (homicide-suicide in … (name of each European country), intimate partner femicide-suicides) on the Internet. Other publications were identified in international repositories of articles or in libraries.

There is little research focused on intimate partner homicide-suicide or intimate partner femicide-suicide written in Europe. The information regarding this type of violence is frequently presented within the broader context of homicide-suicide acts. Literature reviews showed that, until now, only Portugal, the Netherlands, France, Germany, United Kingdom, Finland, Switzerland, Italy, Poland and Spain had made studies which collected complex data on homicide-suicides. In Greece, Turkey and Croatia studies were made only from a forensic perspective, at the regional level and these types of data only allow a limited analysis of the phenomenon.

As can be seen, the European research on the issue was limited mainly to countries located in Western, Central and Northern parts of the continent. The research from Eastern Europe and/or the Balkans had seldom approached this topic. Due to the lack of information on intimate partner femicide-suicides, comparison between Romania and other European countries is limited. So, in this chapter I will focus on intimate partner femicide-suicides from Romania and I will make a comparison with other countries only when the available data allows it.

Incidence of IPFS in Romania

Intimate partner femicide-suicides represented an average of 69.3 per cent of the total homicide-suicides in Romania (2002–2013). The percentage of intimate partner femicide-suicides from the total of homicide-suicides was higher in the period 2002–2009 (average percentage of IPFS was 78.3 per cent). After 2010, the percentage of IPFS from the total homicide-suicides was under the average calculated for the entire analyzed period (42.9–52.1 per cent).

The analysis of data regarding IPFS for the period 2002–2013 showed the fact that the IPFS rate varied between 0.005–0.065 per 100,000 inhabitants. The lowest values of the IPFS rate were registered in 2004, and the highest in 2008 and 2009. The average IPFS rate for the analyzed period was 0.034 IPFS per 100,000 inhabitants. The values of the IPFS rate were lower in the period 2002–2007 (0.018 IPFS per 100,000 inhabitants) than in the second part of the analyzed period (2008–2013 the average IPFS rate was of 0.049 per 100,000 inhabitants) (see Diagram 3.1).

Diagram 3.1 Intimate partner femicide-suicides rates in Romania (2002–2013)

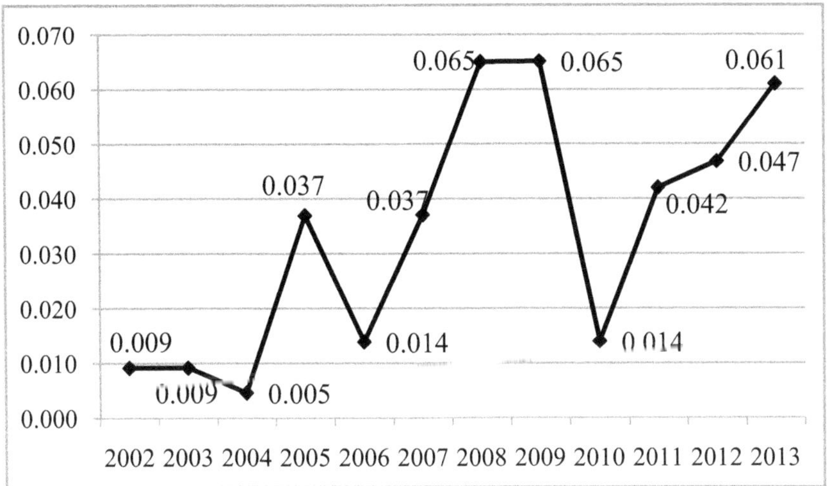

The majority of IPFS cases occurred in Romania (N=76; 86. 4 per cent) with 12 cases occurring in other countries, such as Italy (7 cases), Spain (2 cases), USA (2 cases) and Greece (1). Most IPFS cases were committed between non-emigrants (70.5 per cent) and only approximately one third between Romanian emigrants (29.5 per cent).

Half of all IPFS took place in an urban area, while 42.2 per cent of IPFS happened in the rural area. I did not have data regarding the area where they were committed for 7 IPFS cases.

Incidences of IPFS in Europe

The interest of Finnish researchers for homicide-suicides made the analysis of these cases possible for a large period of time. Therefore, a study which analyzed the period 1960–2000 showed that IPFS represented 29 per cent of intimate partner homicides (Kivivuori and Lehti 2003: 227). On the other hand, the analysis of data from the EHSS showed that all cases of intimate partner homicide-suicides in Finland (1990–2005) were intimate partner femicide-suicides (Liem and Oberwittler 2012). IPFS represents 59 per cent of the total of homicide-suicides (Id. 208). In Switzerland, the percentage of IPFS from the total of homicide-suicides committed between 1991 and 2001 was 74.3 per cent (Panczak et al. 2013).

In the UK, IPFS represented 63.2 per cent of the homicide-suicides registered at a national level for the period 1988–1992 (Barraclough and Harris 2002). A recent study made in the Yorkshire region showed that 76.7 per cent of homicide-suicides were intimate partner femicide-suicides (1993–2007) (Gregory 2012).

Studies regarding homicide-suicides in France were limited to the analysis of the cases from three regions of France: Paris and suburbs, Indre-et-Loire and Loir-et-Cher. The data from the Paris region showed that IPFS represented 85 per cent of homicide-suicides committed between 1991 and 1996 (Lecomte and Fornes 1998). In the other two French regions, IPFS represented 80 per cent of the total of homicide-suicides committed between 2000–2005 (Saint-Martin et al. 2008).

Offender's characteristics

The average age of IPFS perpetrators was 45.1 years (21–74 years). Almost half of the IPFS perpetrators were aged between 40–65 (48.9 per cent). Perpetrators with the age between 26–39 represented approximately a third of the total (30.7 per cent). People younger than 25 and older than 65 represented 7 per cent each.

The information on the level of education was small. I had data about the level of education only for 15 cases. However, I had more information about the jobs of the perpetrators (I did not have information for 30 per cent). Most of the offenders were workers (26.1 per cent), pensioners (13.7 per cent) and without any job (12.5 per cent). Seven perpetrators were policemen and 4 of them were military people. There were also 2 businessmen, 2 managers and 2 engineers among the perpetrators. More than half of them were working in Romania (56.8 per cent) and approximately a fifth were working abroad at the time of the IPFS (19.2 per cent). I did not have information about the country where they were working for 17 per cent of the cases.

Only one out of five perpetrators consumed alcohol (22.7 per cent). Only 8 perpetrators were registered with mental illnesses. However, the information regarding the perpetrators' health state must be cautiously seen as I only had access to data regarding their health state mentioned by journalists, police or prosecutors (I did not have access to medical data from the National Health House). Only 7 perpetrators did not have a criminal background.

Few of the European studies discussed the characteristics of IPFS perpetrators. Most of the studies were limited to describing the profile of homicide-suicide perpetrators and less the profile of IPFS perpetrators. Nevertheless, I found some information regarding IPFS perpetrators in studies made in the UK, Portugal and the Netherlands. In The United Kingdom, the perpetrators' average age was 4 years higher than the victims' age. (Barraclough and Harris 2002). A study made also in the UK for the region of Yorkshire (1993–2007) showed that 87 per cent of the aggressors were employed at the moment of committing the crime and most of them did not have a criminal background (77 per cent without a criminal background) (Gregory 2012). The studies from the Netherlands also showed that the age of perpetrators (an average of 48 years) was higher than the victims' age (average age 43 years) (Liem et al. 2009).

In Portugal, the average age of IPFS perpetrators was 55 years old (Pereira et al. 2010). The authors showed in the same study that the age of perpetrators from the Lisbon area varied between 33 and 79 years (2004–2008) (Id. 243). A recent study of IPFS in Portugal for the period 2005–2007, showed that the average age of IPFS perpetrators was 50 years, and most were employed at the crime moment (da Ponte Martens Graça de Matos 2013: 6). Even in the European studies, data regarding the criminal history of aggressors is missing. Da Ponte Martens Graça de Matos (2013) showed in her study that information about previous criminal records appeared only in three cases of attempted IPFS.

Victims' characteristics

The average age of IPFS victims in Romania was 39.9 years (16–74 years). Victims were 5.2 years younger than aggressors. Most of the victims were aged between 26–39 years (42 per cent) and between 40–64 years (30.7 per cent). Young women aged between 16–25 years represented 12.5 per cent. Very few victims were people older than 65 years (6 victims, 6.8 per cent). The data regarding the victims' level of education was limited to 14.7 per cent of the total of victims. According to the available data, 10.2 victims were university graduates (doctors, teachers, bank clerks, social assistants, engineers). Regarding the victims' professions, most of them were workers (21.6 per cent). Pensioners (12.5 per cent), housewives (9 per cent) and women with a high occupational status (doctors, teachers, engineers etc.) (6.8 per cent) were also victims of IPFS. Most of the victims were employed at the crime moment, and half of them were working in Romania. The rest of the victims (21.6 per cent) were working abroad: Italy (10), Spain (3), Germany (2), the UK (2), Greece (1) and USA (1); 10 victims (11.4 per cent) had consumed alcohol before the IPFS.

The data regarding the IPFS victims from the European space were quite limited. Only the studies made in Portugal and Switzerland analyzed the profile of IPFS victims. The research from Switzerland showed that women who were victims of IPFS were aged between 30 and 39 or over 80 (Panczak et al. 2013). In Portugal, the average age of IPFS victims was 48 years, and the age group of victims was between 21 and 80 years. Victims were younger than aggressors

(Pereira et al. 2010: 243). Another study also made in Portugal confirmed the fact that victims were younger than perpetrators (the victims' average age was 44 years old), most of them were employed (44.8 per cent) (da Ponte Martens Graça de Matos 2013: 6).

Data regarding homicide-suicides

The number of IPFS committed in the urban environment (50 per cent) was higher than IPFS committed in the rural environment (42 per cent). Almost half of the homicides (45.5 per cent) and 20.5 per cent of suicides were committed with a knife. One of five cases was committed through shooting (19.3 per cent). 12.5 per cent of homicides were committed by strangling, while 36.3 per cent of suicides were committed by hanging. 16 per cent of IPFS were committed with witnesses. In 8 per cent of IPFS, the witnesses were members of the aggressor's family, and in 5.7 per cent of the cases, the witnesses were members of the victim's family. Only in two cases (2.3 per cent) the witnesses were neighbors. Most IPFS occurred in places inhabited by the victim and the aggressor (64.8 per cent). The common house is the space in which almost half of IPFS (45.5 per cent) occurred, which made it almost impossible for the presence and actions of witnesses. Few cases happened in the aggressor's house (3.4 per cent) or in the family household (3.4 per cent). A significant number of cases happened outside the space where the victim and aggressor lived (19.3 per cent). These cases were committed on the street either because the victims were trying to escape the aggressor and they were caught on the street, or because the aggressors decided to attack them on the street in moments that they chose (during the night when victims were coming home from work or during the day when victims were alone and left their household to run some errands). In this last case I am talking about aggressors who committed homicide-suicides deliberately and who had been following their partners, from whom they had been separated, for a long time.

The studies made in the European space showed that, in most cases of IPFS, firearms were used (Panczak et al. 2013, da Ponte Martens Graça de Matos 2013, Liem et al. 2009). Studies from Portugal showed that 79 per cent of IPFS were committed with firearms and in the house of the victim (72 per cent) (Pereira et al. 2010: 243). Even in the Netherlands, most IPFS were committed with firearms (43 per cent) (Liem et al. 2009). In these studies there is little information about witnesses, residence environment (rural/urban) where IPFS was committed, consumption of alcohol or other substances. In Portugal, Da Ponte Martens Graça de Matos (2013) shows that even if information regarding the consumption of alcohol or other substances is not registered in documents, there is data which confirms the presence of alcohol consumption in 28.6 per cent of the analyzed IPFS cases. Another study identifies only one perpetrator who had consumed alcohol (Pereira et al. 2010: 243). In the UK, alcohol consumption was signaled only in three cases of IPFS (Gregory 2012).

Motivation

Jealousy (associated with infidelity suspicion) was the main motivation of IPFS committed in Romania (37.5 per cent). Women's desire to separate from their partners was also an important motivation of IPFS (19.3 per cent). I included in this category the wife's filing for a divorce (10.2 per cent), separation by leaving the common house (6.8 per cent) and the wife's departure abroad (2.3 per cent). Conflicts (11.4 per cent) and domestic violence reported or not to the police (10.2 per cent) were other factors which led to the homicide of the female partners. The financial difficulties generated by debts to moneylenders or by bank loans (5 cases), alcohol consumption (5 cases), the aggressors' health issues (one was mentally ill and another one was incurably ill in terminal phase) and the victims' health issues (one victim had cancer) were less mentioned in the police or parquet documents. Only in three cases did the aggressors have confirmation that their wives had cheated on them, and the partners' refusal to come back to their husbands led to their homicide. Two other cases of IPFS were committed because the aggressors did not want to be separated from the partners who their parents refused to accept.

The finding that the majority of HS cases in Romania involved male offenders killing their female intimate partner because of jealousy and pending separation are in line with the international literature on homicide-suicides (Liem and Oberwittler 2013). In Italy, the main motivations of IPFS identified for the period 1985–2008 were jealousy (25.7 per cent), mercy killing generated by the depreciation of the victims' health state (10.3 per cent) and financial difficulties (10.3 per cent) (Roma et al. 2012). Jealousy, separation and conflicts appear as main motivations in the studies made in Portugal. Da Ponte Martens Graça de Matos (2013) showed that half of the IPFS were motivated by jealousy, 27.8 per cent by the victim's separation from her partner and 22.2 per cent by conflicts. The study made by Pereira et al. (2013), also in Portugal, confirms the presence of the three motivations of IPFS. What differs is their percentage in the total of IPFS motivations. This time, separation (38.9 per cent) is the main motivation. It is followed by jealousy and infidelity suspicion (31.5 per cent) and conflicts (22.2 per cent). The victim's separation from the aggressor appears as main motivation also in the cases of IPFS committed in Paris between 1991 and

1996. 45 per cent of IPFS were motivated by the victim's separation from the aggressor (Lecomte and Fornes 1998).

History of previous abuse

Information regarding the status of the relationship between the partners involved in IPFS from Romania was unavailable for almost half of the cases (52.4 per cent). For the cases in which this information was known most of them had the status of current partners (29.5 per cent). Only 18.1 per cent were divorced (6.8 per cent) or separated (11.3 per cent). IPFS happened between partners who had been separated for one year the most (16 cases, 18.1 per cent). The relationships most exposed to the risk of IPFS seem to be the ones up to 10 years long (15 cases, 17 per cent). There was information regarding the history of previous violence for 24.9 per cent of the cases. In 8 cases there were threats of death against victims (6 cases) and victims' relatives (2 cases). In two cases the aggressor threatened to commit suicide.

In Europe, IPFS generally occurred between current partners who were separated at the moment of the crime (Pereira et al. 2013, da Ponte Martens Graça de Matos 2013). Approximately 60 per cent of the partners involved in IPFS in Portugal were separated for one year (57.9 per cent – Pereira et al. 2013; 60 per cent - da Ponte Martens Graça de Matos 2013). The relationships which lasted more than ten years as an average seem to be more exposed to the risk of their ending through IPFS, 34.5 per cent (da Ponte Graça de Matos 2013, Pereira et al. 2013). History of previous abuse was signaled in approximately half of the cases analyzed in Portugal (46.8 per cent – Pereira et al. 2013, 55.2 per cent – da Ponte Martens Graça de Matos 2013). In the UK, history of previous abuse of the female partner was registered in 63 per cent of IPFS (Gregory 2012). Studies from France, even if they were not conducted on a national level and only give information about the Paris area (1991–1996), showed that 50 per cent of IPFS victims were abused by their partners before the homicide (Lecomte and Fornes 1998).

Intimate partner femicide-suicide and migration

Romania has been affected in the last two decades by the external migration of inhabitants of almost all areas of the country to the European and non-European space. The number of Romanians who emigrated into the European Union was higher than 2.3 million people (EUROSTAT 2012). As seen in Balica and Stöckl (2016), the Romanians' external migration seems to have determined discrepancies in the relationships between intimate partners who had the status of emigrants. The recent economic crisis led to the modification of migratory trends, meaning the number of women who left to work abroad increased (Sandu 2006: 31, Stănculescu et al. 2011: 139). The absence of women from their families produced an exchange of female-male roles (men took over women's roles and vice versa) (Anghel and Horváth 2009). In some cases, this led to the multiplication of infidelity suspicion by the husbands who remained home (Anghel and Horváth 2009: 400, Girigan 2011, Lupu (n.d.): 49–51, Torre 2013, Vlase 2011) and to inter-family conflicts and domestic violence (Toth and Toth 2006: 68).

In this context, the analysis of homicide-suicide cases committed in the period 2002–2013 showed that 30 per cent of the cases were committed between Romanian emigrants (Balica and Stöckl 2016). The present study confirmed the presence of cases of homicide-suicide committed between Romanian emigrants for 25 per cent of homicide-suicides (33 cases) registered between 2002 and 2013.

Most homicide-suicides committed between Romanian emigrants were IPFS (78.8 per cent). On the other side, one third of IPFS were committed between Romanian emigrants (26 cases, 29.5 per cent) (see Diagram 3.2). IPFS happened in Romania (53.8 per cent) and a third were committed in Italy (27 per cent). The number of IPFS committed in other countries was smaller: Spain (2 cases), the USA (2 cases) and Greece (1). The number of IPFS grew especially after 2008 (see Diagram 3.2)

Diagram 3.2 IPFS between emigrants and non-emigrants (cases)

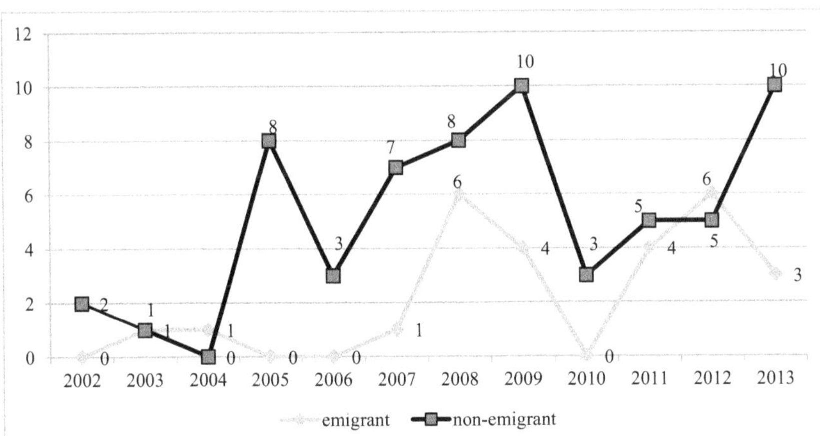

Most cases were committed in the urban environment (76.9 per cent) between current partners (38.5 per cent). Information regarding the duration of the relationship was also limited for IPFS between emigrants. I had information about the duration of the relationship only for 11 cases. In these conditions, the tendency for occurrences of IPFS in relationships that lasted less than 10 years seems to remain the same (5 cases). The other six IPFS between Romanian emigrants were distributed uniformly in the interval 11–15 years and 20–25 years of relationship (three cases for each and every interval). Only in seven IPFS were there witnesses (two cases the victim's family members, three cases the aggressor's family members and two cases neighbors).

IPFS were committed with knives (46.2 per cent), by shooting (23.1 per cent), strangling (15.4 per cent) and in other ways (four cases). The motivation of IPFS between emigrants is similar to that of IPFS in Romania. Jealousy associated with infidelity suspicion (13 cases, 50 per cent), the victim's separation from the aggressor (9 cases) through a divorce, leaving the common house or leaving to live abroad. Financial difficulties (1 case), the aggressor's health issues (depression) (1 case) were also among the factors which determined IPFS. In five cases domestic violence was mentioned (in one case the victim had obtained a restraining order), and in two cases the aggressors had threatened their victims with death. Only six aggressors left messages before committing suicide; four left hand written notes, one aggressor left a message on the victim's body and another one talked on the phone with family members.

Offender's characteristics

The aggressors' average age was 43.4 years. Most perpetrators were aged between 26 and 39 (46.1 per cent) and between 40 and 65 (34.6 per cent). I had little information about the level of education, profession, and health state and alcohol consumption. Due to this I will just say that only three aggressors had consumed alcohol and one had used drugs. Three aggressors were known to have mental issues and 5 aggressors had a criminal background.

Most aggressors were working abroad (17), so they were emigrants: Italy (8 aggressors, 30.8 per cent), the USA (3 aggressors, 11.5 per cent), Spain (2 aggressors, 7.7 per cent), Austria (1 aggressor), Germany (1 aggressor) and Cyprus (1 aggressor). Seven aggressors were working in Romania (26.9 per cent).

Victim's characteristics

The average age of victims of IPFS between emigrants was 37.8 years. Half of the victims were aged between 26 and 39 and 23 per cent were aged between 40 and 65. Only one victim was 23 years old and another one 68 years old. I had information about the level of education of victims only for three of them. These victims were university graduates. Analyzing the professional status, almost half of the victims

(12 victims, 46.1 per cent) had a low professional status (housewives, housekeepers, pensioners). Only two victims had a high occupational status (bank clerk and engineer). I did not have information regarding the professions of 12 victims. Most victims were working abroad, so they were emigrants (19 victims, 73 per cent). Women who were working in Italy seem to be exposed to a greater extent to the risk of being IPFS victims. 38.5 per cent of the victims were working in Italy. Women who were working in other European countries (Spain – 3 cases, Germany – 2 cases, the UK – 2 cases, Greece – 1 case) or in the USA (1 case) present a smaller risk of being killed by their intimate partners.

In Europe, the number of immigrants involved in IPFS seems to have been quite small as information about this type of violence appears quite rarely. Panzack et al (2013) mentioned only the fact that in Switzerland, in the case of foreigners without permanent residence, a higher risk of being a victim of homicide-suicides (1991–2008) was registered. Studies made in the UK drew attention to the fact that, between 1988 and 1992, 9 per cent of the victims (16 victims) of homicide-suicides were not born in the UK (Barraclough and Harris 2002). Among the countries of origin we can mention some countries from Europe (Italy, Germany, Poland, Northern Ireland, Scotland), but also countries from other regions of the world (Canada, Jamaica, Malaysia, Pakistan, Sri Lanka) (Ibid.). Liem et al. (2009) mention in a study for the period 1992–2006 that 7 per cent of homicide-suicide victims registered in the Netherlands were of Surinamese origin (N=10). This was the only information regarding homicide-suicides committed between immigrants from European countries. At least this was the information published in the articles and reports in English and French which I had access to. There might be also some other studies made in national languages to which I did not have access.

Conclusions

The analysis of data regarding IPFS in Romania in comparison with other European countries, for which studies about homicide-suicides were identified, emphasized some particularities of IPFS in Romania. The incidence of IPFS in Romania was closer to the incidence of IPFS in the UK. The percentage of IPFS from the total homicide-suicides in Romania (69.3 per cent) was similar to the percentage of IPFS in the UK from the total homicide-suicides (63.2 per cent) (Barraclough and Harris 2002). The number of IPFS in Romania was smaller than that of IPFS registered by studies in France and much bigger than the number of IPFS in Finland. On the other side, what is interesting is the fact that all cases of intimate partner homicide-suicide identified in Romania and Finland were committed by men, so they were IPFS. This situation was not found in other European countries. The average age of aggressors in Romania was smaller than that of victims and the tendency was valid also for other European countries. The average ages of aggressors and victims of IPFS in Romania were smaller than those registered in other European countries. In all the European countries where studies were made, including Romania, the number of aggressors with a criminal background who committed IPFS was small. I could not make comparisons for other socio-demographic features of victims and aggressors as there was no available data.

IPFS in Romania were committed with knives and firearms, while firearms were used mostly in Europe. Most IPFS in Romania occurred in spaces inhabited by the victim and the aggressor (64.8 per cent). The common house was the place where almost half of IPFS (45.5 per cent) happened. In other European countries, IPFS were committed in the victim's house. Jealousy associated with infidelity suspicion and pending separation were the main motivations of IPFS identified in Romania and other countries. The differences between the data of European studies and that of Romania were given by the percentage that the two types of motivation had in total. The relationships that seem the most exposed to the risk of committing IPFS were those with current partners and those up to 10 years long.

IPFS in Romania is different from IPFS in other countries because of the large number of IPFS committed between Romanian emigrants and because of the lack of IPFS committed between immigrants from Romania. It is true that Romania is affected more by the migration of its population towards other European countries (emigration), than by the migration of population from other countries to Romania (immigration). There are though, some small communities of immigrants in Romania, but the violent acts from inside these communities seem not to have ended with IPFS. From the information that I had, there was just one case of maternal filicide-suicide committed by a Romanian woman married to an Arabic immigrant citizen. The European studies noted just the presence of some cases of homicide-suicide in the communities of immigrants from the respective countries, but they did not analyze the particularities of these cases. Further studies remain to analyze IPFS committed in the communities of immigrants in the European space and to emphasize the particularities of this type of violence between intimate partners.

4. Filicide-Suicides and Familicide-Suicides

Filicide-suicides and familicide-suicides represent two types of homicide-suicide which researchers discussed every time they knew they could mention new elements. However, the number of studies regarding these two types of violence was quite small in the European space. The situation is explained through the reduced number of studies regarding homicide-suicides in Europe. In this context, although I identified a small number of filicide-suicides and familicide-suicides in Romania, I tried to bring into the discussion some elements regarding these two types of homicide-suicide. The present chapter is structured in two subchapters. The first subchapter will present the results of the analysis regarding paternal filicide-suicides and maternal filicide-suicides. The second subchapter will present information regarding familicide-suicides committed in Romania.

Filicide-suicides

In the specialty literature different terms were used in order to refer to murders that had children as victims. Some researchers used the term "child homicide" in order to name "the intentional killing of a child or infant" (Debowska et al. 2015: 1). The term "filicide" was used in order to refer to the killing of a child older than 24 hours (Resnik 1969). Some authors used filicide to term the killing of a child not older than 18 (West and Friedman 2007, Dixon et al. 2014) and other authors used filicide without mentioning limits for the age period (Mariano et al. 2014, Bourget and Gagne 2005). The situation was similar in the case of filicide-suicides. Some researchers defined filicide-suicide as being the homicide committed by a parent against his child without mentioning the child's age limit (Shackelford et al 2008). Other researchers limited the child's age to 18 (Friedman et al. 2005). Regardless of the way in which they defined filicides and filicide-suicides, all researchers tried to analyze them to emphasize the factors that determine filicides and filicide-suicides. In order to have more precise results, some studies tackled the problem of maternal filicide-suicides, others of paternal filicide-suicides or both types of filicide/filicide-suicide. In the European space, studies regarding filicides/filicide-suicides were made only in Austria and Finland (Putkonen et al. 2009), Italy (D'Argenio et al. 2013) and Turkey (Eke et al. 2015). In Italy, the first study which analyzed maternal filicide-suicides committed in this country was published in 2013. The study emphasized a series of particularities of maternal filicide-suicides in Italy between 1992–2010

(D'Argenio et al. 2013). The comparative analysis of the cases of filicide/filicide-suicide committed in Austria and Finland (Putkonen et al. 2009) brought new elements regarding the features of filicide in the two countries. A feature of filicides committed in the period 1995–2005 was mothers' involvement in killing their children to a greater extent than fathers' involvement (Austria maternal filicides – 72 per cent, Finland maternal filicides – 52 per cent) (Ibid.).

Methodology

In order to emphasize the particularities of filicide-suicide cases committed in Romania, I extracted from the Homicide-suicides in Romania database all the cases of maternal and paternal filicide-suicide. Filicide-suicide was defined as the murder committed by one of the parents (mother or father) against a child (regardless of the child's age) followed by the suicide of the aggressor parent a maximum of one week after the homicide. Attempted filicide-suicides (maternal and paternal) were excluded from the analysis. In the end, I identified N=17 cases of filicide-suicides (12 paternal filicide-suicides and 5 maternal filicide-suicides).

All filicide-suicide cases had at least one official institution as data sources (police or parquet). For 8 filicide-suicides, the information was taken from three sources (police, parquet and the media), for 5 filicide-suicides information was found only in official institutions (police and parquet) and for 3 cases I had information from police and the media. 11 of the 17 cases of filicide-suicide were covered and information could be accessed from online media.

Due to the fact that paternal filicide-suicides and maternal filicide-suicides have special particularities, I decided to structure the section regarding filicide-suicides in two parts. In the first part I will present the results of the analysis of data regarding paternal filicide-suicides and in the second phase I will present the characteristics of maternal filicide-suicides.

Paternal filicide-suicides in Romania

Paternal filicides-suicides identified in the Homicide-suicides in Romania database (N=12) were committed in the last five years of the analyzed period (2009–2013). The number of filicide-suicides grew constantly starting with 2009 (1 case). In 2010 two paternal filicide-suicides were committed, and 3 filicide-suicides were committed in 2011. Only in 2012 was the number of filicide-suicides smaller than the previous year (2 cases). In 2013 the most filicide-suicides (4 cases) were committed.

All paternal filicide-suicides happened in Romania. Most paternal filicide-suicides happened in the rural environment (7 cases). Four paternal filicide-suicides were committed during the day (6 am–6 pm), two during the evening (6 pm–10 pm) and four during the night (10 pm–5.59 am). The ways of killing the children were various. A third of the cases were committed with a knife and three cases by hanging. The rest of the cases were committed by ax striking, throwing them from a tall building, hitting and car accidents. Five suicides were committed by hanging and two by stabbing. Other suicides were committed by throwing themselves from a tall building, car accidents and throwing themselves in front of a train. The members of the victims' families were witnesses in two cases of paternal filicide-suicides. In two cases, the aggressors left hand written notes in which they explained the reason for the filicide-suicides. In another two cases, the aggressors spoke on the phone with family members (the children's mothers and the aggressors' parents) before and after killing their children.

The motivation of paternal filicide-suicides was connected with the problems of the relationships between aggressors and their intimate partners (mother of the murdered children) and with the health or financial problems of the aggressors. More than half of the paternal filicide-suicides were motivated by the aggressors' desire to get even with their wives who either had divorced them (5 cases) or kept refusing to come back from abroad and continue the relationship with the aggressors (2 cases).

A paternal filicide-suicide case is the one committed by a father who killed his two children. One of the children was his former wife's and had health problems, the second child resulted from the relationship that he had at the moment of committing the crimes. The depreciation of the aggressor's health state and the increasing conflicts that he had with his current partner caused him to kill his children and then commit suicide (Case A).

Case A: Paternal filicide-suicide as revenge on his former and current partner

L.N. killed two of the three children that he had after two relationships. The victims were a 3-year-old girl and a disabled 16-year-old boy with mental health issues. Each of these two children came from another relationship (one from the relationship with his former wife and one from the current relationship). L.N. also had two jobs because he was trying to pay off big debts that he had to the bank. The divorce from his wife and the financial problems seem to have deteriorated the health state of L.N. who had been diagnosed with depression 2 years ago. The day he decided to kill his two children, the aggressor made a video recording where he announced that he wanted to kill himself and his two children. At the end of the video recording, the aggressor said: "Can you see them playing? You won't see them again." A short time before committing the filicides, the current partner called and told him to bring the 3-year-old boy home. The aggressor's answer was: "you will see what will happen!" The declarations of police representatives said that there were more conflicts between the current partner and the aggressor for which police were called. Moreover, from the partner's declaration it appeared that the aggressor had threatened her and had told her she would be sorry for not listening to him. Hence the conclusion that filicide-suicide would have a connection with the conflicts between the aggressor and the current partner. After the phone conversation that he had before the crime, the aggressor took his two children and drowned them in Tarnița Lake. In order to be sure that the 3-year-old girl would die, the little girl's body was tied to the father's body. The family says that the aggressor had two more suicide attempts in 2009 and 2010. The Medical Center Medstar that did the annual check-up diagnosed him in 2010 with depressive syndrome, and in 2011 recommended some treatment. (Aggressor 49 years old)

Another case of paternal filicide-suicide was committed against a 5-year-old boy. The aggressor had just found out that his wife wanted to leave him. Because they could not decide how to split the family wealth and the boy's custody, the aggressor chose to kill his child rather than risk giving the baby to the mother who was working in Italy (Case B).

Case B: Paternal filicide-suicide committed due to the separation from the wife

B.N. had been married for 6 years to H.N., and they had a 5-year-old boy together. The relationship between B.N. and H.N. was a conflictual one, the family and neighbors confirmed the fact that the two had conflicts quite often. The wife had gone to work in Italy for 3 years from where she was sending money to support the family. BN was not working and he was taking care of the child. The wife usually came back to Romania for two weeks twice a year. In 2012, after the winter holiday, the wife decided to divorce and she let her parents know that she would separate from her husband. Two months later, the husband was informed on the phone by his wife that she wanted to divorce him. Deeply affected by the wife's decision and due to the fact that he did not have a job or a house to move into, B.N. had two suicide attempts after finding out what his wife had decided. The suicide attempts were followed by death threats against the wife's mother. Moreover, B.N. threatened to kill his child, but the witnesses did not believe him. Meanwhile, the wife came back from Italy to divorce him. During discussions with her husband, B.N. threatened to kill his wife. Finally, the two spouses seemed to come to a mutual agreement on how to split the wealth and the child's custody. The two partners decided that the husband should keep the child's custody and remain in the house. B.N.'s refusal to let the child sleep one night with his mother caused her to cancel the agreement. The mother decided to go to court and have the judge decide who would have custody of the child. Upset because of this, B.N. tried to burn the house where his wife and her mother were. Because the women called the police, the aggressor locked himself in the house with his son and threatened to kill him. When the police arrived, B.N. killed his son and then killed himself. (Aggressor 30 years old)

Four filicide-suicide cases were committed because of the depreciation of the aggressors' health state. A Unitarian priest had depression after he found out that his wife was supposed to die soon (she had cancer) and decided to kill his two boys and then commit suicide. Another pastor committed homicide against his child after posting on Facebook messages which announced some health problems of the aggressor. The aggressor had associated on Facebook the image of a knife with the message "Warriors are not always the fastest or strongest people. Force and speed can be developed through training. Warriors are those who choose to stay between the enemy and the enemy's dearest people". Another father killed his child because he had financial problems and suspected his wife of infidelity and another one because he had had a conflict with his son.

Aggressors' characteristics

The aggressors' average age was 39.6 years. The aggressors' age varied between 29 and 59. For two aggressors I had data regarding the level of education (faculty graduates). The occupational status of fathers who killed their children was quite low; Six did not have a job, and three were workers. One aggressor was a businessman and two aggressors were pastors (when I say pastor I mean priest). Four aggressors were known to have mental illnesses. Three aggressors had consumed alcohol before committing the filicide-suicides. Only one aggressor had a criminal history. Most aggressors were working in Romania (10 cases).

Victims' characteristics

The filicide-suicide cases had 17 victims. Seven cases had only one victim and five cases had two victims each. Most victims were boys (11). The majority of victims were minors (14 cases). Ten children were between 1 and 10 years old, and four were teenagers aged between 13 and 16 years. One case had a 31-year-old young man as a victim.

Maternal filicide-suicides

In the Homicide-suicides in Romania database, only five maternal filicide-suicides were identified. Maternal filicide-suicides were committed in the period 2008–2013. Every year of this period one maternal filicide-suicide occurred (except year 2011). All cases happened in Romania. Two maternal filicide-suicides happened in the urban area and three in the rural area.

Three homicide cases were committed with a knife and two by strangulation. Mothers committed suicide by throwing themselves from a tall building (two cases), by hanging themselves (two cases) and by stabbing (one case). Most of them were committed in the house where mothers and their children were living (four cases). All cases were committed without witnesses. Three cases were committed during the day in the time period 6 am–6 pm and only one case during the evening (6 pm–10 pm). Three mothers left hand written messages in order to explain their gesture. One mother talked on the phone with the girls' father before killing the children. In this last case, a Romanian woman married to a Turkish man, settled in Romania, killed both her daughters (aged 5 and 9) and then committed suicide. She left a written message in which she brought up the difficulties that she faced having married a Muslim man. After marriage, the young woman who was Orthodox had to convert herself and become a Muslim, which was not easy. Or at least this is what we understand from her note: "Turkish people don't pray to God… I'm not accusing anyone". Moreover, the husband's family seems not to have accepted her although she had converted to Islam. Family friends also told about the young woman's alcohol consumption, which was also confirmed on the day of the filicide-suicide. After killing the little girls, she called her husband and talked to him on the phone. The message on the phone was un-intelligible for the husband who hurried to arrive home.

In most cases, the motivation of committing homicide against the children correlated with the mothers' or children's health state. A mother killed her mentally ill daughter "in order to end her misery". Another mother killed her mentally ill daughter because she had a breakdown after 29 years of taking care of her without any help from the Romanian institutions. From the husband's statements we found out that the family could not handle the situation any longer: "She wrote that she got tired of all this madness; that the girl was yelling and screaming. She said she wanted to go to Hell, she could not take it anymore, she did not ask for forgiveness, I was spared of two crosses" (She killed her mentally ill daughter after which she committed suicide. What the mother wrote in her farewell note, Stirile Protv.ro, November 19, 2013). A mentally ill mother killed her 17-year-old daughter during a depressive crisis generated by the interruption of the treatment given by doctors after her last hospitalization (5 months prior). The financial difficulties and losing her job caused another mother to kill her daughter.

Aggressors' characteristics

The mothers who killed their children were aged between 30 and 53. The average age of mother aggressors was 40.5 years. Only one was a university graduate. Four of them were housewives and one a teacher.

Victims' characteristics

The total number of victims was six. All victims were girls. The age of the victims was between 1 and 29 years old. Four victims were aged between 1 and 9 years, one victim was 17 years old and another one 29 years old. The 29-year-old victim was mentally ill and in the care of the family.

The analysis of paternal and maternal filicide-suicides committed in Romania emphasized the fact that the two types of filicide-suicide have certain particularities. The number of paternal filicide-suicides was approximately twice as big as the number of maternal filicide-suicides. The motivations of the two types of filicide-suicide were different. Paternal filicide-suicides seem to be committed by the fathers who wanted to get even with their partners who had left them (divorced or left abroad). Maternal filicide-suicides were committed by mothers with mental issues. The financial difficulties represented a smaller risk of committing filicide-suicides regardless of their type. The aggressors' age is similar in the case of both types of filicide-suicides. Small children with an age up to 10 seem to be the victims of the two types of filicide-suicide. The small number of cases of maternal filicide-suicide and paternal filicide-suicide represents a limit of these results. For a greater accuracy of the results, the research must be extended to a larger period of time in order to identify a larger number of cases. Moreover, I consider it necessary that the research regarding filicide-suicides should be extended in more countries from the European space. The cases of filicide-suicide identified in more countries should be included in a common database which allows us to emphasize some significant results for this type of violence.

Familicide-suicide

The term familicide was used most of the time in the specialty literature in order to designate the homicide of an "intimate partner and at least one child" (Liem et al. 2013: 351, Leveillee et al. 2009, Liem and Koenraadt 2008, Wilson et al. 1995). In other studies, parricide (Bourget et al. 2007, Heide 2013, Heide and

Frei, 2010, Marleau et al. 2006) and siblicide (Peck and Heide 2012) were included in the category of familicide. Other studies included in the familicide "children killing one or both parents plus other family members (siblings, grandparents, etc.)" (Fegadel and Heidi 2015). In a recent study, Liem and Reichelmann (2014) showed that "Multiple family homicides is also known as *familicide* or the killing of multiple family members" (p. 44). The same authors identified four types of familicide: Despondent Husbands, Spousal Revenge, Extended Parricide, and Diffuse Conflict (2014: 50).

The term of familicide-suicide was used in the same way as familicide. Hence the difficulty to compare data from more countries regarding this type of violence. Nevertheless, I can notice a recent tendency to designate familicide-suicide as the "multiple killing of family members associated with perpetrator suicide" (Johnson and Sachmann 2014: 100).

Methodology

The cases of familicide-suicide were extracted from the Homicide-suicides in Romania (2002–2013) database. I selected all the homicide cases committed by a member of the family (regardless of his role in the family) against other members of the family (of the first victim/of the aggressor) followed by the suicide of the aggressor a maximum one week after the homicide. I excluded the attempted familicide-suicides. In the analyzed period I identified only N=5 cases of familicide-suicide. Four cases were committed against the female intimate partner and the child. Only one case was committed by the aggressor against the intimate partner's parents and child. The information regarding three cases was obtained from all the sources used for making the database (police, parquet and online media) and for two cases I had information only from the online media.

Familicide-suicides in Romania

The analysis of information regarding the cases of familicide-suicide identified in the Homicide-suicides in Romania (2002–2013) database emphasized the fact that all cases of familicide-suicides (N=5 cases) were committed by men. Only one aggressor was a Romanian emigrant in Switzerland. Four cases happened in Romania and one case happened in a town in Switzerland. Familicide-suicides were committed in the period 2005–2013 (one case per year in five years out of the eight mentioned years). Three cases happened in the urban and two cases in the rural area. Two homicides were committed by shooting, two with a knife and one by arson. The aggressors used almost the same weapons for suicide. Two aggressors committed suicide by shooting, one by stabbing with a knife, one by poisoning and one by arson.

Only in three cases were the witnesses mentioned. In two cases the witnesses were members of the victim's family and in one case the witnesses were members of the aggressor's family. Four familicide-suicides were committed during the day (three familicide-suicides were committed in the period 6–12 am, and one familicide-suicide between 12 am and 6 pm). One familicide-suicide was committed during the night after 3 am.

In three cases, the aggressor left a message before committing suicide in order to explain the violent acts. In two cases, the aggressors left hand written messages and in one case the aggressor spoke on the phone with his friends before committing suicide.

The motivation of familicide-suicides was different. For three cases, the motivations of the acts of violence were directly connected with the relationship between the aggressors and their intimate partners. One aggressor committed familicide-suicide after the divorce filed by the wife had come through. The aggressor decided to kill his former wife and child after being forced to split their wealth after the divorce. Another familicide-suicide case occurred after the girlfriend of one of the aggressors threatened to leave him if he did not end the relationship with the former girlfriend. The third familicide-suicide happened when his wife announced that she wanted to leave him because she had another boyfriend. To get even, the husband killed her child and parents. One case was committed by the aggressor after losing his job. In this case, the aggressor killed his wife and son. The fifth case of familicide-suicide was committed by a husband overwhelmed with the debts that he owed to colleagues and moneylenders. Because he did not manage to find the money and he could not deal with the moneylenders' pressure, he decided to kill his wife and son. In total, four cases had as victims the wives/former wives and children. One of these cases had three victims: the current girlfriend and her child plus his former girlfriend.

I chose as an example two cases of familicide-suicide committed by men because of their desire to get even with the partners who had left them. The first case is the one that had as victims the former partner and the child. This time, the aggressor got even directly with his former partner. Among the victims we can mention the current partner of the former concubine, but he survived the attack (Case C).

Case C: Familicide-suicide as revenge against a concubine and her child

M.R. killed his former partner and his 2-year-old son, only two months after his wife had left him for another man. The fact which determined the violent end of the victims was the woman's decision to move in with her new partner. Thus, three days after the former partner moved together with her son into the house of the new boyfriend, M.R. decided to kill them. The decision came after a period in which the former partner had more conflicts with the new partner. The family friends said that two weeks before the murders, there was a conflict between the woman's former partner and the current partner which ended with the intervention of police and with a fine for the woman's current boyfriend. The neighbors confirmed the fact that the aggressor had a fight with the woman's current boyfriend also the day before the murders, the reason being his desire to visit his son. The homicide of the former girlfriend and of the little boy happened during the night after the aggressor had watched the former concubine and the current partner having sexual relations (according to the notes written by the prosecutor during investigations). The aggressor attacked the three (the concubine, the child and the current partner) with the intention of killing them, but the partner of the former girlfriend survived. Several hours after the crime, he called his manager from his job and some neighbors who he told what he had done and also told them that he wanted to commit suicide. The motivation of the acts was jealousy. (Aggressor 35 years old, shepherd)

The second case of familicide-suicide is a special case because the abandoned partner got even with his wife by killing the other members of her family. The fact that his partner was abroad and she refused to recommence their relationship caused the aggressor to kill her child and her parents who remained in the country. This time revenge made the loved ones suffer. Through this violent act, the aggressor exposed his former partner to two extreme types of violence: murdering all members of the family that remained in the country and exposing her to the public odium (the articles published in the media sanctioned the former wife more than the aggressor who killed her family) (Case D).

Case D: Familicide-suicides as revenge against concubine – killing of her parents and child

C.I. had a relationship of almost 11 years with N.M., a relationship which deteriorated slowly due to C.I.'s jealousy associated with infidelity suspicion. As a result of their relationship, they had a boy whose custody they were fighting for when the boy was 7. The familicide-suicide occurred after N.M. left for Italy with the intention to earn the money necessary to get custody of the child. C.I. suspected that she had another relationship in Italy and, in order to gain revenge, he decided to kill all her family who remained in the country (her child and adoptive parents). Before killing them, the aggressor threatened his girlfriend by sending her text messages. Because she was not answering his messages, the day when they celebrated their 11 year anniversary, he sent her a warning message: "You will be sorry. Everything ends tonight. This evening means a lot to me. Tonight we were supposed to celebrate 11 years of relationship and you will always remember that you transformed my love into revenge. I will sacrifice myself." Two days after this message, the aggressor went to action. During the night of January 1 to 2, he killed all members of N.M.'s family and then sent another message to his concubine. This time, the message announced the death of her loved ones: "It's really serious. Answer me because it all ended with murders. I'm sitting here and crying and wondering why you told me we would make up. In this way a lot of people would have been saved. You can call home, all of them are dead, and nobody is moving anymore." N.M. did not pay attention to this message either, thinking it was just another attempt of the aggressor to make her come home and start their relationship over. A little time after the crime, he wrote a note in which he explained the motivation of his act. Then he wrote a note with the message: "Don't come in, I did a crime. Call 112" which he put at the house entrance. C.I. committed by through hanging. (Aggressor 29 years old, Şag village, January 2, 2012)

Aggressors' characteristics

The aggressors' average age was 41.8 years. Their age varied between 35 and 55 years. The level of education was mentioned only in the case of two aggressors: one was a high school graduate and the other one a faculty graduate. The profession was mentioned for four aggressors. Two aggressors were policemen, one locksmith and another one a shepherd. Only one aggressor had consumed alcohol. Only one aggressor had a criminal history.

Victims' characteristics

The five familicide-suicide cases had 12 victims. Three familicide-suicides had two victims and two cases of familicide-suicide had three victims each. The information regarding victims was quite limited. The victims' age varied between 2 and 57 years. Four victims were minors aged between 2 and 12. Three victims had a high level of education (faculty graduates), and two victims had an average level of education. Another two victims were minors aged between 2 and

5, therefore they might have been at kindergarten. I had information about the profession of seven victims. Three victims had a low occupational status (two housewives and one worker) and two victims had an average status (a nurse and a student). Only one victim had a high occupational status (an accountant).

Conclusions

The familicide-suicide cases are quite rare in Romania. Part of them can be associated with the phenomenon of Romanians' emigration which determined the departure of at least one parent abroad in search of a job. As I mentioned before, only men committed familicide-suicides in Romania. We have no case of familicide-suicide committed by women. When the five male aggressors were confronted with situations in which they were losing control over their intimate partner, they decided to get even with her by killing themselves and their children or by killing the family members. The same happened with the aggressors who were confronted with difficult financial situations. Unfortunately, I did not have information regarding the history of the health state of aggressors and information about their attempted suicides. The small number of cases makes it difficult to emphasize some particularities specific to Romania. I cannot, though, ignore the fact that in the case of familicide-suicides and of filicide-suicides, the children of the families affected by emigration became the people against whom the aggressors directed their criminal acts because they only wanted to punish their partners.

Part II Homicide-Suicides and Online Media

5. Femicide-Suicides in the Romanian Online Media

Although the cases of femicide and femicide-suicide keep being covered by the international press, only few studies analyzed the way in which journalists present these types of violence. Recent studies regarding the media representation of femicide drew attention to the way in which journalists described the cases of femicide and emphasized the journalists' tendency to diminish the aggressors' responsibility through some direct and indirect techniques of blaming the women victims (Meyers 1994, Taylor 2009, Richards et al. 2011, Fairbairn and Dawson 2013). On the other hand, the studies regarding femicide-suicides showed that these cases tend to be presented as newsworthy or routine cases (Nikunen 2011), as romantic love, loss of control by perpetrators (Gius and Lalli 2014) or as related/non-related to prior domestic violence (Richards et al. 2014). Moreover, journalists presented femicides and femicide-suicides as an individual event and not as a social problem and through this they contributed to maintaining a decreased level of intervention and prevention methods (Berns 2004, Carll 2003, Taylor and Sorenson 2002, Fairbairn and Dawson 2013, Richards et al. 2013).

Few studies tried to analyze the media coverage of femicides/femicide-suicides committed in Romania. Some of these studies tackled directly the subject of femicide-suicides (Balica forthcoming), while others placed the subject in the background (Balica and Stöckl 2016, Balica 2016). Each of these studies analyzed just some of the violent acts that are part of the sphere of femicides or femicide-suicides. Some articles discussed femicide-suicides whose victims were immigrant Romanian women offering sexual services legally or illegally (Balica forthcoming). Others brought attention to some aspects of intimate partner femicide-suicides (Balica and Stöckl 2016, Balica 2016). On the other hand, in the international literature studies about the media coverage of femicides and femicide-suicides are only one part of the cases which could have been designated femicides or femicide-suicides. More precisely, they said that intimate partner femicides/intimate partner femicide-suicides are equal to femicides/femicide-suicides. The present chapter will also have the same limit. I will use the term femicide-suicides in order to nominate intimate partner femicide-suicides. Other subtypes of femicide-suicides will be excluded from the analysis.

Methodology

The present chapter was written starting with the analysis of the way in which the online media in Romania covered the cases of femicide-suicide committed in the period 2010–2015. I identified all the articles from the online media which published information about the cases of femicide-suicide committed between Romanian citizens. I selected both the articles about femicide-suicides committed between Romanian citizens in Romania and the articles about the cases committed in other countries between Romanian emigrants. I included in the analysis only the articles published in Romanian. Femicide-suicide was defined as the homicide of the female intimate partner and then the aggressor's suicide (the victim's intimate partner) in a period of time that lasted up to 48 hours. When I am talking about intimate partner, I mean: wife/husband, former wife/husband, concubine, girlfriend/boyfriend. The cases of attempted femicide-suicides and the cases in which the aggressor's suicide happened in a period of time longer than 48 hours were excluded.

In order to identify the articles, I used the following methodology. In the first phase, I used the keywords "he killed his wife and then committed suicide", "he killed his girlfriend and then committed suicide". For a greater precision of my search, I associated the previously mentioned keywords with the years from the period 2010–2015. The keywords associated with the years were introduced in the search engine Google Chrome. After I identified a case of femicide-suicide, I extracted from the respective case other keywords and I continued the search for articles associated with the respective case. Among the extracted keywords from the core of the first article identified for one case, I can mention: surname and first name of the aggressor, surname and first name of the victim, city where femicide-suicide was committed and the way in which the victim was murdered (e.g. he shot her and then killed himself).

In the end, my analysis was made of N=135 articles identified in the online media for N=28 cases of femicide-suicide committed in the period 2010–2015. The articles were published both in online newspapers with national coverage (Adevărul.ro, Libertatea, Spynews.ro) and in online newspapers which published information from certain regions or counties in the country (Jurnalul de Buzău, Sighisoara online.com, voceatransilvaniei.ro, Monitorul de Vrancea). I also identified articles published on news sites (Ziare.com, Hotnews.com) and articles published on websites of TV channels (România tv, Acasatv.ro, Protv.ro).

The objectives of the research were formulated as to permit: 1) identifying the way in which online media in Romania covered victims and aggressors; 2) identifying the sources used by journalists in order to write the articles; 3) the context of the femicide-suicide articles and 4) the analysis of language. The analysis of media coverage of femicide-suicide in Romania proposed, among others, to confirm or inform the aspects emphasized by the study made by Richards et al. regarding the relation between domestic violence and femicide-suicide in media coverage of this subject (2014). During the analysis of media coverage of Romanian online articles, I tried to emphasize the presence or absence of the 4 media frames used by Richards et al.: "1) femicide-suicide by a male perpetrator; 2) femicide-suicide due to loss of perpetrator control; 3) femicide-suicide as a mercy killing, and 4) femicide-suicide due to jealousy" (Richards et al. 2013: 24).

At the same time, I proposed to analyze the way in which the Romanian journalists from the online media present victims and aggressors. I was rather interested in checking whether, through the way in which victims and aggressors were described, journalists blame victims and diminish the role of the aggressors in committing femicide-suicides. More precisely, I wanted to see if the Romanian journalists use the same techniques of blaming the victims of femicides as identified by Taylor in 2009 in the case of a metropolitan newspaper from Florida. The study made by Taylor emphasized the fact that journalists tend to use direct and indirect techniques of blaming the victims of femicides. Among the direct techniques of blaming the victims used by the American journalists, Taylor enumerated: describing victims in a negative way, informing readers about the lack of their actions regarding informing police about the violent acts or the threats to which they were exposed and about their relationships with other men (2009: 33). Describing the aggressor as a man with health or financial problems and informing about the acts of domestic violence without mentioning the role of the aggressor in these violent acts are indirect techniques of passing the responsibility of the violent acts to the victims. (Taylor 2009: 34).

I was of course interested in identifying the socio-demographic features of the victims and the aggressors from the covered cases in order to identify the eventual criteria for selection of cases in order to be published according to the victims' and aggressors' profile.

The analysis of the sources used by the Romanian journalists in documenting their articles about femicide-suicides had as a purpose identifying the types of sources that journalists prefer to use. Moreover, I tried to identify the purpose in which these sources were used (for bringing additional information regarding the motivation of femicide-suicides, for confirming the information obtained from other sources, for giving information about the history of previous abuse). The studies made in other countries showed that the sources of official and unofficial information can be used differently by the journalists who write about femicides and femicide-suicides. The official sources were frequently used by journalists in order to inform about both types of violence. Among these sources police and parquets are most often brought into the discussion (Richards et al. 2014, Taylor 2009). Sometimes, the information picked up from the police, parquets or court houses were used by journalists to directly and indirectly blame the victims of femicide (Taylor, 2009). The victims' and aggressors' families were the sources most often contacted by the journalists who described femicide-suicides (Richards et al. 2014), while neighbors were most often interviewed by the journalists who presented cases of femicides (Richards et al. 2011). Starting from this, I tried in this chapter, to emphasize the way in which the Romanian journalists from the online media described femicide-suicides.

During the analysis, I tried to answer the following questions:

1. What sources were used by Romanian journalists in the coverage of femicide-suicide cases?
2. How were aggressors presented? What was the information about the aggressors (identification data, data regarding health state, criminal background, etc.)?
3. How were victims presented? What was the information about the victims? Did the Romanian journalists try, through the presented information, to blame the victims for femicide-suicide?
4. Was the coverage of femicide-suicides correlated with prior history of domestic violence?
5. How were the cases of femicide-suicide explained by the Romanian journalists? Does media coverage of femicide-suicide cases fit in the media frames identified by Gius and Lalli (2014) for intimate partner femicide (femicide as romantic love or loss of control)?

Description of femicide-suicide cases

The 28 femicide-suicide cases included in the analysis were committed between Romanian intimate partners. Most cases (N=26) were committed in Romania. Only two femicide-suicide cases were committed between Romanian people who were living/working abroad (one case in Germany and one case in the USA).

The journalists' interest in the femicide-suicide cases grew step by step during the analyzed period. Thus, while in 2010 only one case of femicide-suicide was covered, starting with 2011 (five cases) the number of covered femicide-suicides grew until 2013 (seven cases). Furthermore, the number of femicide-suicides registered for 2010 in the Homicide-suicides in Romania database was quite small (three cases). The number of femicide-suicides in Romania tripled in 2011 (nine cases) compared to 2010. We could say that in 2010 journalists covered one out of three femicide-suicides. While the number of femicide-suicides in Romania grew, the number of covered femicide-suicides grew as well. The report was, this time, one covered case out of two registered cases (2011 – nine registered cases – five covered cases). This report remained the same until 2013 (13 registered cases out of which seven were covered).

The cases of femicide-suicide selected to be presented in the online media were treated differently by journalists. Only one article was published for each of five cases. For 69.2 per cent of the cases (N=18) 1–5 articles were published, while for the rest of the cases 6–11 articles were published. As an average, for every case of femicide-suicide, 4.8 articles were published. More than half of the cases were covered for only one day (14 cases). Approximately one third of the cases (seven cases, 27 per cent) were covered for two days, four cases were covered for three days and only one case was presented for four days. The most covered case was committed in 2014 in a village in south-east Romania. The case was covered for more days than other cases because it had elements that took it out of the patterns. This femicide-suicide occurred in "Săptămâna luminată" (the first week after Easter) a period of time with important meaning for Romanian Christians. Moreover, the aggressor was mentally ill and he was 10 years younger than his wife.

The articles in which femicide-suicides were presented varied from short news articles (100 words) to articles of several pages. Approximately 40 per cent of the articles (N=53) were short articles where journalists mentioned the village/town, the relationship between the victim and the aggressors, the age of the two and, eventually, the institutions involved in investigating the case. I included one article of this type in order to give an example.

> A man killed his wife, after which he killed himself, in a house situated in the 1st district, in the Bucureştii Noi neighborhood, according to some sources from the police. The quoted sources said, to Mediafax, that the incident was announced by the neighbors who called the emergency number 112. Most probably the husband, aged 46, cut his wife's throat, aged 55, after which he stuck the knife in his abdomen, said the policemen who reached the crime scene. The police officers from Homicide Service started an investigation which is run under the coordination of prosecutors of the parquet near the Bucharest Court House. (*A man killed his wife after which killed himself, in a house in the 1st district in Bucharest*, Andrei Dumitrescu, Mediafax.ro, November 5, 2015)

When journalists considered that femicide-suicides can draw the public's attention, they wrote long articles where there was also information about the victims and aggressors and the relationship between them.

Official and unofficial sources used for media coverage of femicide-suicides

The analysis of articles emphasized the fact that journalists used more types of sources (official and unofficial) for writing some articles. Official sources were quoted 88 times in articles. Unofficial sources were quoted 137 times. Among the official sources, police (31 per cent) and parquets (24 per cent) were the most quoted institutions (see Table 5.1). Although they presented data which journalists could usually obtain only from official sources (police, parquet, forensic doctors), other articles did not mention the sources (35 articles, 26 per cent). The analysis of articles where sources were mentioned emphasized that journalists usually quoted more sources during articles. I identified, thus, articles in which journalists used more official sources, articles in which more unofficial sources were quoted, but also articles which used both types of sources.

Table 5.1 Official institutions as sources

Type of sources	Institutions/categories of sources	Number of appearances
Official sources	Police: spokesperson, manager of the police unit, press release	42
	Parquet: spokesperson, case prosecutor, press release	32
	Hospital: county hospital, medical unit, hospital manager, spokesperson, doctors	3
	National Institute of Forensic Medicine: forensic doctors, psychiatrist experts	10
	Security company employees	1

Official sources were mentioned so that the information included in the articles would be more verifiable The press releases of the police and parquets were the most frequently quoted in the articles about femicide-suicides. On the other hand, the articles written by journalists are similar in structure and content to press releases or declarations by police officials and parquets. I am saying this as some articles included entire fragments from press releases. Journalists simply preferred to quote directly the official sources without making any effort to take over the information obtained in the press conferences or from releases given by the press offices of the police or parquet. Journalists especially quote information regarding the modus operandi, weapons used and motivation of femicide-suicides.

> We found two spouses who were deceased in their house, we are talking about Marin spouses, she seems to have been killed by her husband, after which he committed suicide.

> Most probably he killed her by strangling after which he stabbed himself around the heart with a knife with a 14cm blade. We did not find any note. We found violent traces only on her, at the level of the neck, the chest and of the hands; it must have been a fight and he committed suicide after that. Most probably, from the information that we have from neighbors, it was a jealousy crisis. The two spouses were found in bed, both in pajamas, he was lying with the knife in his chest next to her. Everything might have happened a day before because the day before yesterday she was at work and yesterday she did not come to work", declared prosecutor Nicolae Ghihaniş. (*Murder followed by suicide, in the block ISEH*, April 6, 2013, Monitorul de Vrancea)

As Taylor noticed (2009) in the case of American journalists, I can notice in the case of Romanian journalists a tendency to use the information from the official press releases of the police/parquet in order to pass the responsibility of violence to the victim. More precisely, from the official press release given by the case prosecutor, the journalist extracted the paragraph in which the motive of the crime was mentioned: jealousy. Then, the journalist informs us that the victim told her husband that she had a boyfriend.

> The case prosecutor, Iulian Avram, declared that the motive of the crime is supposed to have been jealousy. "The woman was murdered with 13 knife strikes, most of them in the neck and chest area. The perpetrator seems to have caught her in a narrow place, between the fridge and the sink, in the kitchen. After the forensic expertise, we will settle if the woman was beaten or not before the crime. (…) The woman had come back to the country two days ago and she told her husband that she had found another man. The entire apartment was a mess. Many traces of blood were found. The knife with which he stabbed her was found also, but there is no farewell note left by the perpetrator", declared the criminal prosecutor Iulian Avram, from the parquet near the Court House Hunedoara. (*Under the terrified eyes of their little boy, a man killed his wife and then hung himself*, Deva.Ziare.com, April 8, 2013)

Journalists sometimes tried to include information from the investigations made in the places where femicide-suicides happened. But these investigations were limited to some elements which could have been picked up during some discussions with neighbors, colleagues or relatives. The journalists did not contact specialists (psychologists, family doctors, social workers) who could have offered an explanation of the causality of femicide-suicides (a more complex and clearer explanation than the one offered by the police or parquet). What is interesting is the fact that the analysis of the way in which homicide-suicides committed by the Romanian policemen (see chapter 7 of this book) were covered emphasized that journalists contacted experts who could offer explanations of homicide-suicides committed by policemen. On the other hand, journalists did not consider it necessary to appeal to the information that experts could have given for the cases of femicide-suicides (see Table 5.2).

Table 5.2 Unofficial sources used by Romanian journalists

Type of sources	Institutions/categories of sources	Number of appearances
Unofficial sources	Relatives of the aggressor	13
	Colleagues and friends of the aggressor	7
	Relatives of the victim	22
	Colleagues of the victim	7
	Neighbors, building administrators	30
	Witnesses	7
	Letters/messages left by the aggressors	10
	The victim's boyfriend	2
	Rumors	3
Media	Press agencies: Mediafax, AGERPRESS	11
	Online newspapers: Realitatea.net, Adevarul.ro, spynews.ro, voceatransilvaniei.ro	15
	TV station website: Antena3, RomaniaTv	7
Social networking sites (SNS)	Facebook	3
No sources		35

Among the unofficial sources used in the articles about femicide-suicides, the most quoted were the neighbors (22.2 per cent) and the victims' relatives (16.3 per cent). These two categories of people are, in general, those who are in the proximity of the place where the violent act happened when the authorities do field research.

In some cases, the victims' relatives were also witnesses or survivors of the homicide. Regardless of the situation, journalists used relatives in order to give readers information about the development of the event or about other elements that happened before the homicide. I am talking here about the information connected to the death threats addressed to victims or their relatives made by the aggressor before committing the violent act. Moreover, when journalists get in contact with the victim's relatives, we find information about the history of the relationship between the victim and the aggressor, or information about factors that speeded the evolution of the relationship towards homicide.

> He kept threatening her with the death, with shooting, but we thought he was joking, those were his jokes. I saw him when he entered the gate, I think he had the weapon behind his back. I could just tell. She got up from the table and told him "I told you not to come because I have work to do". And then he shot her in the mouth and then ran, I think he wanted to shoot the others too, but the children (the victim's cousins) ran from him quickly" said Cristina Adam, the victim's sister-in-law. (December 13, 2013 Adevărul.ro)

The neighbors are sometimes represented by "village old women", who, through their life experience are thought of as credible sources of information regarding the profile of the victim or the motivation of homicide. In fact, old women are those who say honest things and give much deeper information than relatives. Old women, in fact women in close proximity to the families affected by murder, are used to pass the responsibility of murder to the aggressor's family (who did not accept the girl as a partner for their son) and to the victim who refused to leave for Italy with the aggressor.

> The old ladies from the village say Larisa was a working girl, who was taking care of the family household, when her parents were away working in Italy. Larisa is a good, serious girl, she is great. He called her at his place, she said no so he took out his gun and shot her", said a terrified neighbor. "His parents did not want him to take this girl, and now she refuses to go because she was not wanted and look at him, what he has done to her", said another old lady. (Adevărul.ro, December 13, 2013)

Press agencies (8.1 per cent) and online newspapers (11.1 per cent) were other sources which journalists used for writing their articles. Sometimes, when they quote other online newspapers, journalists prefer to present the case only in one short paragraph and then mention the source where the reader can access all the information.

Social networking sites are increasingly used by journalists as unofficial sources. The victims', aggressors' or the friends' posts on Facebook were taken by journalists and included in the articles about the cases of femicide-suicides. In two cases journalists took information from the Facebook pages. I am talking about a case of femicide-suicide committed in the USA by a 72-year-old husband (an American citizen of Romanian origin) against his 35 years younger wife (a Romanian woman). Unsatisfied with the way in which her partner had been treating her lately, the wife found herself another boyfriend and tried to divorce her husband. The wish to separate hurried the tragic end of the young woman. In this case, the information was taken from the diaspora newspapers and from the

Facebook page of the victim's boyfriend. The victim's boyfriend was a member of the Romanian diaspora from the USA also known as a journalist and a poet. His messages and poems from Facebook were taken by the Romanian journalists in order to give more romance to the case.

> Of all God's distances, you'll remain the most beautiful, Ana!
> You told me you had never been so happy and you told me: I love you as I have never loved anyone before in my life, and I let myself be shot with birds in the temples for your sake.
> I promise I will never forget the mornings when we were waking up at 5 to have butterflies derailed in the parking spaces where the fireflies were getting crowded so we could share the light of the light later. (*Passionate crime in the USA. A 72-year-old Romanian murdered his 37 year old wife and then committed suicide. The reason would be jealousy,* Stirile.Protv.ro, November 17, 2015)

In the second case in which information was taken from Facebook, journalists referred to the victim's Facebook page. They went to the victim's Facebook page and took photographs and information from this page because the aggressor wrote on the victim's body the message "Facebook kills!". More information about this case will be presented in chapter 6.

Other journalists preferred to include in their articles parts of the messages written by aggressors before committing suicide. The messages left by aggressors were quoted by journalists in 7.4 per cent of articles. Journalists tried to give credibility to the cases of femicide-suicide with the quoted sources. They tried at the same time to respect the ethical norms of their profession which require that the information be checked by more credible sources. Although some journalists used more sources of information of different types, most articles about femicide-suicides were simple enumerations of information identified in different sources. Only seldom did journalists make complex investigations. When they talk about femicide-suicides, journalists talk only about the respective case, they do not place the information in the general context of the acts of violence committed in Romania. Only in one article did the journalist refer briefly to another case of femicide-suicide. Although the articles about the cases of femicide-suicides are easily accessible on the Internet, journalists do not make connections between the cases published online (sometimes even by the newspapers for which they work). They prove through this fact that they want to attract the reader of the newspaper with articles about femicide-suicides. They are rather interested in the uniqueness and sensational nature of the case and not in the analysis of a type of violence or in the expression of a point of view.

Analysis of titles

When they wrote the titles of articles which presented the cases of femicide-suicide, the Romanian journalists tried to catch the public's attention by including some information about the victim, the aggressor or about the way in which femicide-suicides were committed. The analysis of titles of 135 articles emphasized the fact that 65.2 per cent of the titles (N=88) contain both information about the relationship between the victim and the aggressor and information regarding the type of violence (homicide followed by suicide). In other words, journalists made it clear even from the title that we are talking about femicide-suicides.

> "Shocking case at Hanu Conachi: He killed his wife after which he killed himself", (Teodora Miron, Viața-libera.ro, September 10, 2013)

> "Passionate crime in the USA. A 72-year-old Romanian murdered his 37-year-old wife and then committed suicide. The reason would be jealousy" (Stirile.Protv.ro, November 17, 2015)

> "A young man from Hunedoara killed his wife after which killed himself. What might have made the man do such a gesture?" (Stirile.Protv.ro, October 18, 2015)

> "A man killed his wife and then committed suicide, in a place in the 1st district in Bucharest" (Andrei Dumitrescu, Mediafax.ro, November 5, 2015)

For the rest of articles (N=47, 34.8 per cent), journalists did not give information regarding the relationship between the victim and the aggressor. In this situation, the reader finds out from the title that it is about an act of violence, "a tragedy", "a murder or a suicide". Moreover, in order to emphasize the sensational element of the violent acts, they added information regarding the villages/cities where they happened. The information about villages/cities appeared especially when it was about small villages to which journalists do not generally pay attention. In the titles given to articles, journalists are trying to draw attention to a certain type of event that went out of the patterns and affected small communities where villagers live their lives dealing only with daily problems.

> "Shock! Murder followed by suicide in Lupeni!" (Carmen Cosman-Preda, Ziarul Hunedoreanului, October 18, 2015)

> "Murder or suicide? Two young people were found dead in Lupeni – *A love story ended tragically and saddened a small village from Hunedoara*" (Danilea D, ro.blastingnews.com, October 18, 2015)

> "Tragedy at Tichilești. A couple found dead in the house" (VoxTV Regional, April 18, 2015)

> "Murder followed by suicide at Tichilești" (Brăila.Ziare.com, April 17, 2015)

In their attempt to draw the attention to articles, journalists also included information about the way in which the femicide-suicides were committed. This information was added only when the modus operandi went out of the patterns that were typical for committing homicide-suicides in Romania. As I mentioned in chapter 1 of this book, homicide-suicides in Romania were mostly committed with a knife (homicides – 57.6 per cent, suicides – 39.4 per cent). In the analysis of titles of articles about femicide-suicides, journalists mentioned information about the cases committed by shooting or other methods that were out of the ordinary.

The analysis of titles of articles which described cases of femicide-suicide showed that only 25 per cent of the titles (N=34 articles) included information regarding the way in which femicide-suicides were committed. Besides the information about modus operandi, the titles also gave data regarding the city of residence of the victim or of both murdered partners.

> "He cut her throat, then he did hara-kiri to himself! Horrible murder in the 1st district of capital" (Spynews.ro, November 5, 2015)

> "A young woman from Mehedinți died after her boyfriend shot her in the head. The murderer committed suicide a short time after that" (Adevărul.ro, December 13, 2013)

Another method to attract the reader was to give information about the family children. Children were exposed even if they were not witnesses to the violent acts. Here is an example in which journalists informed the reader about violent acts: "He killed his former wife, after which he sent a message to their child: "I killed your mother. I am going now." (Stirile.Protv.ro, March 3, 2013).

Victims and Aggressors

The articles published online contain mostly little information about victims and aggressors. The names of the victims and of the aggressors and the town/village where they lived were mentioned more often than information regarding age, profession and health state. The age of the victims and of the aggressors was mentioned almost equally (victims 63.7 per cent, aggressors 69.7 per cent). The aggressors' age was given for 23 cases (88.5 per cent) while the victims' age was presented for 21 cases (80.8 per cent). Almost half of the aggressors were aged between 26 and 39, and the other half between 40 and 65 years old. Only one aggressor was 72 years old. The age of the victims of the covered cases was slightly different to that of the aggressors. The cases with young victims seem to be more covered, 66.7 per cent of the victims were aged between 20 and 39. Approximately 30 per cent of the victims were aged between 40 and 55. We can notice that, in general, journalists tend to select coverage cases where the victims are women, children or old people. In the case of this type of violence, journalists do not seem interested in victims older than 55. This time journalists seem to use other criteria than the age of the victims/aggressors for the selection of cases.

The analysis of articles also emphasized the fact that information was given about the victims' and aggressors' profession only in few cases. The victims' profession was mentioned in nine cases (34.6 per cent) and the aggressors' profession in eight cases (30.7 per cent). Only 14 per cent of articles contained data regarding the victims' profession and 17.8 per cent had data about the aggressors' profession. Among the mentioned professions for victims, we can enumerate especially those which could be associated with a low occupational status (workers, housekeepers, waitresses). The victims with a superior status were quite rarely mentioned. One case had a urologist as a victim. On the other hand, the situation was slightly different for aggressors. From the statements regarding the aggressors' profession, we can notice that they preferred to select cases with aggressors with an average status. Policemen (three cases), military personnel (one case), foresters (one case) were those who caught the journalists' attention. Businessmen who killed their partners were also more visible. Therefore, journalists selected the cases with aggressors who had a special status in the communities to which they belonged and aggressors who were more known due to their profession. Thus, journalists were trying to raise the visibility of the cases and of the newspapers where they were writing.

At the same time, journalists offered the aggressor a higher importance for specifying their status every time they thought it necessary to report the victims who were just ordinary people (with a low social status) or whose status was considered so important as to be mentioned. This situation could be appreciated as being an indirect technique of blaming the victim (Taylor 2009).

Femicide-suicides and domestic violence

In the last five years, researchers have oriented their attention to the analysis of the relation between femicides/femicide-suicides and domestic violence (Richards et al. 2014, Gillespie et al. 2013, Fairbairn and Dawson 2013, Richards et al. 2011). All these studies analyzed the way in which the print media covered femicides and femicide-suicides. As far as I know there were no studies about the way in which the online media covered femicides or femicide-suicides. In Romania there was a small interest in the analysis of media coverage of domestic violence, femicides or femicide-suicides. Few studies tried to emphasize the way in which the Romanian media covered the theme of domestic violence (Marinescu and Ştefănescu 2004) and of femicide-suicides (Balica and Stöckl 2016,

Balica 2016, Balica forthcoming). None of the aforementioned studies brought into discussion the relation between domestic violence and femicides/femicide-suicides. In this context, I tried to direct my attention to the way in which the online media covered the relationship between domestic violence and femicide-suicides committed between Romanian people (regardless of the country where they happened).

The first question I asked myself was whether the articles which present femicide-suicides also include information regarding domestic violence. Then I tried to analyze the information given about domestic violence in order to identify the perspective from which the journalists' message is seen by readers (victims are blamed or not, journalists are or are not interested in getting involved in promoting a message meant to stimulate the prevention of femicide-suicides).

From the analysis of articles, approximately one third (28.1 per cent) of the articles which presented femicide-suicides made a connection between femicide-suicides and domestic violence. Some articles said that the aggressors who committed femicide-suicides had also abused their partners (17 articles, 12.6 per cent). On the other hand, other articles just mentioned that there had been acts of violence between the two, without saying who the aggressor was (10 articles, 7.4 per cent). We find out about some women could not stand domestic violence for a long period of time, and the women's decision to separate led to their homicide.

> George and Lili were married for 20 years. They loved each other deeply, say their close friends and family, but the man's violence made his wife become distant. "He was jealous and he told her that, he was always beating her and was telling her to come back, but she did not want this anymore, if they did not get along well, she did not want it anymore", said some acquaintances. (*The man form Mogoşoaia who killed his former wife, found hung in a village near Bucharest after 15 hours of searching*, Stirile.Protv.ro, March 3, 2013)

Among the violent acts prior to femicide-suicides we can mention acts of psychological violence. Some aggressors blackmailed their victims saying they would kill themselves if the women decided to separate.

> In front of the gate, I found also the victim's friend who told us that the man had not been at his first suicide attempt. "Last week he ran after her with the hatchet through the courtyard. She managed to escape and hide at the neighbors'. I told her she should not go back home anymore. But she came back home, because he was threatening to kill himself. He wanted to kill himself also with electrical wires. She stopped him then. I talked to her after that and he seemed to have calmed down", said in detail Dorina Alexe. (*Shocking case at Hanu Conachi: He killed his wife after which he killed himself*, Teodora Miron, Viaţa-libera.ro, September 10, 2013)

Journalists present little information about the victims' actions to protect themselves from the aggressors' violence. Only seven articles presented information about the measures taken by victims after being abused by aggressors. Four victims managed to obtain restraining orders and three victims withdrew their complaints made to the police or court houses. The lack of this information can be the result of the lack of initiative of victims or the lack of journalists' interest for presenting the background of the domestic violence and the measures taken by victims. Both variants may be right as in Romania there is a limit to the protection system designated to victims of domestic violence. Moreover, as I have already mentioned, journalists did not struggle to identify more information about femicide-suicides, but they preferred to take over parts of press releases presented in the first days after the committing of the crime (and not information from the final phase of the investigations of authorities).

The restraining orders did not keep the aggressors away from the victims. This seems to be the message of the four articles which give information about the presence of such a measure. The aggressors kept following their victims even if they separated and even if they obtained a restraining order.

> Neli and George Badea separated two years before, and the woman had obtained a restraining order from a judge against her former husband. Her husband was extremely violent and he was not allowed to come closer than 200m to her. (*He killed his former wife and then he sent a message to their child "I killed your mother. I am going now."* Stirile.Protv.ro, March 3, 2013)

The message transmitted by some journalists to their readers is sometimes ambivalent. Journalists avoid positioning themselves in their reports to the victim or the aggressor. I took as an example an article which presented a femicide-suicide committed in 2013 in a village near Bucharest. If we analyze, for example, the first extract from the article published by Stirile.Protv.ro we can notice that the journalist seems to be on the aggressor's side who tried to rebuild his relationship with the victim ("he took her to Paris"). On the other hand, although she went to Paris, the victim got divorced and made the legal procedures to obtain a restraining order. Until this point, the journalist seems to be on the aggressor's side and he emphasizes the proper behavior of the aggressor. The victim's behavior is blamable because, despite the husband's efforts to rebuild the relationship, she refused to continue their marriage. The second extract emphasizes the inability of the victim's actions to protect herself from the husband. As for the husband, the journalist changes his attitude for a little bit and names him the "individual" in order to mark his distance from the aggressor.

> Lili got divorced half a year ago. George would have tried to fix the relationship and took her to Paris. But Lili did not want to continue. Moreover, she obtained a restraining order because she felt harassed. (*The man form Mogoșoaia who killed his former wife, found hung in a village near Bucharest after 15 hours of searching*, Stirile.Protv.ro, March 3, 2013)

> The paper written by the Court House did not keep the man away. On Wednesday evening, he followed Lili again, and when she remained alone in Mogoșoaia medical clinic, he burst over her. (*The man form Mogoșoaia who killed his former wife, found hung in a village near Bucharest after 15 hours of searching*, Stirile.Protv.ro, March 3, 2013)

The article from which I extracted the above fragments presented the cases of femicide-suicide as a romantic love story where the husband was jealous. In order to support the existence of a special love story, the journalist quotes the confessions of the family friends. The confession of the family friends mentions on one hand the love story, and on the other hand, it finds excuses for the domestic violence generated by the husband's jealousy. This jealousy was the one which determined the domestic violence that lasted for 20 years. Jealousy is thus the excuse for the violent behavior.

Through their speeches, journalists motivated the acts of domestic violence prior to femicide-suicides and femicide-suicides. The motivation of the violent acts was made through information regarding the aggressors' state of health, the alcohol/drugs consumption, the husbands' infidelity, marital discord and money problems. In 12 per cent of the articles there was information about the aggressors' alcohol consumption. The aggressors' health state was brought up in 6.7 per cent of the articles, and data about their infidelity was mentioned in only two articles. What is interesting is the fact that journalists mentioned the women's infidelity more often (16 articles, 11.8 per cent) as reason for the violence prior to femicide-suicides. Marital discord was also mentioned quite often (12.6) without stating who or what generated these conflicts.

Only two articles mentioned money problems as reasons for domestic violence. Through the way in which they motivated domestic violence, but also through the way in which they made a relation between femicide-suicides and prior domestic violence, the Romanian journalists represented femicide-suicides as 1) crime of passion, 2) the result of the husband's jealousy, 3) depreciation of the aggressor's health state and 4) accident. The most frequently used was the one which motivated femicide-suicides with the husband's jealousy (38.5 per cent). Jealousy also appears associated with other types of representations: femicide-suicides as crimes of passion, femicide-suicides as accidents. Femicide-suicides were described as crimes of passion in only 8.2 per cent of the articles. Loss of control by aggressors was mentioned in 5 articles (3.7 per cent), and the perpetrator's mental health issues in 9 articles (6.7 per cent). Only one article described a femicide-suicide as being the result of an accident.

Femicide-suicides as romantic love

The study made by Gius and Lalli (2014) showed that the frame of "romantic love" was used by the Italian press in order to justify violence against women and femicide. The analysis made by the two researchers included in the romantic love frame the articles which associated femicide with crimes of passion, jealousy, separation/divorce, unrequited love, and aggressor/victim in love with the partner (p. 61). Starting with the analysis of Gius and Lalli, I tried to identify the media frames of femicide-suicides in the Romanian online media. The results of the analysis of the 135 articles which presented femicide-suicides showed that Romanian journalists tend to present femicide-suicides as romantic love. Almost half of the articles (46.7 per cent) justified femicide-suicides as being crimes of passion (8.2 per cent) and motivated by jealousy (38.5 per cent). In this context, the aggressor's guilt was diminished. Journalists transferred a part of the guilt towards the victims who either did not return the aggressors' feelings or left them for other men.

Aggressors were presented as men who were trying to keep the relationship with the partners they loved. I chose as an example the way in which a femicide-suicide was committed by a Romanian settled in the USA. The way in which the case was presented is interesting because the victim's guilt is visible in the entire article. The femicide-suicide was defined as a crime of passion even from the title. Then the journalist brought up a passage from the interview with the answer given by the victim's sister to the question regarding the victim's feelings towards the aggressor husband. From the sister's comments we found out that it was rather a marriage of self-interest. In this way, the journalist structures the statement putting the victim in a negative perspective from the beginning (of a relationship based on self-interest and not on love). If, from the title the homicide committed by the husband was associated with a crime of passion generated by jealousy, the victim is the one who did not have the same feelings towards the aggressor husband and took advantage of a marriage with an American citizen of Romanian origin.

> Reporter: "Did she love him?"
> Geta Matei, Ana's sister: "I don't know how much love it was, but she wanted to make herself a future. She was threatened, he was getting drunk, he was violent, he was using bad words. He was very jealous, she was beautiful and young, he was 72, she was 37 years old." (*Crime of passion in the USA. A 72-year-old Romanian man killed his*

> *37-year-old wife, and then he committed suicide. The reason would be jealousy*, Stirile.Protv.ro, November 17, 2015)

Then, the journalist tells us that the story behind the femicide-suicide seems to be a soap opera. The victim had fallen in love with a young Romanian journalist and wanted to separate from her husband. The young woman's feelings were described as being "crazy love", the author of the article saying again the expression "the woman had fallen madly in love" more times during the article. The article kept informing us about the victim's actions that determined the femicide-suicide. We find out that the victim posted her photographs with her new boyfriend on Facebook. This action of the victim was immediately correlated with the husband's jealousy and death threats.

> The woman had fallen madly in love with another Romanian man, who has also moved to the USA, and she let her husband know that she wanted to divorce.
> The whole story seems taken from a soap opera. Although between Ana and Mircea Thomas there was a 35 year age difference, the two got married 9 years before, and she followed her husband to California where he had settled 30 years before.
> Meanwhile, she met another Romanian man in the USA, Florian Silisteanu, with whom she fell madly in love. The man, a poet and a journalist, is known in the community in Sacramento. The two did not hide their love and posted tens of photos on social networks. Blinded by jealousy, the husband threatened them with death several times. (*Crime of passion in the USA. A 72-year-old Romanian man killed his 37-year-old wife, and then he committed suicide. The reason would be jealousy*, Stirile.Protv.ro, November 17, 2015)

The husband's reaction "blinded by jealousy" came after the victim exposed her love story with the young journalist on Facebook after she separated from her husband. The journalist thus diminishes the aggressor's guilt by justifying it with the victim's inappropriate behavior. Only towards the end of the article do we find out that the jealous husband was also violent. All this information though, is presented as the consequence of the victim's actions.

> Lately the woman complained to her relatives from Romania that her husband, at the age of 72, had become suspicious and violent. So she decided to divorce him and moved to a friend's house. (*Crime of passion in the USA. A 72-year-old Romanian man killed his 37-year-old wife, and then he committed suicide. The reason would be jealousy*, Stirile.Protv.ro, November 17, 2015)

Moreover, the victim was also blamed for not taking into consideration the husband's threats and not following the boyfriend's advice to contact the police after being threatened with death. On one hand, the victim is guilty to have generated the husband's jealousy, and on the other hand, that she did not listen to her boyfriend's advice.

> Florian Silisteanu, Ana's boyfriend: "two weeks before, he had threatened to buy a gun and shoot her and I told him this was not a game, and I received other threats in the meantime and we had to call the police." (*Crime of passion in the USA. A 72-year-old Romanian man killed his 37-year-old wife, and then he committed suicide. The reason would be jealousy*, Stirile.Protv.ro, November 17, 2015)

In conclusion, the message of the article seems to be: the victim generated the femicide-suicide through her infidelity towards the partner who loved her and through her non-action when the partner's aggressiveness transformed into death threats. The journalist used in this case the direct techniques of blaming the victim identified by Taylor (2009).

Femicide-suicides as accident in a conflict

Another way to describe the femicide-suicide used by the Romanian journalists was that of associating the crime with an accident that happened during a conflict generated by the inappropriate behavior of the victim. Here is, for example, the case of a femicide-suicide committed by a retired policeman. The journalist tells us that the femicide occurred because of a marital discord generated by the wife's unannounced visit to her partner's work place. Upset because the wife visited him at his job, the husband took her to the basement of the building where he was working in order to have a talk with her. For what followed after that, the journalist presented us with two variants. According to the first variant the husband killed her and then killed himself. The second variant suggests an accident ("in her fall, the woman hit her head on a piece of furniture – this injury provoked her death") preceded by a conflict and a beating where both had been involved ("they started beating each other").

> The man seems to have hit his wife in the head with an object and when he realized he had killed her, he wrote a farewell note and threw himself in front of a train after driving 70km away from the crime scene. This is the first variant. The second variant would be that the retired policeman Marius Simedrea, originally from Oțelu Roșu, might have had an argument with his wife, then they started beating each other and the man hit her. In her fall, the woman hit her head on the furniture – this injury brought her death. The man panicked, got into the car and left for the house of some friends from a neighboring town. On his way to his friends, the man had a mental "declick" and decided to end his days. More precisely, 70km away from his home, he stopped the car at a railway stop and threw himself in front of the first train which went by at that time. (*A former policeman from Oțelu Roșu killed his wife after which killed himself*, InfoCS.ro, October 3, 2014)

In this case too, the journalist is on the aggressor's side rather than on the victim's side. The aggressor is described as being a person appreciated by colleagues and inhabitants of the town for the way in which he had done his job.

> His colleagues and even the other citizens say only good words about the policeman who had worked for years in "public relations", that is an "officer on duty" at the police station in Oţelu Roşu. All the people say that he was a good professional man who also worked in the "traffic police" after which he remained behind a desk. (*A former policeman from Oţelu Roşu killed his wife after which killed himself*, InfoCS.ro, October 3, 2014)

Among the arguments brought in favor of the aggressor policeman, we can also mention the way in which he reacted when his wife had to pay for the damage from her job. He agreed to sell the house and after retiring he went abroad to work there.

> Those who know him say that, in the last 5 years, the Simedrea family had some big difficulties in their life. The policeman's wife had worked at an currency exchange house downtown and some villains, under the pretext of being from an interior design company, managed to break into the currency exchange house and stole a big sum of money. In order to pay for this loss, the Simedrea family sold their apartment from no. 5, Libertăţii street, they also sold everything that could be sold inside the house after which they rented a house. Then, 3 years before, the woman went to work in Germany where she was taking care of an old woman. Their son left for Germany too, and finally, after the policeman retired, he went there as well. (*A former policeman from Oţelu Roşu killed his wife after which he killed himself*, InfoCS.ro, October 3, 2014)

We know about the victim only the fact that she had worked at an exchange house and she was cheated by some crooks for which the entire family had to suffer. On the other hand, the aggressor was not only a good professional and a good husband, but he was described as a member of the International Police Association (IPA), "passionate about competitive fishing" ("He took part in almost all big fishing competitions from the country next to his IPA colleagues and from abroad"). In this case, the journalist also directly blamed the victim for the acts of violence. Although we do not have information about her infidelity or her lack of involvement in preventing the violent acts prior to the femicide-suicide, the victim was described as a rather negative character. The journalist associated "the tough difficulties of life" of the victim's family with the financial difficulties generated by the victim's naivety from the work place. The victim generated financial losses for the entire family, which changed the life of all family members. They all went abroad to work, even the aggressor who had just retired and could have taken advantage of his pensioner status as his pension could have ordinarily offered him everything that he needed. Therefore, the aggressor was described with positive characteristics, and the victim was associated with the financial difficulties and the change of the entire family's life (their transformation into emigrants).

Femicide-suicides as result of depreciation of the aggressor's state of health – a case of mental disease

Among the cases of femicide-suicides presented by the Romanian journalists in the online media, we can notice cases committed by an aggressor with health issues. The case was covered in nine articles, most of them insisting on the health issues of the aggressor. The journalists gave great importance to describing the way in which the aggressor behaved during the days and hours prior to the crime. The sources used by journalists were the aggressor's parents who recounted the events that preceded the femicide-suicide. They talked about the dreams and the messages that their son received in these dreams. They also told about the aggressor's behavior during the day when the violent acts occurred.

> A strange dream made a 35-year-old man kill his partner and after that kill himself. His parents are also convinced of this. They say that lately the young man was absolutely haunted by the images from the dream. [...] Her son could not find his peace for several days. The man could not sleep or eat because of nightmares. Yesterday the man broke down. He took some bottles of alcohol from a neighbor and entered the house with his 45 year old partner. Those were the last moments in which people saw the two alive. (*He killed his girlfriend because of nightmares,* Observator. TV, April 18, 2015)

> He dreamt that Death had visited him. Marcel's parents say that the young man had been haunted by a dream for several days and he could not find out its meaning. A man with a list on which there were the names of all the dead people from the village appeared in his dream and his name was the last on that list. Tormented and frightened, the man did not sleep at all one night before the fatal day. Moreover, on Friday at dawn, April 17 he woke up his parents who were living in the same courtyard, but in another house, telling them that someone had entered his house and told him he would die. Marcel had no peace during the day, looking to understand the dream that had messed up his life. After going to and fro in the courtyard, he went to a neighbor where he bought some bottles of liqueurs and wine and he came back home. Then he was seen alive for the last time. (*SHOCKING details: While his girlfriend was drowning in her own blood, the man from Tichilesti stabbed himself, and then, with another knife, he cut his throat,* InfoBrăila, April 20, 2015)

The aggressor was presented in almost all the articles as a person affected by the nightmares that he had lately and especially by the dream in which he announced he would die: "confused and scared, the man did not close an eye one night before", "he could not sleep anymore and he could not eat because of nightmares" and "he had not had peace for several days". Journalists describe the aggressor as a young man tormented by nightmares who had a period of worries and who, after a week, "broke down". Because he "broke down", he killed his wife and then committed suicide. Or as a journalist says even from the title of the article "he killed his girlfriend because of nightmares". The responsibility of the femicide-suicide was transmitted to nightmares and to the mental issues from which he was suffering. Only one journalist associated the aggressor with "a monster with a human face". The same journalist gave more information about the history of the aggressor's health state and talked about the hospitalizations because of alcohol consumption.

> The monster with a human face, was admitted several times over the years to the psychiatric hospital because of alcohol consumption. (*SHOCKING details: While his girlfriend was drowning in her own blood, the man from Tichilesti stabbed himself, and then, with another knife, he cut his throat,* InfoBrăila, April 20, 2015)

Journalists do not say anything about the fact that, although he had had these disorders for one week, nobody tried to take him to a doctor in order to receive special help and overcome the crisis that he had. Journalists do not use this opportunity in order to include information necessary to the intervention and prevention of the acts of violence generated by the psychic illnesses associated with alcohol consumption. They prefer to explain femicide-suicides through loss of control by the aggressor with health problems. We do not find out anything about the victim and the history of the relationship. The only thing we know about the victim is that she was 10 years older than the aggressor and that "she died in horrible torment".

Femicide-suicides – "the tragic story of a man"

Another way of presenting femicide-suicide was that in which the violent act is described as "the tragic story of a man". We know that the aggressor who killed and then committed suicide was 56 years old and he had just come back from Italy. The journalist gives only some elements about the aggressor and about the femicide-suicide. More precisely, we are informed of the way in which the femicide-suicide was committed and of the fact that he left a note and apologized. See the entire article below.

> Recently returned from Italy, he killed his wife with a hammer and then he committed suicide. This is the tragic story of a 56-year-old man from Iasi. The man left a farewell note, where he did not explain his gesture. He just apologized. After that he ended his life. (Observator.a1.ro, May 19, 2011)

Regardless of the size of the articles which present femicide-suicides committed in Romania, I noticed a focus of the journalists' attention on information regarding the aggressor and modus operandi. The information regarding the aggressor was included in most articles, while the victims were left in the background. The

Romanian journalists decided to catch the readers' attention with the aggressor's profile and the out of the ordinary way of committing the crimes.

Conclusions

The analysis of the way in which the online media from Romania covered femicide-suicides cases emphasized a series of particularities specific to journalists from the online media. The selection criteria of the cases of femicide-suicides for their presence in the online media from Romania were slightly different than those used usually by journalists. In the case of the online media from Romania, journalists tried to catch the readers' attention using different criteria. The common element of the cases seems to be the sensational. They selected cases out of the ordinary either due to the profession of the victim/aggressor, the way in which the cases were committed, the messages left by aggressors or the presence of children at the crime moment. The classical criteria connected to the profile of the ideal victim identified by international studies (Boulahanis and Heltsley 2004, Carrabine et al. 2004) seem to be less used by the Romanian journalists from the online media. The young victims aged less than 25 and older victims are represented very little in the online articles about femicide-suicides. Journalists seem to present the cases which have the same features presented in the statistics of the official institutions and not the cases that are different from the majority through the victim's profile.

The Romanian journalists mostly used unofficial sources for their articles about femicide-suicides.

The most used unofficial sources were the victims' neighbors and relatives. This is a different situation from the media coverage of homicide-suicides in Romania in which official sources were mainly used (Balica and Stöckl, 2016). Regarding the international studies, some of them showed that journalists tend to use official sources (especially police) when they describe femicide-suicides (Richards et al. 2014). Other studies emphasized that journalists tend to use unofficial sources (neighbors) when they write about femicide-suicides (Nikunen, 2011). What was not signaled in the case of the international press, but it appeared in the case of Romanian journalists, is the fact that for 26 per cent of Romanian articles from the online media sources are not presented although the information is similar to that mentioned by other journalists as being given by official institutions (police and parquet).

International studies showed that journalists associate femicide-suicides with domestic violence in 55 per cent of the articles (Richards at al. 2014). The analysis of the way in which the online media from Romania describes femicide-suicides emphasized the fact that only a third of the articles published in the period 2010–2015 correlated femicide-suicides with prior domestic violence. There is a significant difference between how Romanian journalists and journalists from countries with a tradition in preventing lethal violence give attention to domestic violence. On the other hand, regardless of the country in which studies regarding media coverage of femicide were made, the researchers emphasized the journalists' tendency to present these violent acts as the result of jealousy, loss of control of perpetrators (Richards et al. 2014) or as romantic love (Gius and Lalli 2014). This tendency was also prevalent in the case of the Romanian journalists from the online media, and the present chapter emphasized the most important aspects. Femicide-suicides as crimes of passion, the result of jealousy, of depreciation of the aggressors' health state or as accidents were media frames identified in the online media from Romania. The analysis of the way in which Romanian journalists describe femicide-suicides confirmed what other recent international studies emphasized. Journalists tend to diminish the aggressors' responsibility and transmit it to victims who either did not answer the aggressors' attempts to start their relationships over, or decided to separate. Other victims were blamed for not considering the aggressors' threats, for not contacting the authorities or for giving up on protection actions. I am talking about the same direct and indirect techniques of blaming victims which journalists from other countries used and which international studies emphasized (Meyers 1994, Taylor 2009, Richards et al. 2011, Fairbairn and Dawson 2013).

Unlike journalists from other countries, the Romanian journalists proved to be less interested in associating the cases of femicide-suicides with other similar cases or making complex analyses of this type of violence. The Romanian journalists only used official and unofficial sources which gave them standard information about the victim, the aggressor and the way of committing femicide-suicides. The articles from the Romanian online media did not record any analysis made by specialists from the psychology domain, criminology or social work. The Romanian journalists limited themselves to presenting information taken from the institutions which investigated the case and from people from the victim's or the aggressor's social sphere. The articles which present cases of femicide-suicides were in general reduced in length and similar in content. Few articles brought new elements or tried to give additional information about femicide-suicides.

Unfortunately, up to now, we do not have studies regarding the way in which print media in Romania covered femicide-suicides, hence the limits of a comparative analysis with the results of international studies centered on the print media coverage of femicide-suicides. The results of the analysis regarding the online media coverage of femicide-suicides committed in Romania can be used as a landmark for future studies that will analyze the online media. Further studies will bring discussion of the media coverage of femicide-suicides in the Romanian print media or in TV news. The analysis of the way in which the Romanian journalists covered femicide-suicides can offer the necessary landmarks for some actions meant to make the Romanian journalists responsible and cause them get involved in informing and educating readers on the prevention of femicide-suicides and the acts of domestic violence prior to lethal violence.

6. Facebook Kills! A Case Study of Intimate Partner Femicide-Suicides Between Romanian Emigrants

The chapter discusses the way the cases of homicide-suicide committed between Romanian emigrants were made known to the public. The title of the chapter was given by a case that succeeded in drawing the attention of specialists from Romania on the way the aggressor killed his wife and by the motivation of the violent act. At the same time, the case attracted attention over the message written with a red pen on the victim's chest: Facebook kills! Based on this case of homicide-suicide committed between Romanian emigrants, I decided to identify all the cases committed between emigrants and also to identify the way the Romanian press dealt with these cases. I noticed an increase in the interest of journalists to publicize acts of violence where Romanian emigrants are involved over the last years. Thus Romanian journalists brought to the public's attention cases of violence where the Romanians were aggressors (for example: the Mailat case (the young man who raped an Italian woman, robbed her and then killed her) or the burglaries in the luxury shops in Paris) or where the Romanian were victims (an example being the latest case of Romanian women raped by their employers or who had intimate relationships with their employers in order to keep their jobs in Italy). More rarely cases were brought to the public's attention where Romanians managed to impress through their involvement in saving lives and were considered heroes (for example: the case of the nurse Ramona Ianus who saved many lives during the subway accident in Rome, 2006).

In fact, as Beciu himself shows, Romanian journalists had a constant interest for the Romanian migrant as a press subject, the situation becoming even more visible after Romania entered the European Union (January 1, 2007). After this moment, but even before, we could identify in the Romanian press "normal periods" and "intense periods" of written discussions about Romanian migrants. The number of articles from the Romanian press regarding Romanian migrants was growing, especially when positive or negative events happened, such as the ones mentioned in the previous paragraph (2012: 58).

Although online and offline media frequently present information about serious acts of violence from Romania and other countries, there are only few scientific studies on the issue of publicizing almost excessively serious violence through Romanian mass media. There were a few studies which focus on identifying the way written press and television presented the domestic acts of violence (Marinescu and Ştefănescu 2004, Drăgan et al. 2009, Velicu 2011), research on violence in animated cartoons (Velicu 2009) or research focusing on the identification of the types of online violence, especially cyberbullying (Velicu 2014). As for studies which try to identify the way the homicide was promoted we only have a few recent concerns in this area. They include the study regarding the representation of the perfect victim in the online media that publicizes the cases of homicide-suicides in Romania (Balica 2016a) and on the research focusing on the analysis of the violence against emigrant women from Romania offering sexual services in a legal/illegal manner (Balica 2016b). The lack of studies regarding the problem of publicizing the violent crime was one of the reasons that made me identify the way online media presents homicide-suicides. Another reason which made me take this approach was the fact that, although the media informs about acts of violence committed between Romanian emigrants and against them, there is no specific data regarding the violence between Romanian emigrants or studies on the way the media promotes information about serious acts of violence.

Studies regarding Romanian emigrants

Recent studies regarding the way in which Romanian media tackled the problem of the Romanian migrants from the European Union space emphasized a series of particularities connected to the way in which Romanian journalists introduced migrants in the media. In an analysis made at the level of two Romanian (daily) newspapers, Beciu (2012) shows that Romanian migrants are described with some adjectives that refer to their ethnic identity ("Romanian"), social typology (aggressor, victim) and social identity (58–59). Although the research was not focused on identifying the connection between Romanian migrants and violence, Beciu observed that "in general, diaspora is a world of violence, with people who are exactly at the opposed pole, either totally bad, or totally good." (2012: 61) Romanian journalists associate migrants with the status of victim, aggressor or hero. The victim-migrant is, however, the best represented in the Romanian media (Beciu 2012: 62).

Another study made by Borţun (2009) discussed the way in which the Romanian and Italian press presented a serious violent case committed by a Romanian citizen of Romani ethnicity in Italy. The case of the Romanian Nicolae Romulus Mailat, who murdered an Italian woman in 2007, was widely debated in the Romanian and Italian press. The press from the two countries started to debate the issue of Romanian emigrants from Italy who were associated with offenders (even if they did not have any connection to the committed violent acts). Moreover, immediately after committing this violent act, the case was used by the Italian government in order to adopt a government decision through which they could banish any European/non-European citizen from Italy if he represented a public danger. The campaign from the Italian press through which they presented more violent cases committed by Romanian emigrants of Romani ethnicity led to the multiplication of violent acts committed by Italians against Romanians in Italy. The way in which the problem of the respective case was presented and debated by the press from the two countries made Borţun state that the language of the journalists from both countries was xenophobic. In other words, we talked about "a xenophobe speech of the Italians against Romanian immigrants and about Romanians' xenophobia against the Romani people from Italy that affected the image of Romania" (2009: 245–246).

The Mailat case was analyzed by the Romanian Agency of Press Monitoring because the press generated tough reactions from Italian citizens who started to commit violent acts against Romanians from their country. Fotiade, one of the authors of the report made by the Romanian Agency of Press Monitoring, shows that the Romanian press discussed intensely about the Mailat case, thus having the opportunity to present information about the deed, the aggressor's family and other cases of Romani citizens who committed felonies in Italy and cases of Romanians who became victims due to the media campaign (2008: 17). At the same time, Fotiade underlined the fact that journalists broke some deontological norms when they were discussing the case: "they did not respect the benefit of the doubt, they associated the Romani ethnicity with delinquency, they used contradictory or false data and they published information which could have induced panic." (37–39).

Other studies made by specialists in the communication field emphasized the fact that Romanian emigrants represented the subject of some public debates broadcast by Romanian television, especially in the conditions in which emigrants were involved in actions with negative consequences (Beciu 2013a). Although she did not propose herself to identify the way in which journalists widely discussed violent acts committed by emigrants, the author exemplified the way in which Romanian migrants were described in the political talk-shows through a debate generated in which the French press attributed to Romanians the attribute of "offender" starting from widely discussing felonies committed by Romanian Romani (id.).

If we look over the Romanian studies regarding the way in which media present the Romanian emigrant, we can notice that researchers are rather preoccupied with identifying: 1) the way in which non-migrants (Beciu 2013b) or politicians/

journalists relate themselves to Romanian emigrants (Beciu 2013a) and 2) the way in which they try to counteract the association of Romanian emigrants with persons who commit felonies.

Representation of the violence between intimate partners in the Romanian press. Case study homicide-suicide between Romanian emigrants

Methodology

As I mentioned at the beginning of this chapter, what I have in mind is to analyze the way online media took over and publicized the cases of homicide-suicides between Romanian emigrants. As I had at my disposal the Homicide-suicides in Romania database, I decided to analyze homicide-suicides between Romanian emigrants committed in Romania as well as homicide-suicides committed between Romanian emigrants living in other countries. I selected for this analysis all the cases publicized in the online press in Romania in the period 2002–2013.

Firstly, I wanted to identify the way online media (especially online newspapers) had presented these cases. At the same time, I tried to emphasize the measures used by the journalists in order to present these cases (reports, journalistic investigations, using photos and video images etc.). A central place in the elaborated analysis was occupied by the selection criteria used by journalists. I asked myself: What were the criteria at the base of the choice of those cases and their presentation in the online media? Do Romanian journalists have specific selection criteria or use the same criteria as the journalists from the international media? Are there any differences between Romanian online and offline journalists?

For this reason, I tried to identify the types of homicide-suicides that were taken over by journalists, the period of time when the cases had been publicized, the cases that had been publicized for a longer period and which of them determined complex journalistic investigations. I also decided to identify the profile of the perfect victim and the profile of the aggressor in the cases selected to be publicized. The information about the acts of violence (the motivation, the weapons that were used, and the place of homicide-suicides) were also chosen in order to emphasize the criteria used by the journalists for the selection of cases.

Secondly, I decided to identify 'the primary definers' of the situations. In other words, I tried to identify the sources used by the journalists to elaborate the media materials. I wanted to know if the journalists use data from official sources (the police, the prosecutors, the forensic laboratories), unofficial sources (witnesses, relatives of the affected families, direct or indirect victims, neighbors) or none of the sources mentioned above; they just take information published by another journalist.

The basis of the analysis was created by the 27 homicide-suicide cases where Romanian emigrants were involved (HSRE). The cases were identified in the Homicide-Suicides in Romania database. These cases had a mutual element; the fact that at least one of the protagonists of the act of violence was a Romanian emigrant. Thus, I included in the HSRE sample 25 cases committed between Romanian emigrants and two cases where just one of the protagonists of the acts of violence was a Romanian emigrant (a case where the aggressor was a Romanian emigrant and the victim was Italian and a case where the aggressor was Italian and the victim was a Romanian emigrant). Just eight cases had as an only protagonist of the act of violence an emigrant (6 cases where just the victim was an emigrant and 2 cases where the aggressor was an emigrant). In the other 19 cases, the victims as well as the aggressors were emigrants. Just three of the cases we dealt with included a Romanian who had emigrated for a long time and was established in the USA (2) and Switzerland (1 case).

On the other hand, I noticed that in the analyzed period Romanian journalists have presented 14 cases of homicide-suicides committed in Romania and 13 cases of homicide-suicides committed in other countries (Italy – 7 cases, Spain – 2 cases, the USA – 2, Greece – 1, Switzerland – 1). I included in the analysis all these cases in order to emphasize the possible characteristics of the way online media presents these categories of cases.

After choosing the homicide-suicides cases that were included in the HSRE sample, I detected the materials from the online media where they had been presented. In the first phase, I used the Homicide-suicides in Romania database which contained the information regarding the media material where the homicide-suicides cases had been presented. In order to have a clearer image of the way they were publicized, while elaborating this chapter (June 2015) I restarted the investigations regarding the online media materials where the HSRE cases had been publicized.

As there are not any online archives for all the online or offline newspapers in Romania, I decided to use another method, which is more adapted to the Romanian realities in order to identify the articles where the HSRE cases had been promoted. Thus, my investigations started from a few keywords that I chose from the titles already existing in the database for each of the registered cases (for example: A Romanian committed homicide in Italy and then he killed himself). For some cases, I used keywords such as “the name of the aggressor and the victim”, information regarding the whereabouts of the homicide-suicide or, even the profession of the aggressor/victim (in the cases of the titles from the media materials from the

HSR database where there was information about the profession). Thus, I identified 192 media materials (articles, news, posts on blogs, online TV news, videos on YouTube etc.) where these 27 cases had been promoted. The analysis of the content elaborated at the level of media materials was based on a structure analysis grid so that it can allow us obtain information regarding the homicide, the suicide, the victim and the aggressor. In these sections, I added a special section including information regarding the period of time when the case was promoted, the type of media material and the presence/absence of photos and videos.

The distribution in time of the cases of homicide-suicides promoted in the online press

The data analysis of the number of cases of homicide-suicides promoted in the online press every year in the selected period of time (2002–2013) has emphasized the fact that journalists were interested in publicizing the cases committed between emigrants mainly after 2008. In fact, the year 2008 recorded an increase of the total number of homicide-suicide cases registered in Romania and presented in online media (Balica 2015). The growing interest of journalists for HS cases between emigrants meant that in the period 2008–2013, this type of case represents around one third of the cases published in the online press. The distribution of the cases of homicide-suicides (HSR), presented in the online media, and of the cases of homicide-suicides, between Romanian emigrants (HSE), are presented in Diagram 6.1.

Diagram 6.1 Distribution of the homicide-suicide cases (HSR) and of homicide-suicide cases between emigrants (HSE) in online media, in the period 2002–2013

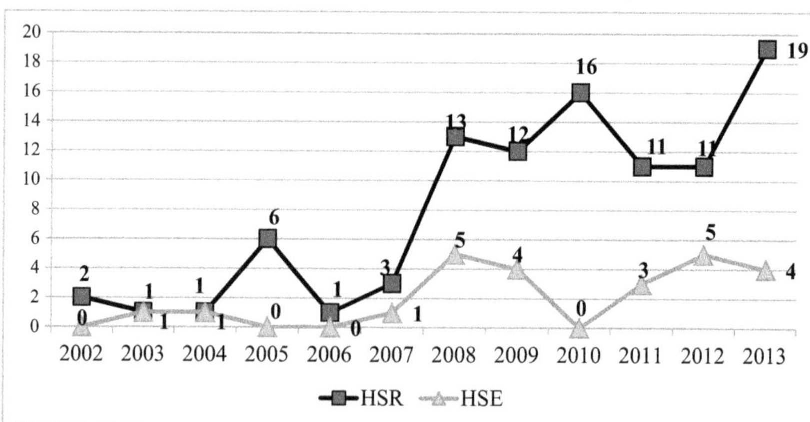

Online publications where cases of homicide-suicides between emigrants have been presented

The information about the cases of homicide-suicides between emigrants was promoted in several types of online media: news aggregator (for example: hotnews.com, ziare.com), national newspapers (adevarul.ro, romanialibera.ro), regional or local (tion.ro), newspapers of the Romanian diaspora in the countries where the acts of violence were committed (gazetaromaneasca.com, stateleunite.net), websites of the TV channels (Antena3.ro, Primatv.ro), personal blogs of the journalists and videos on YouTube.

The frequency of publishing information regarding the cases of homicide-suicides between emigrants

Almost half of the cases (16) were promoted in 1–5 press materials. The other cases had appeared in several articles, but just six cases were promoted in more than 10 media materials (See Table 6.1). One single case was publicized more than the others. I refer to a case presented in 57 media materials, during 28 days in three years (2010–2013). It was the case of a young woman painter well known in the town where the act of violence occurred. The information regarding the way the case was publicized was presented in a recent work. At that moment I was emphasizing the fact that the journalists had chosen to bring this case to the public's attention and to keep it in the public's attention due to the celebrity status of the victim and of the victim's family (Balica 2015a).

Table 6.1 The frequency of publishing information regarding the cases of homicide-suicides between emigrants

Number of articles	Number of cases	Cases distribution over the years
1	5	1/2003,1/2004,2/2009, 1/2011
2	3	2/2008, 1/2009
3	4	1/2007, 2/2008,1/2012
4	3	1/2008; 2/2012
5	1	1/2011
6	3	1/2011; 2/2013
7	1	1/2012
9	1	2010
11	3	1/2010,1/2012, 1/2013
13	1	1/2013
15	1	2010
57	1	2010

As expected, the cases committed during the years at the beginning of the analyzed period (2002–2007) were less promoted. The number of articles where the cases of homicide-suicides between emigrants had been presented increased as we approach the end of the years from the sample period. This indicates, on one hand, the increase of the journalists' interest in the situation of the respective period. On the other hand, we cannot ignore the fact that as the global economic crisis increased more and more newspapers had to choose how to reduce costs related to printed publications and to produce online versions of the newspapers. Consequently, towards the end of the analyzed period we have a bigger number of online publications, a higher number of homicide-suicides and a higher number of publicized cases of homicide-suicides between emigrants. Even in this context, we can notice that not all the cases committed after 2008 were promoted as much as the others. Even during the period 2008–2013 there were differences regarding the number of articles published for each of the cases of homicide-suicides between emigrants (see Table 6.1).

The timeframe when the cases were promoted

One third of the cases were promoted for one day, and one third of the cases for 2 days. The rest of the cases were presented in the articles published in a period of time, which fluctuated from 3 to 28 days (See Table 6.2).

Table 6.2 The timeframe when the cases were promoted

Number of days	1 day	2 days	3 days	4 days	5 days	7 days	28 days
Number of articles	10	10	2	2	1	1	1

Types of homicide-suicides between emigrants

All the promoted cases occurred between persons united by family ties (husband/wife, sons/daughters, cousins, brothers/sisters, grandparents). The great majority of the cases (89%) occurred between current or former intimate partners (spouses, concubines, lovers). There have been just a few cases when the victims were the sons or daughters of the aggressors (filicide-suicide) or other members of the extended family (cousins, brothers, sisters or grandparents) (see Table 6.3).

Table 6.3 Types of homicide-suicides between emigrants

Types of homicide-suicides between emigrants	
Intimate Partner Homicide-suicides (spouses, concubines, lovers)	23
Filicide-suicide (daughters or sons)	3
Kinicide-suicide (cousins, brother and sister or grandparents)	1

The interest of the journalists from the online media in promoting cases of homicide-suicides between emigrants where the victims were women having intimate relationships with the aggressor acknowledges the results registered in the previous research regarding the representation of the homicide-suicides cases in the online Romanian media. The research has shown that online media in Romania focused on presenting homicide-suicide cases committed between intimate partners and that women are mostly the victims (Balica 2015).

The Romanian emigrant as aggressor

Over the research I have asked myself whether journalists preferred to discuss cases where Romanian emigrants were aggressors or victims. The results of the analysis showed that two thirds of the discussed cases (18) had Romanian emigrants as aggressors and victims no matter the country where the violent acts occurred. Only six aggressors were non-emigrants and only in three cases the aggressors alone were Romanian emigrants. We can notice that the majority of the aggressors presented in the media were Romanian emigrants (21 cases). On the other side, if we take into account the data regarding the victims, we can notice that the number of Romanian emigrant victims is bigger (24) than the number of aggressors (21). We could say that journalists preferred to discuss the acts of violence where Romanian emigrants were victims and not aggressors. The differences are small but they can show a modification of the journalists' perspective towards the Romanian emigrants, especially when they committed violent acts in the European and non-European space.

In order to have more information about the Romanian emigrant aggressor I decided to go further and identify the aggressor's profile. The data collected with the help of the analysis board allowed me to obtain, starting from the online articles, information regarding gender, age, professional status and residence. I noticed that almost all media articles presented information regarding gender (27), age (26) and status of the aggressor (20). Furthermore, the majority of articles contained the name of the aggressor, which allowed me to connect data from the press with data from penal files when we made the Homicide-suicide in Romania database (see Chapter 1). The information regarding the aggressor's level of education (3), health state (3) and alcohol (6) or drug abuse was less discussed.

The analysis of information regarding aggressors showed that all aggressors from the cases selected by journalists to be presented to the public were men. More than half of them were men aged between 25 and 39. We can notice the fact that journalists took over homicide-suicides between Romanian emigrants who had a low occupational status and the aggressors were younger than the non-emigrant aggressors.

How was the Romanian emigrant aggressor described?

Journalists from the online media present the emigrant aggressor differently. Some of them, due to the fact that they want to attract as many readers as possible and to punish the aggressor's behavior describe him as "a monster" or "a murderer". To my astonishment, the number of articles where aggressors are described with negative attributes was quite small.

> "His appetite for sex and his blood thirst transformed the 22-year-old Romanian into a monster." (*A Romanian man terrified Spain. He mutilated and killed his girlfriend and then committed suicide*, www.antena3.ro, August 5, 2012)

What is interesting is the way in which some journalists present information about the aggressor who is mentally ill. For example, we have a special situation in an article about a case of homicide-suicide committed in Romania by a husband over his emigrant wife. In the first part of the article the aggressor is described as being "a man from Craiova", and then he is "Ion" (the aggressor's first name). Then the journalist describes the way in which the aggressor murdered his wife and the weapon used. Immediately after we find out that he murdered his wife, the aggressor becomes "the murderer". What is more interesting is the fact that, towards the end of the article, before and after we are told that he was mentally ill, the journalist decides to speak of the aggressor as being Ion or part of the phrase "the Sârbu couple".

> On Sunday evening a man from Craiova murdered his wife and afterwards committed suicide. [...] At a certain moment, Ion became as mad as a March hare and lost his temper; he took a kitchen knife and stabbed his spouse's neck. [...] The murderer telephoned his parents who live in Goicea village and told them what he had just done. [...] After his "confession" the murderer found in his house a rope and hung himself over the door handle. [...] The murderer was medically retired due to his mental illness. (*The mad Ion murdered his wife and then he hung himself over the door handle*, Andreea Adam, www.curierulnational.ro, July 8, 2003)

The majority of articles are short, similar in style to minutes or to speeches of police spokesmen, where journalists blankly present information about the aggressor (mostly a man named X and aged Y… from Z village), the victim (a woman or a child named X, aged Y, with residence in Z village) and the way in which the acts of violence are committed (he murdered with weapon A and committed suicide by X). In very few cases we have journalists who make investigations and write complex articles about the homicide-suicide case. Irrespective of the size of the online article, journalists prefer only to mention the name of the aggressor or to associate attributes such as "the 37-year-old man", "the father", "the husband", "a Romanian". The situation was seen mostly with journalists from diaspora (the USA – Realitatearomaneasca.ro, Italy – gazetaromaneasca.com), in the case of journalists from the local or regional newspapers or from TV stations from Romania (ProTv.ro)

Romanian emigrants as victims

As I mentioned in the section regarding aggressors, journalists were more likely interested in selecting the cases according to the victims' particularities, resulting in the profile of an ideal victim specific to the online media of Romania. Journalists brought to the attention of the public the cases where victims had certain particularities or the cases that were out of the pattern of committing violent acts.

Journalists preferred to present to a larger extent the cases of HS where women were victims (86 percent of victims were females). On the other hand, the aggressors' female intimate partners, aged between 25 and 39 represented almost half of the victims of discussed cases. This profile of the victim from the Romanian online press is similar to the profile of an ideal victim from the written press as shown by studies made up to now by communication specialists in Romania: the majority of victims are women and intimate partners of the aggressors (Marinescu and Ştefănescu 2004). Although they were few (8 cases), all the cases with more victims were published in the online media knowing that violent acts with more victims are more attractive to the audience. Through this tendency to talk more about the cases with more victims, Romanian journalists come closer to the selection criteria used in the international media. Studies showed that journalists tend to talk more about cases of murder with more victims (Boulahanis and Heltsley 2004, Gruenewald et al. 2009).

How was the Romanian emigrant victim described?

As I noticed a special interest for victims when journalists selected the cases they wanted to discuss, I decided to also analyze the way in which victims of homicide-suicides were described. Emigrant/non-emigrant women and emigrants' children are the majority of the victims of violent cases selected by journalists. Each of these categories of victims was described by journalists with the help of technical means adapted to the specific victim and to the need to catch attention.

Emigrant's child as a victim

The cases of filicide-suicides were tackled in a higher number of articles (6 articles; 11 articles and 13 articles) than other types of homicide-suicide. In order to have a greater impact on readers, when a child was the direct victim of the aggressor, information about the victim was associated directly with the way in which the child was murdered and only afterwards journalists gave information about the age of the child:

> "Massacre in Neamț – A man cut his child's neck with a chainsaw and then committed suicide!" (Wowbizz.ro, August 13, 2013)
>
> "What a drama! She listened on the telephone while her husband was killing her children" (click.ro, Nicoleta Livezeanu and Andreea Mitrache, July 5, 2013)
>
> "He killed his child too in order to get even with his wife" (m.click.ro, July 5, 2013)

Journalists give special attention to the cases in which children are witnesses of violent acts and become indirect victims. I chose as an example the case in which a four-year-old child was a witness to violent acts. This time, journalists chose to describe in detail the image of the child witness even from the first sentences:

> Investigators settled that the events which occurred on Saturday morning, in Hunedoara, when a man stabbed his wife with multiple knife strikes and then hung himself, happened in front of their four-year-old child who went out in the hallway of their building with his clothes stained with blood. (*The four-year-old child of the man who killed his wife after which hung himself was the witness of the tragedy*, mediafax.ro, April 16, 2013)
>
> "Mummy and daddy are no longer alive!"- the shocking message of the 3-year-old little boy, witness to scenes which will mark him for the rest of his life" (*In front of the eyes of their terrified little boy, a man killed his wife and then hung himself*, Ramona Ștefan, April 8, 2013)

Moreover, these articles are much more ample, they quote more official or unofficial sources and they give information about the persons affected by violence, including the child witness or other children in the family. Journalists used in the case of articles which discuss filicide-suicides, two specific techniques in order to draw the public's attention to the murder cases that they were discussing: a) they chose the child as an ideal victim, knowing that through this they will catch attention and b) they chose to include information regarding the shocking way in which the murder was committed in the title. Besides this, many researchers underlined the fact that journalists tend to select the "rare" violent cases in order to gain the public's attention; in this category of rare violent acts the above mentioned criteria are also included: the child as a victim and the special way in which the murder was committed (Boulahanis and Heltsley 2004, Carrabine et al. 2004, Gruenewald et al. 2009, Gekoski et al. 2012).

Romanian emigrant woman as victim

As I mentioned before, the majority of discussed cases were intimate partner homicide-suicides, and wives/former wives were the victims. This situation confirms the results of studies made in other countries from which we can see the fact that murders, with women as victims, are more widely tackled than cases in which men are victims (Boulahanis and Heltsley 2004).

Women as victims are most of the time described with the help of some attributes that give information about the victim's characteristics ("the wife", "the x year old young woman", "first and last name") or that refer to a personality from the community where the event occurred ("the daughter of the former director of Weapons Service IPJ Dolj").

The cases for which I identified only one or two online articles (a third of the cases) were cases presented in small articles (10 lines at the most) where journalists included information about the aggressor, the victim and the way in which the murder or suicide was committed. Information regarding the victim appears even from the title:

> "A man from Voluntari killed his wife and then committed suicide" (Gândul.info, August 22, 2011)

> "He killed his wife and then hung himself next to the dead body. The children were inside the house." (Stirileprotv.ro, January 19, 2011)

However, there are situations in which, although the articles are small, journalists decide to give as much information about the victim as possible even from the first sentence of the article:

> "A 41-year-old woman, wife and mother, was beaten to death… (*He beat his wife to death and then committed suicide*, Stirileprotv.ro, August 22, 2011)

When we talk about more victims, the number and complexity of media materials depend on the place where the violent acts were committed. If we talk about homicide-suicides committed abroad, then the media materials are most of the time taken from the press of Romanian communities of diaspora or from the media of the country where the homicide-suicide was committed. If we talk about a case that happened in Romania, then journalists investigate and try to bring as much information as possible from official sources (case prosecutors and police representatives) or from unofficial sources (local people, businessmen from the neighborhood). Regardless of the place where the homicide-suicide was committed, information regarding the number of victims is given even from the title of articles in order to emphasize the criterion that transforms the respective case into an out of the ordinary case:

> "He killed two persons and then committed suicide" (Gds.ro, April 16, 2008)
>
> "Bloody murder: A Romanian from Italy killed his wife and his wife's friend and then committed suicide" (eMM.ro, May 16, 2013)
>
> "Shots in the street: a man shot two people and then committed suicide" (mediafax.ro, May 19, 2012)

The analysis of information regarding victims showed that the great majority of victims were women (85.7 percent) and half of the women victims had a low occupational status. The statement made in the case of aggressors regarding the lack of information about the level of education of aggressors and health state is valid for victims as well: journalists give this type of information for very few cases.

As Beciu noticed, journalists bring to the public's attention little information regarding the socio-professional status of emigrants and when this information appears, it is used "more to legitimate a media speech about 'heroes', 'victims' and 'guilty people'" (2012: 61). In the case of homicide-suicides we talk about emphasizing the case and catching the attention either through the victim's features or through the aggressor's profile.

Information regarding weapons used

Online articles contain information regarding the weapons used for committing the murder or the suicide. We can notice the fact that journalists chose to discuss equally about cases committed with firearms, knives or hanging. What is interesting is the fact that they published both cases that were out of the patterns, i.e. cases committed with firearms (in Romania it is illegal to possess a firearm; only police officers, army personnel, hunters and people who have a gun permit can have a firearm) and cases in which aggressors used weapons specific to the violent acts committed in Romania: knives. Weapons used for committing homicide-suicides are also used by journalists in order to emphasize the uniqueness of the case and in order to make it more interesting for the public. Due to this fact weapons and ways of committing murder were described even from the title:

> "Massacre in Neamţ – A man cut his child's neck with a chainsaw and then committed suicide!" (Wowbizz.ro, August 13, 2013)

> "He killed his wife with 38 hammer and knife strikes" (adevarul.ro, March 26, 2010)

"Primary definers" of the situations

In the specialty literature 'primary definers' are known to be all sources that give "initial definition or primary interpretation of the topic in question" (Hall et al. 1978: 58). In other words, 'primary definers' are all those primary sources on the basis of which journalists write articles or stories and with the help of which they argue or express the position towards the violent act that they tackled. Specialists from the communication field showed that media articles launched through means of communication transmit messages which can influence the opinion of the public and can generate different reactions towards a subject. When we talk about covering some violent acts, journalists can describe reality differently with the help of 'primary definers'. The difference is given by the type of the message transmitted through the primary source (Meyers 2014, Korn and Efrat 2004, Klein 2012, Auxéméry and Fidelle 2010). Studies showed that most of the time journalists used as primary definers for violent cases experts or representatives of some official institutions: police officers, judges or prosecutors (Hall et al. 1978, Beckett 1997, Hogeveen 2005, Schlesinger et al. 1991). The result of this direct relationship between journalists and police or penal system representatives was that of making media articles from a perspective that suggested solving problems created by crimes through improving the system of social control (Beckett 1997, Welch et al. 1997/1998, Cheliotis 2010).

Some studies showed that when representatives of non-official institutions are used as 'primary definers', more precisely intellectuals, the message of the article written by journalists is centered on explaining the causality of the violent act and on identifying some non-punitive solutions (Beckett 1997, Welch et al. 1997, 1998). Other studies showed that messages transmitted through 'primary definers' can sanction the victim's behavior and tolerate the inappropriate behavior of the aggressor. Studies made in more countries have already shown the different way in which the media, with the help of some 'primary definers', presented the same type of violence (rape) committed against some young women who were different through race, ethnicity or social class. Meyers (2014) emphasized the way in which journalists managed to justify violence against a poor young black woman and sanction violence against a white middle-class young woman.

Other studies showed the fact that the media can, through the way in which they present the reality of the violent acts, induce a fear of crime in the readers (Reiner 2007, Korn and Efrat 2004), and induce a multiplication of violent acts through adopting a tolerant perspective towards the aggressor and promoting the idea of the victim's guilt (Meyers 2014) or through the way in which information regarding some violent acts is given (for example information regarding the way in which the suicide of Auxéméry and Fidelle happened, 2010). At the same time, the large number of media articles regarding a type of violence can induce in the public the idea of the necessity of some new measures regarding the citizens' protection, even if the violent acts selected by journalists to be discussed are not so frequent (Signorielli 1990).

Bringing the discussion even closer to the subject of this chapter, i.e. making homicide-suicides between Romanian emigrants known to the public, I have considered it important to analyze the message that the online journalists transmitted through the media articles where they presented the cases of homicide-suicide. The questions I asked myself were: What type of message have Romanian journalists transmitted through the articles from the online media? Have Romanian journalists adopted the point of view of the institutions of the penal system (police office, parquet, court house, and forensic medicine) and have they inserted in the press articles only the point of view of the representatives of the official institutions empowered to instrument the respective cases? What is the percentage of the official sources and how much do the non-official sources represent from the total of 'primary definers' used by Romanian journalists? Have Romanian journalists limited themselves to discussing the cases of homicide-suicide between emigrants as news which can be included in the section *fact of life*, or have they tried to debate and offer a perspective meant to show the need for imposing some measures capable of preventing some homicide-suicides? For all these questions I have tried to find answers over the analysis made at the level of online articles identified for the cases of homicide-suicides between Romanian emigrants.

'Primary definers' for homicide-suicides between Romanian emigrants

Official institutions as primary definers

The analysis of media articles identified for the 27 cases of homicide showed the fact that Romanian journalists most of the time limit themselves to taking information regarding the violent acts between Romanian emigrants from a main official source: the police office. The parquet (through the case prosecutors) is the second institution which offers information regarding the case of homicide-suicide. More rarely, journalists solicit and bring to the readers' attention information from the Institute of Forensic Medicine, the county or local hospital.

> On December 29, current year, around 21.00, the dispatcher of capital police was made aware that in an apartment in the 5th district, there were two dead bodies. A complex team formed of a prosecutor of the parquet near the Bucharest Court House, police officers from the 5th district and specialists from the homicide and criminologist services went to the incident place and settled the following:
>
> In the apartment they found the dead bodies of two young people, aged 28 and 32, husband and wife respectively, with residence in Bacău county, and without any legal forms for the address where they were discovered. They presented injuries on their heads, bodies and limbs. The wounds were produced with a cutting-stinging object. (*He killed his wife and the committed suicide*, amosnews.ro, December 30, 2012)
>
> "As the investigation shows, at least from the data found up to now, the man killed his sister-in-law first and then his concubine. He killed his sister-in-law with two shots in her abdomen. Farcaş Ladislau had a criminal record, he committed several similar acts 25 years ago" declared Prosecutor Dan Ursu, from the parquet near the court house in Arad. (*Three dead people in Arad county. He shot his former girlfriend and his sister-in-law and then committed suicide*, Ana Zidărescu and Marian Păvălaşc, evz.ro, May 19, 2012)

There are also cases for which more official sources were used and journalists seem to adopt the position of a person interested in identifying the evidence from the file in order to classify the violent act as a road accident (and identifying the guilty parts) or as a suicidal act. I chose as an example a case of filicide-suicide committed in Romania. The children's father, upset that his wife did not want to return from Spain, decided to punish her and kill their children. He chose as a way of committing the homicide-suicide a suicidal road accident: he smashed his car which his two children were in into a TIR truck. For this case journalists used as sources: the road police from Dolj, the parquet near Dolj Court House, the psychologist of the the Service of Complex Evaluation of DGFP Dolj, the mayor from the village where the aggressor lived and the witnesses (the driver of the truck and a witness). Seen from a general perspective, the article resembles minutes, where all the facts and evidence are presented.

> The police officers of the Road Service Dolj sent more teams to the place of the accident, and after the first examination they clarified that the Opel Astra car went in the opposite direction of the traffic and crashed into a truck that was driven according to the regulations. Cristian Nelu Roşu, who was driving the Opel car from Leu to Craiova, went the

opposite way on the road and crashed into a truck coming from the opposite direction according to the regulations by Marian Stan Ruţă, aged 37, from Sadova village. Due to the impact, the Opel car smashed entirely and the driver and his daughter died instantly. Andrei, Roşu's 5-year-old son lived for several minutes after the impact. The police officers from the Road Police Office tried to settle exactly how the road accident happened and, after the first examination of the declarations of some witnesses, reached a shocking conclusion: Cristian Nelu Roşu crashed his car into the truck deliberately and committed suicide. (*He got his children into the car and drove them to death*, Gazeta de Sud, July 5, 2013)

THE DRIVER OF THE TRUCK: "This assumption was supported not only by the declarations of the driver of the truck and by the declarations of Cristian Nelu Roşu's father, but also by the fact that at the place of the accident no brake tracks of the Opel car were found. Marian Stan Ruţă explained that he saw how the Opel overtook another car and after that he continued to go in the opposite way some hundreds of meters. "He overtook another car long before and after that he did not come back into his lane and crashed directly into me. I applied the brakes and I swerved to the right as much as I could, but I had no choice" said the driver of the truck. (*He got his children into the car and drove them to death*, Gazeta de Sud, July 5, 2013)

Taking into consideration the declaration of Cristian Roşu's father and due to the fact that police found another witness who said that Cristian Nelu Roşu got his children into the car and murdered them, the investigations were taken over by the prosecutors of the parquet near the Dolj Court House. "Today (yesterday) a penal cause was registered at the parquet near Dolj Court House, in which an investigation is being made into the felony of first degree murder. At this time there are clues that the driver deliberately got his children into the car and went the opposite way where he crashed his car into the truck", declared Prosecutor Magda Bădescu, the spokesperson of the parquet near Dolj Court House. (*He got his children into the car and drove them to death*, Gazeta de Sud, July 5, 2013)

In fact, all the sources are used by the journalist for judicially classifying the act of violence. Towards the end of the article he uses the mayor of the village as a source, also presenting the idea of a material help that City Hall could offer for the funerals of the victims.

"I do not know in detail the situation of the family, but, as I have understood, the boy had asked for his father's forgiveness after which he got into the car and left with his two children. What happened next is a tragedy that confused us all. The daughter Alexandra was a student in 8th grade and had graduated with 8.38, so she was a good child. The little boy was at kindergarten. We have already started a social investigation because our (local authorities) involvement is needed in order to support Cristian's father with everything that is necessary", declared the mayor Iulian Cristescu. (*He got his children into the car and drove them to death*, Gazeta de Sud, July 5, 2013)

Furthermore, the journalist also wants to describe the consequences of the violent act for the road traffic from the neighborhood:

> Due to the road accident, the traffic on DN6 was interrupted for approximately two hours. The police officers from the road police department deviated the traffic to the streets that go behind the edge of DN6, but only part of the drivers took the risk of going on those streets. The other ones waited in a line until the truck and the Opel car were taken off the road. (*He got his children into the car and drove them to death*, Gazeta de Sud, July 5, 2013)

At the end of the article the journalist brings information given by the psychologist from the Department of Complex Evaluation of DGFP Dolj:

> In general people make such gestures out of revenge. This man was sure that his wife was interested more in their children than in him, so he decided to take revenge, to make her suffer. The children became collateral victims; they were used for revenge. It is clear that this man had a personality imbalance." explained Claudia Măciucă. (*He got his children into the car and drove them to death*, Gazeta de Sud, July 5, 2013)

International press agencies or newspapers of the diaspora as primary definers

When we talk about a case of homicide-suicide committed abroad, the sources used for presenting the cases are the articles from the newspapers from the Romanian diaspora or the articles given by the press agencies and the newspapers of the country where the violent acts happened. If the case covered proves to be interesting for the public and, in the respective period there are no other important events (I refer to political events because these are the ones which catch the journalists' attention), journalists try to complete the information with data from other sources. But, as Codreanu and Fotiade (2008) have shown, Romanian journalists prefer to take information from the international press agencies or from the countries where the homicide-suicides happened.

I will tell you how journalists covered a case which happened in Greece and which did not get too much interest from the Romanian journalists (it had only 4 articles in two days, it was not illustrated with images). All the four appearances of the case had the same title and the same content. All the articles quoted the Greek press agency ANA and only two articles quoted the Greek press agency ANA and the international agency Agence France Press (AFP) as sources. The content of the article was each and every time the one below and the title was the same in three cases: "A Romanian man from Crete shot two persons and then committed suicide." Only one article had a slightly different title: "He killed two persons and then committed suicide" (Gazeta de Sud. Ziarul oltenilor de pretutindeni, gds.ro)

> A Romanian man shot and killed the girlfriend that had just left him, also a Romanian girl, and a man who accompanied the girl, before committing suicide on Monday night, in Crete, announced today the Greek press agency ANA, quoted by AFP. Aged 36, the Romanian man was following the victim and opened fire on her while she was getting into a car where there were two Greeks, in the center of Heraklion city. The woman and the driver of the car died instantly. The second man who was in the car and who was suspected to be the new boyfriend of the woman was slightly injured. The aggressor went away from the crime scene and committed suicide. (*A Romanian man from Crete shot two persons and then committed suicide*, Realitatea Românească, April 15, 2008)

The Romanian journalists limit themselves to the information from abroad. Although, given their proximity to the space where the two actors of violence lived together until the moment of the violence, they could have brought up more information regarding the violent acts precursory to the homicide-suicide. They could have also informed other victims found in the situations precursory to the fatal violence about the high risk to which they were exposed due to not telling others about the frequent acts of domestic violence.

Regardless of the source used, the great majority of media articles are simple presentations of data without too many journalistic investigations meant to offer information regarding the reasons for the violent acts, the consequences of the violent acts for the members of the family or the measures taken to prevent this type of violence.

Unofficial sources as primary definers

Journalists use information from unofficial sources for very few cases: witnesses, relatives of the affected families, direct and indirect victims, neighbors. When they use unofficial sources, journalists try to update information regarding the case of homicide-suicide. In other words, unofficial sources are rather secondary and not primary sources. Information picked up from unofficial sources refers to the violent background of the relationship or to facts about the aggressor or the victim.

> Ladislau Farcaş lived in Austria, but every time he came to Romania – and he came once a month, state the villagers from Pecica […] The woman's neighbors say that Maria had presumably left Ladislau a few days ago because he was beating her. […] The sellers from the food shop in front of which the tragedy happened told the investigators that they were not alarmed when they heard the noise because they thought there were children throwing with firecrackers. (*Update: Massacre on a street in Arad! He killed his concubine and his concubine's sister-in-law and then committed suicide*, www.libertatea.ro, May 19, 2012)

They were together for many years, but lately he kept getting drunk and was beating her, I could see her with bruises on her face all the time, once she needed surgery so she complained to the police and asked for a restraining order", said Olga, Maria's sister. (*The seller who assisted to the murder from Arad: "A 3-year-old child was a witness to the slaughter"*, Cristian Dan, www.libertatea.ro, May 21, 2012)

The discussions about the information sources of the Romanian journalists use in order to write the articles regarding the homicide-suicide cases can continue with an analysis of the way in which the writing style of the media articles has evolved in the case of serious violent acts. A simple review of the analyzed corpus emphasizes some modifications in the way of writing the articles; we are witnesses to a multiplication of sources used over the analyzed period of time (2002–2013). This diversification of sources is, of course, due to the fact that we could also face a diversification and multiplication of the types of media communication means. The Internet made the multiplication of the number of online newspapers possible and it also contributed to the increase in the speed of updating the information regarding the tackled cases of homicide-suicide.

Social media networks (Facebook, Twitter) led to the transformation of any person found in the proximity of the case into a possible unofficial source. Moreover, the reduced costs of making an online newspaper made possible the appearance of some local or regional online newspapers set up by journalists who had their headquarters close to the area where the event happened. In this way, online/off-line newspapers and national television stations had the possibility to take over information regarding the cases committed abroad or in villages from Romania, which did not present any interest for the journalists from the written press or from television before the development of the Internet. With all these modifications, Romanian journalists remain dependent on official sources. This relationship of dependence between a journalist and the representatives of the police or parquet led both to adopting a new judicial perspective over cases and to a lack of a perspective, which can emit signals meant to lead to modifications in the behavior of the possible victims, aggressors or witnesses. Readers are thus transformed into receivers of shallow messages similar to a description by the police where events, wounds and weapons used are presented and described. Journalists do not offer information regarding the measures which could be taken by a person found in a situation similar to the person who had just been killed, they do not launch messages through which Romanians are encouraged to notice in advance threats or developing conflicts, they do not present efficient ways of intervention from the witnesses or the people found in the proximity of cases.

'Facebook kills!' – Case study

The case selected to be discussed is a case of intimate partner homicide-suicide between emigrants. The way in which journalists covered this case was a bit different from the other cases of homicide-suicide. The case was covered for 3 days (May 6–8, 2012) in 27 press articles. The majority of articles were published on the first day (17 articles) and only a third on the second day (8 articles). On the third day (May 8) only 2 press articles were published. It is interesting that two reportages regarding this case made in 2012 by the TV station Antena 1 were posted on YouTube in February 2015 by a person who had the pseudonym of Bamilian Tenn.

As a matter of fact, the way in which the aggressor decided to kill his wife was a special one. What made this case of homicide-suicide be totally different? The fact that after killing his wife, the aggressor wrote in a red pen on the victim's chest: "Facebook kills". Through this, the aggressor got closer to the way serial criminals leave their signature at the place of the deed or people who commit suicide leave a message to the other members of the family. From this particularity, journalists went further and made a connection with other cases of suicides which were announced on Facebook a few days before being committed. In other words, journalists used this case to draw attention to messages on Facebook by certain persons before suicide. The connection of this case with the social network Facebook was made also due to the appearance of information according to which the aggressor suspects the victim of having a relationship with a man she met on Facebook. As a consequence, journalists transmitted two messages regarding Facebook: the first in which Facebook is associated with the socializing network, where people who commit suicide post messages before suicide, and the second, according to which Facebook is the network where you can start new relationships. Beyond these two associations, journalists created press articles slightly different from the ones written for the cases of homicide-suicide.

As I have already said, this case was tackled differently by journalists. First of all, journalists placed many photographs from the family archive in the published articles. Most of the photographs had the aggressor as the main character and photographs were either from Romania or from the countries where he had worked. In some photographs the aggressor appears with all the members of the family: wife and two young children (3 and 4 years old). When they published some images with the children of the family, some journalists did not respect the deontological norms and published the images of the two children without being protected as the current law demands.

Secondly, journalists brought information regarding the aggressor's and victim's Facebook accounts and the messages posted by the aggressor before the homicide-suicide. The messages from the victim's account were used by a local TV station, Hunedoara TV in order to begin the reportage dedicated to the case and posted on YouTube on May 8, 2012. Find below the message taken from the victim's account:

> We lived together because we loved each other… I forgave many unforgivable mistakes. I did many things on impulse… I was deceived by persons about whom I did not think they would ever do this. I smiled when my heart was crying…I made eternal vowels. I happened to mistake the way, but I moved forward *("Facebook kills" Shocking murder in Deva*, Hunedoara TV/YouTube, May 8, 2012)

If the victim's Facebook account was used after two days from the murder by the local TV station in order to make the reportage regarding the homicide-suicide case, the aggressor's Facebook account was used even from the first day by journalists and online newspapers in order to better illustrate the case.

> Colesniuc did not list his wife at the relationship status on Facebook, but he posted more photographs with her and their two children. In one of them he swore eternal love to his wife: "I love you my dear until we grow old (my sweet (sic!) and beautiful)". Iulian Colesniuc had made a Facebook account some time before, in March 2012. *("Facebook kills" The dreadful message found on the dead body of a woman from Deva*, Realitatea.net, May 6, 2012)

Thirdly, the case is different through the way in which information sources were used. Unlike other cases, one of the first quoted sources was the Deva Court House from where journalists took also information regarding the divorce trial of the two. The Deva Court House is the first official source which appears in the first article published by Realitatea.net. Journalists included in this first article a print screen of the web page of the Deva Court House where information regarding the divorce file between the victim and the aggressor was published.

> The divorce was initiated by Diana Mirela Colesniuc, Iulian's wife, in February 2012. However, on March 14, 2012, the court house states the end of the divorce action through "the making up of the two parties". *("Facebook KILLS": The murderer from Deva strangled his wife after two months from their MAKING UP*, May 6, 2012, Realitatea.net)

Then, also on the first day, another source which appears more rarely in other cases: the Institute of Forensic Medicine in Deva. With the help of this source, the first information regarding the manner of committing murder and suicide was given.

> "During the night, we were called about a person who threw himself from the upper floor. In the apartment we found the dead body of his wife. She had injuries in the cervical zone, injuries produced by strangulation. We will make the autopsy and we will settle everything with certainty", declared Dan Mărculescu, manager of the Institute of Forensic Medicine, Deva. (*Murder after murder! A man from Deva killed his wife in front of the terrified eyes of their children, and then committed suicide*, Larisa Ciută and Ionuț Chiperiu, Click.ro, May 6, 2012)

As we have also seen in other cases, the police office and the parquet were two of the official sources the most often quoted by journalists during the first and second days. The information given by the spokesperson of Hunedoara Police Department comes to complete the history of the relationship between the victim and the aggressor.

> The victim called the police and said that her husband had cut the Internet cable and had addressed her and her family with bad words. In the written complaint made to the police, the woman said that she did not want the policemen to do an investigation at the marital residence, but she asked that a policeman speak with her husband. The second day, the woman withdrew her complaint and said that her husband had left the country. No investigation was made", declared the spokesman of Hunedoara Police department. (*"Facebook kills!" The young woman from Deva killed by her husband had made a complaint to the police, but she withdrew it"*, May 7, 2012, Realitatea.net)

The information supplied by the case prosecutor contains references to the violent acts preceding murder. As a matter of fact, the case prosecutor appears in most of the press articles made by the TV journalists (10 TV reportages) or in most of the online written press.

> According to the prosecutor Iulian Avram from the parquet near Hunedoara Court House, the 37-year-old man strangled his 28-year-old wife, then committed suicide, throwing himself from a tower block near the one where he had lived together with his family. He said that, most probably, it was about a murder followed by suicide and was explaining the fact that the man, who was working abroad, threatened his wife on the telephone on more than one occasion, and on Saturday he returned home and during the night they had a fight after which everything happened. (*"Facebook kills! The young woman from Deva killed by her husband had made a complaint to the police, but she withdrew it*, Realitatea.net, May 7, 2012)

What is interesting is the way in which journalists use the official institutions in order to bring information from unofficial sources. For example, when journalists use the declarations made by prosecutors in order to give information regarding the history of the aggressor's relationships. We find out that the aggressor had been married before and according to his former wife quoted by the prosecutor, the aggressor had previously attempted suicide after the divorce from his first wife.

> "After the hearing of the former wife, she declared that he had previously had a suicide attempt, when she separated from him, many years ago. Also after the hearings, it was settled that between the two spouses (the murdered woman and her husband) previous disagreements followed by violence had happened", declared the prosecutor. (*"Facebook kills! The young woman from Deva killed by her husband had made a complaint to the police, but she withdrew it*, Realitatea.net, May 7, 2012)

The unofficial sources were less used over the media articles, if we consider Facebook an exception. Some references to neighbors and the son of the aggressor from another marriage had been made, especially when the articles were published by newspapers or local TV stations. Although this case was discussed more than other cases of homicide-suicides between Romanian emigrants and more diverse sources were used, we can notice that journalists limited themselves to giving information regarding the victim, aggressor, family and the history of their relationships. Journalists did not make connections with other cases of homicide-suicide, they did not contact experts from inside or outside the justice system who could have offered information regarding causality and did not suggest ways of intervention and prevention of some other cases of this type. The public also received information about the ways of committing violent acts and, although they mentioned the domestic violence acts from the history of the relationship, journalists did not transmit the necessary messages for potential future victims. No information regarding measures that could have protected the victim and could have made the murder impossible was mentioned. Although the case was intensely discussed and could have been used as a good opportunity to bring into discussion the way in which women (victims of domestic violence) should act in order to protect themselves and to be protected by the specialized institutions (police department, shelters for victims), I did not identify any of these messages in the 29 media articles. Journalists did not bring up other cases of domestic violence ending with the death of the victim, but they treated the case as isolated. Hence the lack of involvement of journalists in making investigations and connections with other violent acts.

Beyond these limits, it is important that journalists decided to bring to the readers' attention such cases which occurred between persons with the status of emigrants. In this way, they drew attention to violent acts committed between emigrants and to Romanian temporary emigrants who were in Romania or abroad. Authorities from Italy and Spain and from other countries too signaled the increase of the number of immigrants involved in serious violent acts on their territory. Specialists from Spain, for example, drew attention to the percentage of murders committed by immigrants in the total number of murderers committed against women from Spain and proposed measures of preventing these violent acts (Vives-Cases et al. 2008/2013). The intense tackling of the homicide-suicides which happened in Romania can become an alarming signal for the institutions empowered to interfere and prevent their multiplication. Romanian journalists have the task to go further with investigations and to try to overcome the phase of writing articles like they were minutes from the police or parquet. In order to do this, they need a change of vision in the way they tackle the violent acts. The violent acts do not have to become life facts or something that brings more readers, but they must become an opportunity for debates centered on identifying the causes and the measures necessary for their prevention.

7. Media Representations of Homicide-Suicides Committed by Policemen

The analysis of data regarding the cases of homicide-suicide in Romania showed the fact that a significant percentage of people who committed homicide-suicide were represented by policemen, military personnel and/or security agents (15 per cent). Almost all cases had as a purpose the murder of the life partner, but there were also some that had a victim's superior military personnel or other people from the aggressor's proximity. In the first part of the chapter I will present information regarding particularities, risk factors, motivations and characteristics of victims and aggressors. In the second part I will discuss the way in which the online press takes information about these cases and presents it in press articles.

Homicide-Suicides committed by police in Romania

Among the homicide-suicide cases registered in the Homicide-Suicides in Romania (2002–1013) database, I identified 20 cases committed by police officers and warrant officers, military personnel and agents of some protection and security services. Police warrant officers and officers (one retired) committed nine homicide-suicides. Military warrant officers and officers committed five homicide-suicides and security agents committed six homicide-suicides.

Homicide-suicides committed by policemen occurred in the period 2005–2013. In this period of time, the number of cases was uniformly distributed (one case per year), except 2008 and 2011 when two cases were registered. All cases happened in Romania. Homicide-suicides committed by policemen were: intimate partner femicide-suicides (3 cases), familicide-suicides (2 cases), paternal filicide-suicide (1 case), parricide-suicide (1 case), matricide-suicide (1 case), and in one case the policeman committed homicide against his colleague.

Offenders' characteristics

All perpetrators were men. No woman committed homicide-suicide in the analyzed period of time. The average age of policemen who committed homicide-suicides was 32.1 years. The policemen's age varied between 25 and 55. Most cases were committed by men aged 25–34 years (8 cases). Only one policeman was 55. Two of the policemen had consumed alcohol and one drugs. We had information of mental illness (depression due to the separation from his wife) for one policeman.

Victims' Characteristics

Homicide-suicides committed by policemen had 13 victims. The victims' average age was 34.7 years. Their age varied between 5 and 58. Most of the victims were women (10) and all of them were the policeman's relatives (wives, mothers, daughters). Three victims were people with professions similar to the perpetrators': a military policewoman, a police officer, and a security agent. Two other victims had an average occupational status: a clerk at a warehouse, a clerk in the City Hall. One victim was a student, one a pensioner and another one a worker. All victims were working in Romania. Only one victim had consumed alcohol and another one drugs.

Characteristics of Events

Five cases had only one victim and four homicide-suicides had two victims each. Only one case occurred in the rural environment, the rest were committed in the urban area. Most of the cases were committed by shooting (6 homicides and 7 suicides). Among the weapons used for the crime, there were knives (2 cases) and heavy objects (1 case). Two of the suicides were committed with a knife. More than half of the homicide-suicides happened in places that were accessible to the perpetrators (3 homicide-suicides in the common house of the victims and policemen and 2 in the victims' houses). Only two homicide-suicide cases were committed with witnesses (the victim's or the aggressor's family members).

The analysis of data from the Homicide-suicides database showed that the homicide-suicides committed by policemen were generated by jealousy associated with infidelity suspicion (3 cases), by conflicts related to the divorce and separation of goods (2 cases) or by conflicts generated by unpaid debts to work colleagues or moneylenders (1 case).

Two homicide-suicides were motivated by the refusal of the policemen's parents to accept their sons' relationships with the chosen partners. One case was about a relationship between a policeman and a married woman who had a child. The second case was that of a policeman in love with a Roma woman who the parents did not want to accept. As we can clearly notice, most of the victims of homicide-suicides committed by policemen were people from the family. Only one case was incongruent to this pattern; a case in which a policeman killed his colleague and then himself. After talking to their colleagues, we found out that the policeman was frequently humiliated by his co-worker and this was the reason why he committed the homicide and then the suicide.

The motivation of homicide-suicides committed by policemen does not seem to be different from the one of other types of aggressions. Besides the factors that seem to be already known, policemen are also exposed to the daily professional stress generated by the specific work that every policeman does.

The analysis of data regarding intimate partner femicide-suicides committed by policemen (3 cases) and regarding familicide-suicides (2 cases) showed that policemen killed, in most of the cases, the partners who were already separated from them (4 cases). Homicide-suicides occurred in a short period of time after the separation (from several days to 2 months). Only one victim was married to the policeman who committed homicide against her. Witnesses mentioned the presence of frequent verbal conflicts between the partners for three cases. The domestic violence acts to which she was exposed forced another victim to file a complaint to the police against her husband who was a policeman. In one case the policeman even threatened his partner with death.

Only three policemen left messages before their suicide (one left a note and two wrote text messages on their mobiles). One policeman spoke on the phone with friends and relatives before committing the homicide-suicide. Three homicide-suicides committed by policemen happened during the day, between 6 am–12 am. Four cases were committed between 6 pm – 10 pm and 2 cases happened during the night (10 pm–5.59 am).

The information regarding homicide-suicides committed by policemen in Romania is quite limited. Furthermore, the number of cases seems to be limited as well. The analysis of these cases requires special attention and can also take into consideration information which police units have about the respective policemen, about their health state and annual psychological evaluations made in their police units. However, this data was not available until the writing of this book. Moreover, I did not have access to the penal files (indictments) of some cases because they were instrumented by the Military Parquet.

No studies regarding homicides or suicides committed by policemen from Romania have been made until now. Even studies about homicide-suicides among Romanian police officers have not been made until this date. The number of international studies regarding homicide-suicides committed by policemen is very small. Some studies refer especially to the cases committed in the USA (Violanti 2007, Leenaars 2010) and bring information regarding motivations of homicide-suicides, modus operandi and other particularities of homicide-suicides among policemen. The results of these studies have some elements that are common with homicide-suicides committed in Romania. I am talking, for example, about the fact that most homicide-suicides analyzed in the USA were committed by men aged up to 40, and the firearms from their jobs were the most frequently used for violent acts (Violanti 2007). The policemen's intimate partners and families seem to be the most frequent victims of homicide-suicides committed by policemen (Violanti 2007, Leenaars 2010). The motivation of homicide-suicides the most frequently expressed during the studies was divorce or estrangement (Violanti 2007, Klinoff et al. 2015). The relationships between policemen and their wives were often affected by domestic violence and abuse, which eased the committing of homicide-suicides by policemen (Violanti 2007, Leenars 2010, Klinoff et al. 2015). Due to this, researchers maintained their opinion according to which we have to interfere in order to reduce the risk of abuse against the policemen's wives. This could lead to reducing the number of homicide-suicides committed by police (Leenaars 2010). Studies from the European space regarding homicide-suicides are even more difficult to identify. We have some information about homicide-suicides committed by police in a study made in Portugal. However, there is very little data about these cases. We find out only the fact that, for the period 2005–2007, researchers identified two homicide-suicides committed by police officers (1 retired) (Ponte Martens Graca de Matos 2013: 8).

Media representations of intimate partner homicide-suicide committed by police officers

The online media in Romania have presented in the recent past more and more cases of violence committed by policemen against members of their family. Cases of murder committed by policemen against their wives or girlfriends and the cases of murder committed against their parents were intensely covered, especially after "the murder in Perla" committed in 2012 by a policeman in a hairdressing salon in a high-class part of Bucharest (ending with the death of the wife and the wife's friend and the injury of another 6 people). After this event, journalists became more interested in discussing acts of violence committed by policemen. Acts of domestic violence, murders and suicides committed by policemen became a subject more prominently presented through online media. A simple search with Google Chrome.ro and some keywords such as "a policeman killed his wife" sends us to 21 articles regarding cases of policemen who killed their wives in the first three pages. At the same time, if we use keywords like "a policeman committed suicide" we reach 29 articles about suicides of Romanian policemen or policemen from abroad.

The interest of journalists for covering these cases is explainable. As I have also shown in chapter 6, journalists select for discussion serious violence cases that break patterns either due to characteristics which victims or the aggressors have, or due to the particularities of the violent acts. In the case of murders and suicides committed by policemen, we have more elements which transform these cases in the press. We are talking, firstly, about violent acts committed by persons who, due to their profession, are supposed to ensure the protection of people and not murder them. Moreover, we have a violent act committed in a special way, with the help of a weapon owned by the policeman. I say it is a special way of committing the murder or the suicide because in Romania the great majority of murders were committed with hard objects that were handy for the aggressors or victims (Institute of Forensic Medicine, 2003–2014). Regarding suicides, studies have shown that most of them were committed through hanging (Ibid.). Moreover, I have to mention the fact that in Romania citizens are forbidden by law to own weapons. Only certain professions are allowed to own weapons and they have a gun permit: policemen, military personnel, hunters and security agents or employees who transport great sums of money or very valuable objects. These two issues made the murder or suicide cases into subjects of interest for the articles from the written press, television and on-line media.

The cases of homicide-suicide have some extra particularities if compared with the cases of murder or suicide: the great number of victims and the type of violence: the murder followed by the aggressor's suicide, in our case the policeman. These particularities have transformed the cases of homicide-suicide into the most covered press subjects. The analysis made at the level of online media for the last ten years showed that not all the cases of homicide-suicide were covered. Why were they not covered? Even if, at the level of communities where they happened, there was information regarding these cases, they did not reach the attention of journalists from the central or local newspapers. We assume that, as I showed in chapter 6, journalists have policemen and case prosecutors as their main sources of information. We can also assume a reluctance of policemen towards discussing cases where the aggressors were their colleagues (you will see further in this chapter the way in which cases of homicide-suicide were covered with the help of information given by different police units). This is one of the consequences of using mostly the official institutions as 'primary definers'. More precisely, the journalists' dependence on information given by policemen leads to covering only the cases which institutions choose to cover.

Methodology

The present chapter tries to bring information regarding the way in which the online media from Romania discussed the cases of homicide-suicide committed by policemen. I gave special attention to the cases of intimate partner homicide-suicides, but given the little number of cases covered, I also considered it necessary to discuss cases of homicide-suicide committed against other members of the family of the policeman.

In the first phase of the research that was the basis of writing this chapter, I selected the cases of homicide-suicide which occurred between 2002 and 2013. These cases were extracted from the Homicide-suicides in Romania database. In the second phase, starting with the cases of homicide-suicide identified for the analyzed period in the database, I looked for all the media articles published online for each of the cases.

Finally, the corpus of my analysis was made of 116 media articles identified in the online environment for seven cases of homicide-suicide committed by policemen between 2008 and 2013. I have to mention that, although my investigations regarding the cases of homicide-suicide committed by policemen targeted the period between 2002 and 2013, I identified only seven cases of homicide-suicide covered in the online press. All these cases were covered after 2008 (two cases in 2008, one case in 2009, two cases in 2011, one case in 2012, and one case in 2013). This situation can be explained through: 1) the increase in the number of cases of homicide-suicide committed by policemen; 2) the increase in the interest of the journalists from the online media for this subject after 2008; 3) the development of online media due to the economic crisis which generated the reduction of costs of offline publications and 4) a change in the attitude towards policemen and transforming policemen from "heroes" into "aggressors". This last assumption of the change in the attitude towards policemen can be valid especially after September 24, 2010, a day in which over 6000 policemen from Romania took to the streets and protested against the measures initiated by the president of Romania and taken by the government against policemen (dismissing personnel, reducing salaries, financing the system) ("Leave the country, son of a bitch!". *The revenge of Băsescu against the policemen who asked for his resignation has effects even after 28 months*, January 21, 2013, Jurnalul.ro). After the events of 2010 when thousands of policemen from all over the country started an unauthorized march towards the presidency headquarters, there was a series of measures sanctioning the leaders of the police and the ones who participated in marches and indignation meetings.

Types of homicide-suicide committed by policemen presented in the online media

The online media in Romania covered between 2008 and 2013 seven cases of homicide-suicide committed by policemen. The discussed cases had as a common denominator only the fact that the aggressor was a policeman, and the weapon with which they murdered their victims was a firearm. As for the rest, journalists chose to present cases which had one or more family members (wife, child and parents) among the victims (see Table 7.1).

Table 7.1 Types of homicide-suicide committed by policemen presented in the online media

Year when the homicide-suicide was committed	Relationship between victim and aggressor	Period of time when it was covered	Number of articles
2008	wife and son	24.04.2008–17.11.2010	8
2008	wife	2.10–27.12.2008	9
2009	girlfriend	17.12–20.12.2009	8
2011	wife and daughter	13.04–19.04.2011	21
2011	parents	15.06.2011–1.08.2013	17
2012	mother	31.03–7.06.2012	22
2013	girlfriend	23.03–27.03.2013	31

As seen in Table 7.1, only three cases were intimate partner homicide-suicide (the victims were wives and girlfriends). Two other cases had both intimate partners and family children as victims. Two of the most tackled cases had the parents of the aggressor as victims (mother and both parents).

Period of time when the cases of homicide-suicide committed by policemen were covered

The most covered case was the one in which a policeman from Dâmbovița killed his girlfriend and then committed suicide (31 articles in 5 days). This case was picked up by more online publications because the victim was the daughter of a gypsy leader who had recently been involved in an intensely covered story (his son, a well-known footballer, had died of cancer). In addition, it was a relationship between a policeman and a young woman of Romani ethnicity, a relationship which seems to not have been accepted by the policeman's parents. Another intensely covered case was one which had the mother of a former policeman from Constanta as a victim (22 articles in 3 months). Journalists showed interest in the case because the policeman was a well-known person in his village. He had been convicted and sent to prison for attempted rape and he was a drug user. The case of a policeman (the former leader of Service of Weapons and Munitions of the County Police Office, Dolj) who had shot his wife and daughter was tackled for 7 days (21 articles). This case was more discussed than a case where a policeman killed his wife and son (8 articles in 7 months).

The fact that he was a policeman – a former leader of Service of Weapons and Munitions and current leader of the hunters' association in the village transformed this case into a more interesting one for the public. In addition to this, it is also interesting that the daughter survived the attack and journalists wrote about the experience of the young woman in hospital. Another case of violence, committed by a policeman, was one which had as victims a mother and father who were against a relationship which the young man had with a married young woman, who had also a child from her previous marriage. The case was among the ones presented in more online publications (17 articles).

These four cases were the most covered cases of homicide-suicide committed by policemen. We can notice the fact that there are four types of homicide-suicide: intimate partner homicide-suicide, matricide-suicide, familicide-suicide and patricide-suicide. The rest of the cases (2 intimate partner homicide-suicides and one familicide-suicide) were less covered (8–9 articles) (see Table 7.1).

'Primary definers' of homicide-suicides committed by police

The analysis of media articles referring to the cases of homicide-suicide between Romanian emigrants has shown that journalists use most of the time 'primary definers' as the official institutions component of the penal system of justice (police and parquet). Because they want to have more information regarding the sources journalists use for their press articles, I decided to identify the main sources used for writing the media articles regarding the cases of homicide-suicide committed by policemen. The analysis of the 116 on-line articles identified for the cases in which policemen were aggressors has shown a series of particularities.

Official institutions as primary definers

Journalists used as information sources for the articles regarding the cases of homicide-suicide committed by policemen: official institutions (55.4 per cent), unofficial sources (30.3 per cent) and other types of sources (14.2 per cent – experts, media, social networks). Over the analysis I also identified articles for which sources were not mentioned (20 articles).

Official institutions were this time also the most often mentioned, and from these the components of the justice system in particular (police department, parquet, court houses, penitentiaries, National Institute of Forensic Medicine) were the main sources for the documentation of the articles. Police, parquet and judicial sources (there were no precise statements regarding institution) were quoted over more press articles (see Table 7.2).

Table 7.2 Official institutions as primary definers

Type of sources	Institutions/categories of sources	Number of appearances	Total
Official sources	Police: spokesperson, manager of the police unit, press release	33	148
	The manager of Romanian Inspectorate of Police	1	
	Minister of the Interior	1	
	Parquet: spokesperson, case prosecutor, press release	30	
	Hospital: county hospital, medical unit, hospital manager, spokesperson, doctors	38	
	National Institute of Forensic Medicine: forensic doctors, psychiatrist experts	4	
	SMURD: coordinators and doctors	7	
	Direction for Child Protection	1	
	Court House: portal of court houses, minutes of the judge	3	
	Penitentiary: spokesperson	1	
	Judicial sources	24	
	Unions of policemen: leaders of Pro Lex & SNPPC	4	
	Mayor	1	

Spokespersons, chiefs of territorial units and case prosecutors gave information regarding the cases committed by policemen. It is interesting that some materials had even high level representatives, managers of the institutions involved in instrumenting the cases as sources. Given the importance of violent cases committed by policemen for the image of the police institution, the representatives of the county units (the top managers at the territorial level), the manager of the General Inspectorate of Police (the top managers at the national level) and even the minister of the Ministry of Internal Affairs were contacted or had press conferences where they gave information regarding the cases of homicide-suicide committed by policemen. The information extracted by journalists from the police representatives was: information regarding the violent act (who committed the deed, reason, age of victim and of aggressor), weapons used, results of annual psychological exam for the respective policeman, the history of the activity of the policeman and the status of the policeman (active, retired, dismissed from police). High level representatives of the police office (chief of the General Inspectorate of Police or the minister) appeared in front of the public after the homicide-suicide only when it was about cases in which the policeman who committed the deed had an important position in the police office. The messages transmitted by the Minister of Internal Affairs and the chief of the General Inspectorate of Romanian Police wanted to inform the public about the measures taken by the managers of the institution after the case and to bring to the attention of the public that the aggressor had not been a policeman for two years (he was retired). What is interesting is the fact that, although the aggressor was a retired policeman, the Minister of Internal Affairs declared that "this character" no longer belongs to the police. We can notice a clear detachment of managers from the former employees involved in the violent acts.

> A team of specialists from the Direction of Internal Control from the General Inspectorate of Romanian Police goes to the Inspectorate of County Police Bihor, as it was announced by the General Inspectorate of Romanian Police. (*A policeman killed his parents and shot himself in the head*, June 16, 2011, Ziare.com)

> "It is regrettable what happened today at Craiova. This character has not belonged to our structures for approximately two years", declared Traian Igaş, Minister of Internal Affairs." (*Shocking case at Craiova: A former policeman shot his wife and daughter and then committed suicide* April 13, 2011, Realitatea.net)

The parquet was represented by the spokespersons, prime prosecutors or case prosecutors. Journalists maintained the connection with this institution during the investigations until finalizing the stories. The court houses were less quoted as this institution was to a small extent involved in prosecuting the cases. The official portal of court houses was quoted by journalists when they wanted to bring more information about the history of the relationship between the aggressor and the victim. They included information about divorce files or actions taken in the court house by victims or aggressors or they brought information about any penal records of policemen.

The hospitals which gave medical care to the victims or to the aggressors who survived for a period of time, or the hospitals which were involved in treating the aggressors were other frequently quoted sources. The case of the policeman who committed suicide after killing his parents was the case which generated an increased interest from journalists, especially after the policeman's sister donated the organs of the policeman. On this occasion, journalists identified more medical units involved in organ transplant and took information regarding transplants made by people who benefited from a transplant.

The medical-legal and psychiatric expertise of the forensic doctors from the National Institute of Forensic Medicine or the doctors' reports of SMURD (special unit of interventions for emergency cases formed of doctors, firemen and policemen) that reached the crime scene were also used as sources for the cases that were more covered.

The leaders of unions of policemen from Romania (Pro Lex and SNPPC) were also approached by journalists, their declarations being explanations of the violent acts. Union leaders took advantage of coverage of homicide-suicide and connected to these cases to problems faced by policemen in general. They emphasized that these violent acts were the result of the measures of policemen's salary decrease (25 per cent) and of announced dismissals (5000 policemen).

> Vasile Lincu, president of Pro Lex, declared, after the discussions of Defense Commission from the Chamber of Deputies, that "there should be more psychiatric check-ups, employees should be checked if they still correspond with this point of view." Nevertheless, he said that we should notice the fact that "even the stress to which people are exposed since this law first appeared (…)" regarding dismissions of the Ministry of Internal Affairs is the reason for these unhappy events. (*Unions comment on the murder in Craiova: Policemen are stressed at work*, April 13, 2011, Ziare.com)

> At his turn, Marian Gruia, chief of SNPPC, said that these cases came to happen also because of the situation employees were in, together with their families, the stress in which they work, financial debts that they have and, especially now, at this time when salaries decreased, the prospect of being dismissed. "We caught the attention of the Defense Commission that part of those who will be dismissed might become future criminals. They have information, they have the criminal environment in which they had worked. And, at the moment when we will dismiss them without any right, we wonder what those people will do" said Gruia. (*Unions comment on the murder from Craiova: Policemen are stressed at work*, April 13, 2011, Ziare.com)

Unofficial sources as primary definers

The media articles published for homicide-suicides committed by policemen also had information from unofficial sources. Journalists tried to bring morc information about policemen and their families and looked for sources in the proximity of the aggressor or the victim. The persons found in the proximity of the aggressor (parents, relatives, friends, colleagues) were more often quoted as sources than the persons found around the victim (see Table 7.3). We can say that journalists were more interested in the aggressor and in identifying some elements to catch the readers' attention. This statement is confirmed also by the fact that all press articles referred to the aggressor defined by his profession of "policeman" and associated with "he shot" or "he killed".

Table 7.3 Unofficial sources as primary definers

Type of sources	Institutions/categories of sources	Number of appearances	Total
Unofficial sources	Parents of the aggressor	7	81
	Relatives of the aggressor	13	
	Colleagues and friends of the aggressor	11	
	Parents of the victim	7	
	Relatives of the victim	4	
	Colleagues of the victim	8	
	Neighbors, building administrators	19	
	Witnesses	3	
	Letters/messages left by the aggressors	7	
	Interview with the victim before being murdered	1	
	Priest	1	
Experts	President of the Association of Security Firms	1	9
	Psychologist, criminologist	5	
	Doctor of Ambulance Service and chief doctor UPU	2	
	Criminology expert	1	
Media	Press agencies: Mediafax, AMOSnews	12	26
	Online newspapers: Ziua de Constanta, Observatorul de Constanta, Evenimentul zilei, Realitatea.net, Independentonline.ro, Incomod media	12	
	TV station website: Protv, RealitateaTv	2	
Social networking sites (SNS)	Facebook	1	3
	Hi5	2	
No sources		20	20

Experts

Among the quoted persons there were also a few experts: criminologists, criminologist psychologists (former police officers), experts from Security firms and doctors. All these persons were contacted by journalists in order to give information regarding the psychological or professional profile of policemen. Very few of these experts were people recognized for their expertise. More precisely, only two former police officers, one criminology expert and another criminologist psychologist were people known in the public eye. Given the fact that he was a carrier policeman, one of the experts had a strict opinion about the policeman who murdered his girlfriend: "He should not have become a policeman!"

> "An unbalanced young person, mentally unstable who did not succeed to merge personal life with the pressures of the policeman job. He was a ticking bomb, anyone could see that he was about to commit a tragic gesture. A man who kept his problems hidden and who chose the craziest and the most damaging solution to solve them. He should not have become a policeman!" explained Butoi. (*Portrait: "The murderer policeman was a ticking bomb"* Cătălina Slujitoru and Adrian David, Click!, December 19, 2009)

From these violent cases committed by policemen, the criminologist expert Tudorel Butoi suggested modifying the way of selecting people who wanted a job in police units.

> "People who cannot deal with the challenges of this job come in our institution. And when they cannot combine their personal life with their job such tragedies happen. Police should adopt the occidental model, FBI type, and keep policemen under supervision for a trial year. If they are not good, the police should let them go", explained Butoi. (*The murderer policeman planned the killing of his girlfriend*, Adevărul.ro, December 18, 2009)

As we can notice, the experts contacted by journalists were persons who had connections with the penal system of justice. The opinions expressed by them were used to describe the personality of the policeman or to give information regarding the weapons used or the premeditated character of the act of violence.

> "He is a former police officer; we are talking about a qualified person who did nothing else but to test, evaluate and release gun permits. He was a professional who knew what owning or using a gun means. He knew how to use a gun. As long as they are active all personnel from the Ministry of Internal Affairs are psychologically tested at regular periods of time in order to see if they can use weapons. The event would rather lead me to the idea that it is a serious momentary mental imbalance which cannot be identified at a regular check-up. I do not think it is a premeditated action", declared Adi Baciu, president of the Association of Security Firms. (*Shocking case in Craiova: A former policeman shot his wife and daughter and then committed suicide*, Realitatea.net April 13, 2011)

Media as information sources

A fifth of the media articles used national press agencies, TV sites or other online publications as information sources. Journalists preferred to take information from the press agencies or to quote other media sources in their first articles about the cases. After publishing their first articles about the cases they completed them with information from other sources identified by the journalists of the respective newspaper. But there were also newspapers which limited themselves to taking the news from the press agency.

Social networking sites (SNS)

Facebook and Hi5 were also mentioned as sources by journalists who wrote about the cases of homicide-suicide. The messages posted on the personal Facebook accounts by the victim and the aggressor before the violent events were also quoted in articles. Although they did not explicitly say, journalists drew attention to the fact that the aggressors had expressed their intentions to the victims on social networking sites. Here we have an example of the discussion between a policeman and his girlfriend before killing her:

> Policeman: You will see in two weeks… I will astonish everybody. I will take you before so that you cannot party anymore.
> AP: Ah… I feel such a pity for you, you are a sick person, I swear I feel pity because you were my man …
> Policeman: You may consider this a disease … but you do not know what happens in my heart and this you want to believe so that you can become more distant.
> AP: You do not even have a heart, you live in another world
> Policeman: I know… I did not have one… but for the moment I lived with you…
> AP: All I want is to be left alone
> Policeman: Do not ask for anything… you will not get rid of me, I swear this to you
> AP: Yes… I arrived home at 9 am, big party
> Policeman: Well, you have one week left … maybe two… after that you will disappear from the landscape
> AP: This is what you think, wait and see what you will hear about me on Saturday
> Policeman: Well then I will take you from Saturday, so I can know a thing, I would rather be in jail than know that a handicapped takes advantage of you.
> (*A policeman shot his girlfriend. The last discussion that the two had on Facebook*, Realitatea.net, March 28, 2013)

We can notice the fact that the policeman had threatened his girlfriend, but the latter did not mind the transmitted message. It is interesting that journalists took this discussion and included it in their articles. But it lacks the message which had to have accompanied this piece of information. Journalists do not inform and do not educate the public regarding the fact that threats made by aggressors represent one of the elements which announces the violent act. In general, Romanian journalists only describe the violent act and give information regarding the victim or the aggressor.

The journalists do not manage to go beyond this pattern and really discuss all these cases of serious violence. They do not make connections between the violent cases of the same type; they do not discuss statistical data regarding the violent acts committed by policemen against their family members. The public does not have information regarding the volume of the violent acts committed by policemen. Their number can be small, but the fact that the media intensely presents the violent cases committed by policemen can lead to the fact that they are much more numerous. On the other side, journalists do not inform the readers about the elements that should make them be more serious about the threats, the acts of domestic violence or the acts of less serious violence that precede murder cases. Journalists do not assume the role of informing and educating with the purpose of preventing acts violence.

Conclusions

International studies show that, in general, policemen are presented by journalists as professional people/heroes who do their job (Barak, 1994, Beckett, 1997). The violent acts committed by policemen are described as being legitimate and executed according to legal regulations even if we are talking about lethal violence (Hirschfield and Simon, 2010). Victims are described in contrast with the positive portrayals of policemen. In most cases, they present information about the criminal history or violent manifestations of victims (Hirschfield and Simon, 2010). In other words, policemen's violence is justified by the media.

The analysis of the way in which Romanian journalists covered the cases of homicide-suicide by policemen emphasizes the fact that journalists avoid justifying the violence of policemen who commit homicide-suicides. The policemen-aggressors are presented as bad cops. A policeman who commits homicide-suicide seems to be a man who does not fit the general profile of the policeman who does his job for the citizens' advantage and who protects them. Romanian journalists contribute to separating the case of criminal policemen from the rest of policemen. The policemen-aggressors who kill their families or other people who are in their proximity are different from the others. Journalists support this idea with arguments of the experts who are quoted during articles, the official police reports or the results of their investigations. They are different policemen because they kill innocent people (family members) who have no connection with the current activities of their job (they are not dangerous criminals who threaten their lives). In this case of unjustified violence of policemen against close people, almost nobody mentions the professionalism that described their career as a policeman. There are few cases where, during media articles, we have information (due to some witnesses/family friends) about positive characteristics of policemen. Further studies will analyze the way in which Romanian journalists present policemen in general or policemen who express their violence against people with whom they have had contact due to their profession.

References

A

Adams, David: *Why do they kill? Men who murder their intimate partners.* Vanderbilt University Press, 2007.

Adinkrah, Mensah: "Homicide–Suicide in Ghana: Perpetrators, Victims, and Incidence Characteristics". *International Journal of Offender Therapy and Comparative Criminology* 58(3), 2014, pp. 364–387.

Adinkrah, Mensah: "Intimate partner Femicide-Suicide in Ghana: Victims, Offenders, and Incident Characteristics". *Violence against Women* 20(9), 2014, pp. 1078–1096.

Adinkrah, Mensah: "Spousal homicides in contemporary Ghana". *Journal of Criminal Justice* 36(3), 2008, pp. 209–216.

Adler, Jeffrey S.: "If We Can't Live in Peace, We Might as Well Die: Homicide-Suicide in Chicago, 1875–1910". *Journal of Urban History* 11/26(1), 1999.

Alvarez, Alex and Bachman, Ronet: *Murder American Style.* Belmont, CA: Wadsworth, 2003.

Anghel, R. G. and Horváth, I.: "Migration and its consequences for Romania". *Südosteuropa* 57(4), (2009), pp. 386–403.

Asal, Victor and Harwood, Paul: "Search engines: Terrorism's killer App". *Studies in Conflict & Terrorism* 31, 2008, p. 7.

Auxéméry, Y and Fidelle, G.: "Impact d'Internet sur la suicidalité. À propos d'une "googling study" sur la rétro-information médiatique d'un pacte suicidaire échafaudé sur le Web". Annales Medico-Psychologiques 168(7), 2010, pp. 502.

Averi, R. Fegadel and Heide, Kathleen M.: "Offspring-Perpetrated Familicide: Examining Family Homicides Involving Parents as Victims". *International Journal of Offender Therapy and Comparative Criminology* 2015, pp. 1–19.

B

Balica, Ecaterina: "Homicides-suicides dans la presse roumaine en ligne". In: Drăgan Ioan et al. (eds.): *Jurnalisme et transformations sociales: des ancienes aux nouveaux medias.* l'Harmattan, 2016.

Balica, Ecaterina: "Le féminicide et les médias en ligne. Études de cas: les femmes roumaines émigrantes qui offrent des services sexuelles légaux/illégaux". In: Marinescu Valentina and Branea Silvia (eds.): *Society, Media and Politics.* Cambridge Scholars Publishing 2016, in press.

Balica, Ecaterina and Stöckl Heidi: "Homicide-suicides in Romania and the role of migration". *European Journal of Criminology*, 2016, pp. 1–18, retrieved 4.3.2016, from DOI:10.1177/1477370816633258.

Balica, Ecaterina: "Violent Crimes in Romania. Significant Results of the Statistical Analysis". In: Balica, Ecaterina and Decarpes, Pascal (eds.): *Violence and Crime in Europe. Social Interventions and Research Methods*. Ars Docendi. 2012, pp. 89–101.

Balica, Ecaterina: "The Homicides: Difficulties and Limits of the Research Methods Used in Romania". In: Balica, Ecaterina and Decarpes, Pascal (eds.): *Violence and Crime in Europe. Social Interventions and Research Methods*. Ars Docendi. 2012, pp. 101–125.

Balica, Ecaterina and Decarpes, Pascal (eds.): *Violence and Crime in Europe. Social Interventions and Research Methods*. Ars Docendi, 2012.

Balica, Ecaterina: "Filicidul maternal şi paternal în România: tendinţe şi factori de risc/Maternal and paternal filicide in Romania: trends and risk factors". *Sociologie Românească* 3, 2010, pp. 97–106.

Balica, Ecaterina and Banciu, Dan: "Agresori în spaţiul familial – particularităţile agresorilor implicaţi în acte de violenţă care determină solicitarea serviciilor de medicină – legală/Aggressors in domestic area – particularities of aggressors involved in violence acts that determine request of forensic services". In: *Asistenţa socială în context European/Social Work in the European Context*, Editura Universităţii din Piteşti: Piteşti. 2009, pp. 84–98.

Balica, Ecaterina: "Murder committed by parents against children". *Prevenirea Criminalităţii* 1, 2009.

Balica, Ecaterina: *Criminalitatea violentă. Tendinţe şi factori de risc/Violent Crime. Trends and risk factors*, Oscar Print: Bucureşti, 2008.

Balica, Ecaterina: "Socio-demographic features of murder offenders in Romania". In: Constantinescu, Cornel (ed.): *Sociologie juridică şi a delincvenţei/Legal and delinquency sociology*, Editura Universităţii din Piteşti: Piteşti. 2006, pp. 129–149.

Barak, Gregg: "Between the Waves: Mass Mediated Themes of Crime and Justice". *Social Justice* 21(3), 1994, pp. 133–47.

Barraclough, Brian and Harris, Clare E.: "Suicide preceded by murder: the epidemiology of homicide-suicide in England and Wales 1988–92". *Psychological Medicine* 32, 2002, pp. 577–584.

Beciu, Camelia: "Diaspora şi experienţa transnaţională. Practici de mediatizare în presa românească". *Revista Română de Sociologie* 1–2, 2012, p. 49–66.

Beciu, Camelia: "Reprezentări discursive ale migranţilor în talk-show-urile politice din România". *Revista Română de Sociologie* 1–2, 2013a, pp. 41–62.

Beciu, Camelia: „Aici“ şi „Acolo“. Strategii identitare în dezbaterile despre migraţia forţei de muncă". *Revista Română de Sociologie* 5–6, 2013b, pp. 369–386.

Beckett, Katherine: *Making Crime Pay: Law and Order in Contemporary American Politics*. Oxford University Press: New York, 1997.

Berman, A. L.: "Dyadic death: A typology." *Suicide and Life Threatening Behavior* 26, 1996, pp. 342–350.

Berns, N.: *Framing the victim: Domestic violence, media and social problems*. Hawthorne: NY Aldine de Gruyter, 2004.

Borţun, Dumitru: "Les role des medias dans la gestion des differences culturelles. Deux exemples de xénophobie: la presse de Roumanie et la presse d'Italie sur les immigrés roumains en Italie (2007–2009)". In: Communautés, Frontiers, Medias. Colloque bilatéral franco-roumain en SIC 16ème édition – juin 2009, University of Bucharest Publishing House, 2009, pp. 238–247.

Boulahanis, J. G. and Heltsley, M. J.: "Perceived fears: The reporting patterns of juvenile homicide in Chicago newspapers". *Criminal Justice Policy Review* 15, 2004, pp. 132–160.

Bourget, D., Gagné, P., and Labelle, M.-E.: "Parricide: A comparative study of matricide versus patricide". *Journal of the American Academy of Psychiatry and the Law Online* 35, 2007, pp. 306–312.

Bourget, D., and Gagne, P.: "Paternal Filicide in Quebec." *Journal of the American Academy of Psychiatry and Law* 33, 2005, pp. 354–360.

Bourget, D., Gagne, P., and Moamai, J.: "Spousal Homicide and Suicide in Quebec". *Journal of the American Academia for Psychiatry and Law* 28, 2000, pp. 179–182.

Bridges, F. and Lester, Stephen David: "Homicide-suicide in the United States, 1968–1975". *Forensic Science International* 206.1, 2011, pp. 185–189.

Brookman, Fiona: *Understanding homicide*. Sage Publications Ltd: London, 3rd edition, 2011.

Browne, A., Williams, K. R., and Dutton, D. G.: "Homicide between intimate partners". In: Smith, M. D. and Zahn, M. A. (eds.): *Studying and preventing homicide*. Sage. Thousand Oaks, CA, 2011, pp. 55–78.

C

Campbell J.: "If I Can't Have You, No One Can: Power and Control in Homicide of Female Partners". In: Radford, J. and Russell, D. E. H. (eds.): *Femicide: The Politics of Women Killing*. Buckingham: University Press, 1992.

Carll, E. K.: "News portrayal of violence and women". *American Behavioral Scientist* 46, 2003, pp. 1601–1610.

Carrabine, E., Iganski, P., Lee, M., Plummer K. and South, N.: *Criminology: A Sociological Introduction*. Routledge: London, 2004.

Cengija, M., Cuculic, D., Petaros, A., Sosa, I. and Bosnar, A.: "Homicide-Suicide events in Southwestern Croatia, 1986–2009". *Medicine, Science and the Law* 52(4), 2012, pp. 217–222.

Centro Studi E Ricerche IDOS: *Caritas e Migrantes, Dossier Statistico Immigrazione 2012*. Raporto–Non sono numeri. 2012. http://www.dossierimmigrazione.it/docnews/file/2012_Dossier_Scheda.pdf.

Chan Ching Yee Aris: "Hostility in Homicide-Suicide Events: A Typological Analysis with Data from a Chinese Society, Hong Kong, 1989–2003". *Asian Criminology* 2, 2007, pp. 1–18.

Cheliotis, Leonidas K.: "The ambivalent consequences of visibility: Crime and prisons in the mass media". *Crime, Media, Culture* 6, 2010, pp. 169–184.

Cod de Procedură Penală publicat în Monitorul Oficial nr 78 din 30 aprilie 1997 - actualizat 2011–2012.

Codreanu, Ionut and Fotiade, Nicoleta (eds.): *Cazul Mailat în presă. De la crimă la criză. Raport de analiză media (1–10 noiembrie 2007)*. Agentia de Monitorizare a Presei. 2008, available at http://www.activewatch.ro/Assets/Upload/files/Cazul%20Mailat%20in%20presa_Feb08.pdf.

D

Daly, M. and Wilson, M.: *Homicide*. Aldine de Gruyter: New York, 1988.

Da Ponte Martins Graça de Matos Sara: *Intimate femicide-suicide in Portugal*. (Integrated Master in Medicine 2012/2013 Scientific Dissertation). Available at: https://repositorio-aberto.up.pt/bitstream/10216/72059/2/93382.pdf

D'Argenio, Alberto, Catania, Giorgia and Marchetti, Marco: "Murder Followed by Suicide: Filicide–Suicide Mothers in Italy from 1992 to 2010". *Journal of Forensic Sciences* 58(2), 2013.

Dawson, Myrna: "Intimate Femicide followed by suicide: Examining the role of premeditation". *Suicide and Life threatening Behaviour* 35(1), 2005.

Debowska, Agata, Boduszek, Daniel and Dhingra, Katie: "Victim, perpetrator, and offense characteristics in filicide and filicide–suicide". *Aggression and Violent Behavior* 21, 2015, pp. 113–124.

Dixon, Shane, Krienert, Jessie L. and Walsh, Jeffrey: "Filicide: A gendered profile of offender, victim, and event characteristics in a national sample of reported incidents, 1995–2009". *Journal of Crime and Justice* 37(3), 2014, pp. 339–355.

Dogan, KH., Demirci. S., Gunaydin, G. and Buken, B.: "Homicide-Suicide in Konya, Turkey between 2000 and 2007". *Journal of Forensic Sciences* 55, 2010, pp. 110–115.

Dobash, Emerson R. and Russell P. Dobash: "What Were They Thinking? Men Who Murder an Intimate Partner". *Violence Against Women* 17(1), 2011, pp. 111–134.

Drăgan, I., Ştefănescu, P., Povară, A. and Velicu A. (eds.): *Reprezentarea violentei televiziuale şi protecţia copilului*. Editura Vanemonde, 2009.

E

Easteal, P.: "Homicide-suicides between adult sexual intimates: An Australian study". *Suicide and Life-Threatening Behavior* 24(2), 1994.

Eurostat: *Statistici privind Migraţia şi Populaţia*. 2012. Retrieved from: http://epp.eurostat.ec.europa.eu/statistics_explained/index.php/Migration_and_migrant_population_statistics/ro; European Commission

Eurostat: *Statistici privind migraţia şi populaţia migrantă*. European Commission. 2012, http://ec.europa.eu/eurostat/statistics-explained/index.php/migration_and_migrant_population_statistics/ro.

F

Fairbairn, Jordan and Dawson, Myrna: "Canadian News Coverage of Intimate Partner Homicide: Analyzing Changes Over Time". *Feminist Criminology* 8(3), 2013, pp. 147–176.

Friedman, Susan Hatters et al.: "Common Factors in Parents Who Kill Their Children and Themselves". *Journal of American Academy of Psychiatry and the Law Online* 33(4), 2005, pp. 496–504.

G

Gauthier, D. K. and Bankston W. B.: "Who kills whom" revisited: A sociological study of variation in the sex ratio of spousal killings". *Homicide Studies* 8, 2004, pp. 96–122.

Gekoski, A., Gray, J. M. and Adler, J. R.: "What makes a homicide newsworthy? UK national tabloid newspaper journalists tell all". *British Journal of Criminology* 52, 2012, pp. 1212–1232.

Gillespie, Lane Kirkland, Richards, Tara N., Givens, Eugena M. and Smith Dwayne M.: "Framing Deadly Domestic Violence: Why the Media's Spin Matters in Newspaper Coverage of Femicide". *Violence Against Women* 19(2) 2013, pp. 222–245.

Girigan, G.: "Efecte socio-economice ale migraţiei după 1989. Studiu de caz: Feldru/Transilvania/Socio-economic effects of migration after 1989. Case study: Feldru Transylvania". *Sfera Politicii* 166, December 2011.

Gius, Chiara and Lalli, Pina: "I loved her so much, but I killed her". Romantic love as a representational frame for intimate partner femicide in three Italian newspapers". *ESSACHESS. Journal for Communication Studies* 7(2), 2014, pp. 53–75.

Gregory, Marilyn: "Masculinity and homicide-suicide". *International Journal of Law, Crime and Justice* 40(3) 2012, pp. 133–151.

Gregory MJ. and Milroy, CM.: "Homicide and suicide in Yorkshire and the Humber: 1975–1992 and 1993–2007". *American Journal of Forensic Medicine and Pathology* 31(1), 2010, pp. 58–63.

Gruenewald, J., Pizarro J. and Chermak, S. M.: "Race, gender, and the newsworthiness of homicide incidents". *Journal of Criminal Justice* 37, 2009, pp. 262–272.

H

Hall, S., Critcher, C., Jefferson, T., Clarke, C., and Roberts, B.: *Policing the Crisis: Mugging, the State and Law and Order*. Macmillan: London. 1978.

Harper, D. W. and Voigt, L.: "Homicide followed by Suicide an Integrated Theoretical Perspective". *Homicide Studies* 11, 2007, pp. 295–318.

Heide, K. M.: *Understanding parricide: When sons and daughters kill parents*. Oxford University Press: New York. 2013.

Heide, K. M., and Frei, A.: "Matricide: A critique of the literature". *Trauma, Violence, & Abuse* 11, 2010, pp. 3–17.

Hillbrand, M.: "Homicide-suicide and other forms of co-occurring aggression against self and against others". *Professional Psychology: Research and Practice* 32, 2001, pp. 626–635.

Hirschfield, Paul J. and Simon, Daniella: "Legitimating police violence". *Theoretical Criminology* 14(2), 2010, pp. 155–182.

Hogeveen, B. R.: "If We Are Tough on Crime, If We Punish Crime, Then People Get the Message: Constructing and Governing the Punishable Young Offender in Canada During the Late 1990s". *Punishment & Society* 7(1), 2005, pp. 73–89.

I

Instituto Nacional De Estadistica: *Population Figures at 1st January 2014. Migration Statistics 2013*. 2014, Retrieved from: www.ine.es/en/prensa/prensa_en.htm.

Institutul National de Medicina Legală/National Institute of Legal Medicine: *Rapoarte anuale/Annual Reports 2003–2014*. Available at http://www.legmed.ro/?doc=1237824528.

Institutul Național de Statistică: *Anuarul Statistic al României/Romanian Statistical Yearbook*, 2007.

Institutul Național de Medicină Legală "Mina Minovici": *Rapoarte anuale de activitate 1998–2014*. Available at http://www.legmed.ro.

Irimescu, G. and Lupu, A. L.: *Home Alone!, Study made in Iasi area on children separated from one or both parents as result to parents leaving to work abroad Alternative Sociale*. Iasi. 2006, Retrieved from: http://www.childrenleftbehind.eu/wp-content/uploads/2011/05/2006_AAS_CLB_Romania.pdf.

J

Johnson, Carolyn and Sachmann, Mark: "Familicide-suicide: from myth to hypothesis and toward understanding". *Family Court Review* 52(1), 2014, pp. 100–113.

K

Kivivuori, Janne and Lehti, Martti: "Homicide Followed by Suicide in Finland: Trend and Social Locus". *Journal of Scandinavian Studies in Criminology and Crime Prevention* 4(2), 2003, pp. 223–236.

Klein, Carolina A.: "Live Deaths Online: Internet Suicide and Lethality". *The Journal of the American Academy of Psychiatry and the Law* 40, 2012, pp. 530–6.

Klinoff, Vera A., Van Hasselt Vincent B. and Black, Ryan A.: "Homicide-suicide in police families: an analysis of cases from 2007–2014". *Journal of Forensic Practice* 17(2), 2015, pp. 101–116.

Korn, Alina and Shivan, Efrat: "The Coverage of Rape in the Israeli Popular Press". *Violence Against Women* 10(9), 2004, pp. 1056–1074.

Koziol-McLain, Jane, Webster, Daniel, McFarlane, Judith, Block, Carolyn Rebecca et al.: "Risk Factors for Femicide-Suicide in Abusive Relationships: Results From a Multisite Case Control Study". *Violence and Victims* 21(1), 2006, pp. 3–21.

L

Legea 295 din 28 iunie 2004 privind regimul armelor și al munițiilor, Monitorul Oficial nr. 425 din 10 iunie 2014. Available at http://www.dreptonline.ro/legislatie/regimul_armclor_munitiilor.php.

Legea nr 135/2010 privind Noul Cod de Procedură Penală, Monitorul Oficial, Partea I, nr 486 din 15 iulie 2010 intrat în vigoare la 1 februarie 2013.

Legea nr. 395 din 16 decembrie 2005 privind suspendarea pe timp de pace a serviciului militar obligatoriu si trecerea la serviciul militar pe baza de voluntariat, Monitorul Oficial nr 1155 din 20 decembrie 2005.

Leenaars, Antoon: *Suicide and Homicide-suicide among police.* Baywood Publishing Company, Inc. Amityville: New York, 2010.

Leveillée, S., Lefebvre, J., and Marleau, J. D.: "Profil psychosocial des familicides commis au Quebec – 1986 à 2000". *Annales Médico-psychologiques, revue psychiatrique* 167, 2009, pp. 591–596.

Liem, Marieke and Reichelmann, Ashley: "Patterns of Multiple Family Homicide". *Homicide Studies* 18(1), 2014, pp. 44–58.

Liem, Marieke, Levin, Jack, Holland, Curtis and Fox, James A.: "The Nature and Prevalence of Familicide in the United States 2000–2009". *Journal of Family Violence* 28, 2013, pp. 351–358.

Liem, Marieke, Ganpat, Soenita, Granath, Sven et al.: "Homicide in Finland, the Netherlands, and Sweden: First Findings from the European Homicide Monitor". *Homicide Studies* 17(1), 2013, pp. 75–95.

Liem, Marieke and Oberwittler D.: "Homicide followed by Suicide in Europe". In: Liem, M. and Pridemore, A. (eds.): *Handbook of European Homicide Research. Patterns, Explanations and Country Studies.* Springer, 2012, pp. 197–217.

Liem, Marieke and Nieuwbeerta, Paul: "Homicide Followed by Suicide: A Comparison with Homicide and Suicide". *Suicide and Life-Threatening Behavior* 40(2), 2010, pp. 133–145.

Liem, Marieke, de Vet, Renée and Koenraadt, Frans: "Filicide followed by parasuicide: A comparison of suicidal and non-suicidal child homicide". *Child Abuse & Neglect* 34(8), 2010, pp. 558–562.

Liem, Marieke: Homicide–parasuicide: a qualitative comparison with homicide and parasuicide, *The Journal of Forensic Psychiatry & Psychology* 21(2), 2010, pp. 247–263.

Liem, Marieke: *Homicide followed by suicide. An empirical analysis.* (Unpublished doctoral dissertation). Utrecht University, Netherlands, 2010.

Liem, Marieke, Postulart, Marieke, and Niewbeerta, Paul: "Homicide-Suicides in the Netherlands. An Epidemiology" *Homicide Studies* 13(2), 2009, pp. 99–123.

Liem, Marieke and Roberts, Darryl W.: "Intimate Partner Homicide by Presence or Absence of a Self-Destructive Act". *Homicide Studies* 13(4), 2009, pp. 339–354.

Liem, Marieke and Koenraadt, F.: "Homicide-suicide in the Netherlands: A study of newspaper reports, 1992–2005". *The Journal of Forensic Psychiatry & Psychology* 18(4), 2007, pp. 482–493.

Lindqvist, P. and Gustafsson, L.: "Homicide followed by the offender's suicide in northern Sweden". *Nordic Journal of Psychiatry*, 49, 1995, pp. 17–24.

Logan, J., Hill, H., Black, M. L., Crosby, A., Karch, D., Barnes, J., et al.: "Characteristics of Perpetrators in Homicide – Followed – by – Suicide Incidents: National

Violent Death Reporting System – 17 US States, 2003–2005". *American Journal of Epidemiology* 168(9), 2008, pp. 1056–1064.

Lupu, A.: "Importanţa redistribuirii rolurilor în familiile de migranţi/The importance of redistributing roles in migrant families". In: Cojocaru, M. et al.: *Migraţia şi efectele ei în Plan Familial. Suport de curs. «Irregular migration and traffiking in unaccompanied minors: urgent measures for minors in situations of extreme vulnerability*. 2006. Retrieved from: http://singuracasa.ro/_images/img_asistenta_sociala/pentru_profesionisti/resurse_asistenta_sociala_copil_singur_acasa/abilitati/Migratia_si_efectele_ei_in_plan_familial_OIM2006.pdf.

Lupu, A.: "Importanţa redistribuirii rolurilor în familiile de migranţi [The importance of redistributing roles in migrant families]". In: Cojocaru, M. et al.: *Migraţia şi Efectele ei in Plan Familial. Suport de curs*. Irregular Migration and Traffiking in Unaccompanied Minors: Urgent Measures for Minors in Situations of Extreme Vulnerability. International Organisation for Migration.

Lecomte, D. and Fornes, P.: "Homicide Followed by Suicide: Paris and its Suburbs, 1991–1996". *Journal of Forensic Sciences* 43(4), 1998, pp. 760–764.

M

Mariano, Timothy Y. et al.: "Toward a more holistic understanding of filicide: A multidisciplinary analysis of 32 years of U.S. arrest data". *Forensic Science International* 236, 2014, pp. 46–53.

Marinescu, V. And Ştefănescu, S.: *Mediatizarea violenţei în familie studiu de caz: ziarele centrale româneşti*. CPE, 2004.

Marshall, Ineke Haen and Summers, Diana L.: "Contemporary differences in Rates and Trends of Homicide Among European Nations". In: Liem, M. and Pridemore, A. (eds.): *Handbook of European Homicide Research. Patterns, Explanations and Country Studies*. Springer. 2012, pp. 39–69.

Meyers, Marian: "News of battering." *Journal of Communications* 44(2), 1994, pp. 47–63.

Meyers, Marian: "African American women in the news: Gender, race & class in journalism". Routledge: New York, 2013.

McClure, Kyla N.: "When do people pay attention? Violence and nonviolence in political movements and the differential media attention provided". *Critical Studies on Terrorism* 7(3), 2014, pp. 394–410.

Milroy, C. M., Dratsas, Magdalene and Ranson, D. L.: "Homicide-suicide in Victoria". *Australia American Journal of Forensic Medicine and Pathology* 18(4), 1997, pp. 369–373.

Ministerul Internelor si Reformei Administrative: *Statistica principalelor activitati desfasurate de Politia Română in perioada 2006–2014*. IGPR. Available at http://www.politiaromana.ro/ro/utile/statistici-evaluari/statistici/arhiva-statistici.

Malphurs, J. E. and Cohen, D.: "A newspaper surveillance study of homicide-suicide in the United States". *American Journal of Forensic Medicine and Pathology* 23, 2002, pp. 142–148.

Mathews, Shanaaz et al.: "Intimate femicide-suicide in South Africa: a cross-sectional study World Health Organization". *Bulletin of the World Health Organization* 86(7), 2008, pp. 552–58.

Morton, E. et al.: "Partner homicide-suicide involving female homicide victims: A population-based study in North Carolina, 1988–1992". *Violence and Victims* 13, 1998, pp. 91–106.

Marleau, J. D., Auclair, N. and Millaud, F.: "Comparison of factors associated with parricide in adults and adolescents". *Journal of Family Violence* 21, 2006, pp. 321–325.

Mercy, J. A. and Saltzman, L. E.: "Fatal violence among spouses in the United States, 1976–85". *American Journal of Public Health* 79, 1989, pp. 595–599.

Mucchielli, Laurent: "Homicides in contemporary France". In: Liem, Marieke C. A. and Pridemore, William Alex (eds.): *Handbook of European Homicide Research. Patterns, Explanations, and Country Studies*. Springer, 2012.

N

Nikunen Minna: "Murder-suicide in the news: Doing the routine and the drama". *European Journal of Cultural Studies* 14(1), 2011, pp. 81–101.

P

Palermo, G. B.: "Murder-suicide: An extended suicide". *International Journal of Offender Therapy and Comparative Criminology* 10, 1994, pp. 106–118.

Paulsen, D. J.: "Murder in black and white: The newspaper coverage of homicide in Houston". *Homicide Studies* 7, 2003, pp. 289–317.

Pereira, A. R. et al.: "Intima te partner homicide-suicide a 5-year case review (2004–08)". Imprensa da Universidade de Coimbra. International Academy of Legal Medicine. Available at http://hdl.handle.net/10316.2/31818.

Pereira, A. R., Vieira, D. N. and Magalhães, T.: "Fatal intimate partner violence against women in Portugal: A forensic medical national study". *Journal of Forensic and Legal Medicine* 2013.

Pritchard, Colin: "Family violence in Europe, Child homicide and Intimate Partner Violence". In: Liem, Marieke C. A. and Pridemore, William Alex (eds.):

Handbook of European Homicide Research. Patterns, Explanations, and Country Studies. Springer, 2012.

Panczak, R. et al.: "Incidence and Risk Factors of Homicide–Suicide in Swiss Households: National Cohort Study". *PLoS ONE* 8(1): e53714, 2013.

Putkonen, Hanna et al.: "Filicide in Austria and Finland – A register-based study on all filicide cases in Austria and Finland 1995–2005". *BioMedCentral Psychiatry* 9(74), 2009.

Peck, J. H. and Heide, K. M.: "Juvenile involvement in fratricide and sororicide: An empirical analysis of 32 years of US arrest data". *Journal of Family Violence* 27, 2012, pp. 749–760.

R

Reiner, R.: "Media made criminality: The representation of crime in the mass media". In: Maguire, M., Morgan, R. and Reiner, R. (eds.): *The Oxford Handbook of Criminology*. Oxford: UK: Oxford University Press. 2007, pp. 302–337.

Roma, Paolo et al.: "The epidemiology of homicide–suicide in Italy: A newspaper study from 1985 to 2008". *Forensic Science International* 214, 2012.

Resnick, P. J.: "Child murder by parents: a psychiatric review of filicide". *American Journal of Psychiatry* 126, 1969, pp. 325–334.

Richards, Tara N. et al.: "An Examination of the Media Portrayal of Femicide–Suicides: An Exploratory Frame Analysis". *Feminist Criminology* 9(1), 2014, pp. 24–44

Richards, Tara N. et al.: "Exploring News Coverage of Femicide: Does Reporting the News Add Insult to Injury?". *Feminist Criminology* 6(3), 2011.

Russell, D. E. H. and Harmes, R. A.: *Femicide in global perspective*. Teachers College Press: New York. 2001.

S

Saleva, O. Et al.: "Homicide-suicide – an event hard to prevent and separate from homicide or suicide". *Forensic Science International* 166, 2007, pp. 204–208.

Shon, Chong Ho Phillip and Roberts, Michael A.: "An Archival Exploration of Homicide -Suicide and Mass Murder in the Context of 19th-Century American Parricides". *International Journal Offender Therapy and Comparative Criminology* 54(1), 2010, pp. 43–60.

Signorielli, N.: "Television's mean and dangerous world: A continuation of the cultural indicators perspective". In: Signorielli N. and Morgan M. (eds.): *Cultivation analysis: New directions in media effects research Newbury Park*. CA: Sage. 1990, pp. 85–106.

Schlesinger, P., Tumber, H. and Murdock, G.: “The media politics of crime and criminal justice”. *British Journal of Sociology* 42, 1991, pp. 397–420.

Stack, S.: “Homicide followed by suicide: An analysis of Chicago data”. *Criminology* 35, 1997, pp. 435–454.

Showalter, C. R., Bonnie, R. J. and Roddy, V.: “The Spousal Homicide Syndrome”. *International Journal of Law and Psychiatry* 3, 1980, pp. 117–141.

Saint-Martin, P., Bouyssy, M. and O'Byrne, P.: “Homicide-suicide in Tours, France (2000–2005) – description of 10 cases and a review of the literature”. *Journal of Forensic and Legal Medicine* 15(2), 2008, pp. 104–109.

Sara da Ponte Martins Graça de Matos: *Intimate Femicide-Suicide in Portugal.* (MA dissertation), University of Porto, Biomedical Sciences Institute Abel Salazar, 2013, available at: https://repositorio-aberto.up.pt/bitstream/10216/72059/2/93382.pdf.

Sandu D. (ed.): *Locuirea Temporară în Străinătate. Migrația Economică a Românilor: 1990–2006.* Bucharest: Fundația pentru o Societate Deschisă, 2006.

Stănculescu M., Stoiciu, V., Alexe, I. and Moțoc L.: *Impactul crizei economice asupra migrației forței de muncă din România [Impact of the Economic Crisis on Romanian Labour Migration].* Bucharest: Friedrich Ebert Stiftung, 2011.

Murat, Salih Eke et al.: “Maternal Filicide in Turkey”. *Journal of Forensic Sciences* Vol. 60(S1), 2015.

Stöckl, Heidi et al.: “The global prevalence of intimate partner homicide: a systematic review“. *The Lancet* 382(9895), 2013, pp. 859–865.

T

Taylor, R.: “Slain and slandered: A content analysis of the portrayal of femicide in the news”. *Homicide Studies* 13, 2009, pp. 21–49.

Taylor, C. A. and Sorenson, S. B.: “The nature of newspaper coverage of homicide”. *Injury Prevention* 8(2), 2002, pp. 121–127.

Torre, A. R.: *Migrant lives. A comparative study of work, family and belonging among low-wage Romanian migrant workers in Rome and London.* (PhD thesis). Department of Sociology, London School of Economics and Political Science, 2013. Available from: http://etheses.lse.ac.uk/693/1/Torre_Migrant_lives.pdf.

Toth, A. and Toth, G.: “Relații de familie [Family relations]”. In: Sandu, D. (ed.): *Locuirea Temporară în Străinătate. Migrația Economică a Românilor: 1990–2006.* Bucharest: Fundația pentru o Societate Deschisă, 2006.

V

Velicu, A.: “Reprezentarea violenţei televizuale pe canalele pentru copii”. In: Drăgan, I. Et al. (eds.): *Reprezentarea violentei televiziuale şi protecţia copilului* Editura Vanemonde, 2009, pp. 173–217.

Velicu, A.: “Moduri de mediatizare în presa scrisă a problemei violenţei televizuale”. *Revista Română de Sociologie* 5–6, 2011, p. 449–479.

Velicu, A.: “Bullying-ul online şi offline: victime versus agresori”. *Revista Română de Sociologie* 1–2, 2014, pp. 19–36.

Violanti, John: “Homicide-suicide in Police Families: Aggression full circle”. *International Journal of Emergency Mental Health* 9(2), 2007, pp. 97–104.

Vougiouklakis, T. and Tsiligianni, C.: “Forensic and Criminologic Aspects of Murder in North-West (Epirus) Greece”. *Journal of Clinical Forensic Medicine* 13, 2006, pp. 316–320.

Vives-Cases, C. et al.: “Mortalidad por Violencia del Compañero Intimo en Mujeres Extranjeras Residentes en España (1999–2006)”. *Gaceta Sanitaria* 22, 2008, pp. 232–235.

Vives-Cases, C. et al.: “Social and Immigration Factors in Intimate Partner Violence among Ecuadorians, Moroccans and Romanians Living in Spain”. *The European Journal of Public Health,* 24(4), 2013, pp. 605–612.

Vlase, I.: “Migraţia de întoarcere a românilor din Italia. Studiu de caz în Vulturu, Vrancea/Return migration of Romanians from Italy. Case study in Vulturu, Vrancea”. *Calitatea Vieţii*, XXII 2, pp. 155–176.

W

West, D. J.: *Murder followed by suicide*. Cambridge: Harvard University Press. 1965.

West, S. G. and Friedman, S. H.: “Filicide, A research update”. In: Browne R. C. (ed.): *Forensic Psychiatry Research Trends*. Nova Science Publishers: New York, 2007.

Weizmann-Henelius, Ghitta et al.: “Gender-Specific Risk Factors for Intimate Partner Homicide – A Nationwide Register-Based Study”. *Journal of Interpersonal Violence* 27(8), 2012, pp. 1519–1539.

Westerlund, M., Gergo H. G. and Wasserman, D.: “The Representation of Suicide on the Internet: Implications for Clinicians”. *Journal of Medical Internet Research* 14(5), 2012, e-122.

Wilson, M. I. and Daly, M.: “Till Death us Do Part”. In: Radford J. and Russell D. E. H. (eds.): *Femicide: The Politics of Women Killing*. Buckingham: Open University Press, 1992.

Wilson, M., Daly, M. and Daniele, A.: “Familicide: The killing of spouse and children”. *Aggressive Behavior* 21, 1995, pp. 275–291.

Index

G

H

I

www.ingramcontent.com/pod-product-compliance
Ingram Content Group UK Ltd.
Pitfield, Milton Keynes, MK11 3LW, UK
UKHW021842100926
8556IPUK00019B/998

9 783631 667224